STRATEGIES
FOR THE
SECOND HALF
OF LIFE

Strategies for the Second Half of Life

by Peter Weaver

FRANKLIN WATTS
New York/London/Toronto/Sydney
1980

Library of Congress Cataloging in Publication Data

Weaver, Peter, 1925–
Strategies for the second half of life.

Includes bibliographies and index.
1. Middle age—United States.
2. Finance, Personal.
3. Middle age—Health and hygiene—United States.
4. Middle age—Family relationships.
5. Happiness. I. Title.
HQ1059.5.U5W4   305.2′4   80-10589
ISBN 0-531-09921-0

TABLE OF
CONTENTS

**PART II
YOUR HEALTH:
TIME FOR A TUNE-UP**

PART III
YOUR HAPPINESS

PART IV
YOUR PARENTS

INTRODUCTION
TO THE
SECOND HALF

You may not realize what is happening. There is no band playing, and no speeches. But, somewhere in your forties, you pass into the second half of your life. You are probably too busy working, raising a family, coping, to think about it or even recognize it. You might notice some subtle changes in the way you look at your life. Instead of counting up from the day you were born, or the first days you can remember, you almost imperceptibly begin to count back from some vague, future end of your life. Sometimes you count the years, usually giving yourself a full measure, and come up with figures that add up to 75, 80 or 85. You pick some ripe old age you think you might live to and then subtract your current age. This gives you the Number of Years You Have Left, which usually ranges from 25 to 30 years or more, depending on your current age and your optimism-pessimism quotient. I'm an optimist—some say I'm an almost pathological optimist. I'm in my mid-fifties, so I calculate that I might have some 25 to 30 years left.

Life Expectancy in the United States (in years)			
Year	Males	Females	Difference
1910	46.3	48.3	2.0
1920	53.6	54.6	1.0
1930	58.1	61.6	3.5
1940	60.8	65.2	4.4
1950	65.6	71.1	5.5
1960	66.6	73.1	6.5
1965	66.8	73.7	6.9
1970	67.1	74.6	7.5
1974	68.1	75.8	7.7
1976	68.9	76.7	7.8
1977	69.3	77.2	7.9

Source: U.S. Division of Vital Statistics, Public Health Service

When you start thinking this way it's official: You're in the second half, and it's going to be quite different from the hectic first half you've successfully played through. In the first half, you had to deal with all sorts of upheavals:

• Education and adolescence. You made it through your parents' control, you made it through school and you made it through the sometimes anxious "dating game." And, most important, you didn't get killed in an auto accident or in a war (which is no mean feat when you look at the nasty statistics).

• Marriage. You took the big step. You may have taken it two or three times. Or, you might have remained single. No matter. You set up a household.

• You raised a family and went through all the laughter and tears that come with parenthood.

• You pushed and pulled, climbing the career ladder. Maybe you changed careers once or twice.

• You no doubt struggled with home ownership, mortgages, taxes, insurance, repairs, moving—the whole hassle.

- You probably paid for much of your kids' education, which might have left you with a shrunken or nonexistent nest egg.

But, you got through it. I got through it. We can take a bow. It was quite an accomplishment. Now we're in the second half and, if we play it right, it could be the better half (there's my optimism creeping in). But I'm not the only one who's optimistic about the possibilities. Dr. Bernice Neugarten, a nationally-known authority on aging and Professor of Human Development at the University of Chicago, says: "The *second half* is a period for parents who have seen their kids go out into the world and it begins in your forties.... There's a long interval that follows when physical vigor remains high, family responsibilities are diminished and commitment to work continues."

For single people, it could be a time when a career plateau may have been reached and there's a casting about for something better or different to do.

In most games, as in life, halves are often broken down into other halves or quarters. And, in the second half of your life, sure enough, there is a third quarter and a fourth quarter. Mind you, they don't have to be equal amounts of time. If you're smart—and lucky—you should have a lot more time in the third quarter than the fourth. A lot depends on your mental attitude and physical fitness. But, in general, the most crucial time in your second half is the third period. It's a time when many a game is won or lost. If you insist on putting it into measurable terms, you might say it runs from some time in your forties on into your sixties, perhaps your seventies. Statistically, it covers more than 53 million people. When you will not work or cannot work because minor ailments have become major ailments, you might say the fourth quarter has

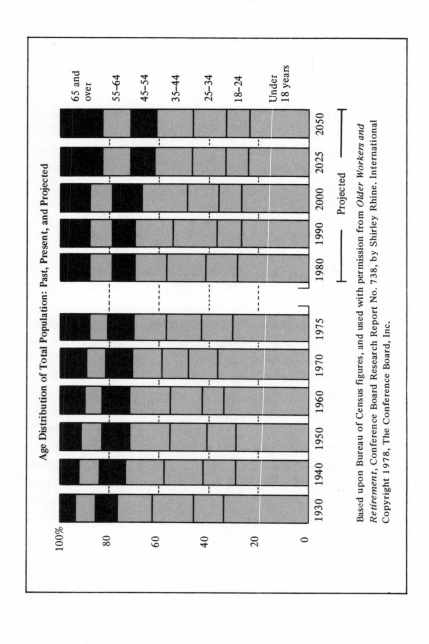

Age Distribution of Total Population: Past, Present, and Projected

65 and over

55–64

45–54

35–44

25–34

18–24

Under 18 years

100%

80

60

40

20

0

1930 1940 1950 1960 1970 1975 1980 1990 2000 2025 2050

—— Projected ——

Based upon Bureau of Census figures, and used with permission from *Older Workers and Retirement*, Conference Board Research Report No. 738, by Shirley Rhine. International Copyright 1978, The Conference Board, Inc.

begun. And, of course, many games are won or lost in the fourth quarter too. But that's another story we'll get to later.

Right now, we're going to concentrate on the "long interval when physical vigor remains high"—the interval that Bernice Neugarten spoke about. How you fare in your later years, or whether you even get to your later years, depends a lot on decisions you make right now—this week, this month, this year. Because the longer you live, the more you find that the major decisions in your life are all too often made by other people—such as your employer, your husband or wife, your government and eventually, even your own children.

WHY RETIRE?

Many people have written about the second half in terms of *retirement*. I'm not one of them. This book is *not* a book about retirement. If anything, it's an anti-retirement book. If you want a real downer, take a look at what Webster's Third Dictionary has to say about the word *retirement*: "A retreat...A withdrawing into seclusion...Withdrawal from office, active service, or business...A place of seclusion...."

Well, to hell with that. If that's retirement, I don't plan to do it very soon—if at all. I want to die with my boots on, working at what I do best. I'm not talking about working to exhaustion (or boredom). I'm talking about figuring a way to work—for pay—at something you like to do for as long as you can, at the pace that suits you best.

Actually, I was initially asked to write a book about retirement. The very thought of it turned me off. Then I started doing some research. I spent days looking through more than a hundred books and "studies" on retirement. The libraries operated by the National Council on Aging and the American

Association of Retired Persons (a few blocks from each other in Washington, D.C.) are filled with books on retirement. They ooze from the shelves.

There must be a better way to live in the second half without "retirement." Yet the vast majority of retirement books take it for granted that everyone must retire and should even look forward to it as some sort of "reward." The reward, of course, is that magnificent, phony word: *leisure*. The trouble is, leisure depends heavily, almost totally, on having plenty of money.

Classic economist Thorstein Veblen coined the term "leisure class" to describe those in this situation, but the definition has changed over the years. The leisure class in the old days were the very rich. They worked at leisure, studied it and applied themselves well. Veblen's leisure class learned French, horseback riding, tennis, and yachting and spent considerable time traveling around the best spots in this country and Europe. But times changed. Now, the so-called leisure class (retired people) has less money than the working class.

Yes, leisure depends on having money. And, to have leisure without sufficient funds—as many retired people live today—is the pits. They can call it what they want, but it's the pits pure and simple.

I expressed my gloominess with the word retirement and the concept it defines to Mike Batten, management consultant and expert on aging and the workplace. He admitted that I had reason to be gloomy and said: "You've got to get to people before they start making decisions about retirement . . . You've got to convince them that they should seriously consider retiring later or even not retiring at all." Working longer, he explained, "is a hedge against inflation, if nothing else."

WORKING AS
A WAY OF LIFE

Dr. Harold Sheppard, co-author of *Work in America* (M.I.T. Press) and *The Graying of Working America* (Free Press) and a Senior Research Fellow of the Center on Work and Aging at the American Institutes for Research, picks up where Batten leaves off and explains: "There's going to be mounting pressure to stay working. The way inflation is going, many people can no longer afford the life of leisure that retirement promises. Few, if any, private pension plans provide for inflation-proof benefits (in 10 years at 7% inflation per year, the purchasing power of pension checks will be cut in half). Someone in relatively good health, with steady employment, will have to think twice before jumping into the economic fool's paradise of early retirement."

If individuals may not be able to afford early retirement, or even "on-time" retirement, Dr. Sheppard says our government can't afford it either. Because people have been living longer and retiring earlier (see charts on page xviii and xix), Social Security funds are under considerable pressure. Congress voted higher withholding taxes to help bolster the Social Security system, and it isn't sitting well with younger workers and employers who have to foot the bill. "Social Security," Dr. Sheppard warns, "may have gone about as far as it can go."

When Batten and Sheppard suggest we start thinking about working longer, some of us feel cheated. What about that world of leisure we were promised at the end of the rainbow? The leisure pot of gold is hard to give up. Physician-gerontologist Alex Comfort, in a report to the Council of State Governments, urges a different view: "Leisure is a con. Leisure should occupy an occasional

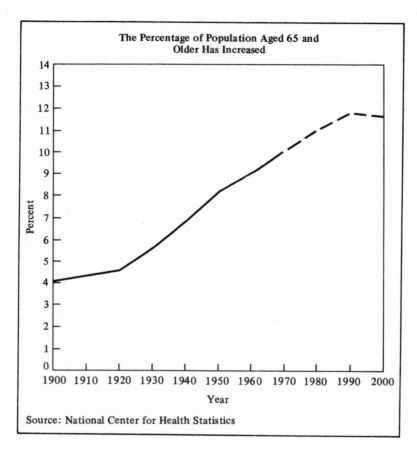

The Percentage of Population Aged 65 and Older Has Increased

Year

Source: National Center for Health Statistics

afternoon, not twenty years. People need some interesting work, not compulsory leisure. If you pay attention to some occupation, leisure in the right sense will follow."

Dr. Comfort, in his fine book, *A Good Age* (Simon and Schuster), expands his thoughts on leisure with these words of warning:

"Retirement is another name for dismissal and unemployment. It must be prepared for exactly as you would prepare for

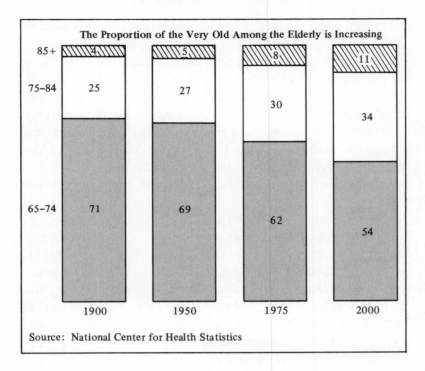

The Proportion of the Very Old Among the Elderly is Increasing

	1900	1950	1975	2000
85+	4	5	8	11
75–84	25	27	30	34
65–74	71	69	62	54

Source: National Center for Health Statistics

dismissal and unemployment. You'll be poorer than you think at a time when you'll need a lot more than now. So, prepare, if you can. Best of all, stay in paid, useful work.... Two weeks is about the ideal length of time to retire. Beware of hobbies. For most people, working actively in society is a great deal better.

"The real curse of being old is the ejection from citizenship which is traditionally based on work. It is a demeaning idleness, nonuse, not being called on any longer to contribute, and hence being put down as a spent person of no public account, instructed to run away and play."

Not only will you need the money that comes from paid work,

but you'll need the stimulation and propensity for good health that seems to come from it.

Speaking for the American Medical Association in testimony before a Senate Labor Subcommittee, Dr. Albert E. Gunn said: "The sudden cessation of productive work and earning power of an individual, caused by compulsory (even voluntary) retirement often leads to physical and emotional illness and premature death. It seems clear that the longer older persons apply themselves to some particular activity that affords a challenge and mental stimulation, the better off they are."

According to Mike Batten, "If you can make it through the 55-to-65 year health danger zone, you'll be better able to continue working and, more than likely, will want to continue working." Apparently, having an interesting job or occupation and good health are intimately related. This is why Parts I and II of this book are devoted to Money (with the emphasis on getting it through an investment in your workability) and Health (with the emphasis on maintaining it so your workability won't be impaired).

But, you ask, what about getting some rest? You've worked hard in your twenties and thirties and well into middle age. Maybe you do deserve a rest. If so, take it now—in digestible bites. And, then press on, plotting and planning to keep at some form of interesting work as long as possible. Invest in yourself and your workability. Otherwise, you risk becoming old before your time. And who wants that? Sigmund May, M.D., author of *The Crowning Years* (Lippincott) sums it up this way: "Too many people, convinced that five or six decades of hard work entitle them to rest on their laurels, discover too late that they cannot sit back and be content. No one should ever presume that he (or she) has earned the right to laziness and luxury. It is a universal, gerontological experience that this kind of wishful thinking leads inescapably to physical and mental decline. If achievement is not made a continuous performance, it atrophies. To stay still is to retrogress and become rigid. Adaptation to change is the secret which preserves the forward-looking aspect of youth."

Maggie Kuhn, the firebrand head of the activist Gray Panthers, puts it even more bluntly: "For God's sake, get off your asses!" She then relents a bit, saying: "Of course, some rest is essential. But, resting as a way of life is deadly."

And, from Richard Bolles, a career-change counselor and author of *What Color is Your Parachute* and *The Three Boxes of Life* (both published by Ten Speed Press): "Retirement normally alludes (in its more general sense) to the beginning of our disengagement from work, or (in its more general sense) to the beginning of our disengagement from life. Which is why death (the completion of that disengagement) often comes so abruptly and early to those who do, indeed, retire and just sit around."

All this talk about doing away with leisure and working on into the sunset may come as pretty heavy stuff to many people who look forward to more time to enjoy their lives after already working so many years. Don't be discouraged. Just be forewarned that stopping work might not be the answer. This doesn't mean you have to stick with a tedious job until you're in your seventies. You should be able to slow down, to take more time off for travel and other interests. You might even be officially "retired" from one job and move right into another one better designed to let you mix business with pleasure.

In *The Three Boxes of Life* (education, work, retirement), Richard Bolles says you should enjoy a little bit of retirement all through your life and not try to lump it into your last few years. You have to start planning and plotting right now to take more control of your life. That's what this book is all about. You're going to see how it's possible to do a lot better with your money as you go into your forties and beyond by finding ways to keep your workability tuned up. Of course, the ideal might be the ability to work in some field that you really enjoy—and get paid for it. It's not a pipe dream. It's possible. We'll look at ways it can be done in Part I on Money.

Part I
Your Money: Will There Be Enough?

CHAPTER 1

THE INFLATION SQUEEZE

Most of us have vague, often romantic, notions of how much money we're going to have when we don't want to work any-more or can't work.— "I've got a pension," we say. It sounds comforting. With the pension you'll also be getting something from Social Security and maybe even some income from your investments. It makes you feel secure and your mind wanders off toward more current matters at work and at home. But you may be laboring under a false sense of security.

Let's see what kind of money you're really going to have when you want to stop working and take it easy. You read about inflation. You see it on TV, and you know what's happening to the monthly price of cars, houses, food, and fuel bills. But your income is probably keeping up fairly well and you're far from starving.

THE RULE OF 72

What you don't realize is that inflation may be wrecking your long-range plans about pension, Social Security and investment income for retirement. James Bly, a financial counselor and senior partner of Bly-McGehee & Company in McLean, Virginia, advises us to "learn the Rule of 72—and learn it well. Otherwise, you'll be out of touch with reality when it comes to financial planning for your later years."

The Rule of 72 works this way:

Pick the rate of inflation you think will be the average over the upcoming years and divide it into 72. Some economists say a 9 percent, long-term inflation rate is a conservative estimate. It could be worse. But, let's divide 9 into 72. You get 8. This means, Bly says, that your present dollar purchasing power will be cut *in half* in eight years. Therefore, if it costs you $20,000 to pay for everything this year, it will cost you $40,000 eight years from now.

When most of us figure out our pension and other benefits, we think in terms of today's dollar and don't realize we'll need more—a lot more—when it really counts: five, ten, fifteen years from now. Bly, whose consulting firm analyzes the financial needs of business people, professionals, and others, says it's a dangerous guessing game to use today's dollar needs to plan for taking it easy in the future. He cites this example:

"BUT HAVEN'T
WE EARNED IT?"

Joe and Jane are in their mid-fifties. They think they want to stop working and move to a sunny spot when they're 65—eight years from now. They feel they've got it made. No real worries. Between the two of them, their total income is $30,000 a year. This nets around $25,000 after taxes. They like their style of living and want to stick with it when they retire. Why not? "Haven't we earned it?" But the world doesn't owe us a living, even if we think we've "earned" it.

Joe and Jane read an article in a magazine that said you won't need as much income in retirement as you do now. It is true that expenses for such things as commuting and business clothing do go down. In addition, you get a series of income tax breaks from Uncle Sam when you turn 65. In some areas, depending on your income, you might get a break on property taxes. On the other hand, you might encounter more travel and recreation expenses. Remember, leisure costs money.

In general, though, people who work in the field of retirement planning say you should be able to live fairly well on two-thirds of your pre-retirement income. Unfortunately, statistics show that, after five years of "leisure" and retirement, many people are living on less than half their pre-retirement purchasing power.

Nevertheless, Joe and Jane, who say they're living well off with $25,000 after taxes, are counting on two-thirds of this amount to keep them happy in retirement. Two-thirds of $25,000 comes to around $18,000 a year, and this is what they're aiming for as spendable, after-tax income when they call it quits at work.

This $18,000 a year would serve them well, they believe, and they feel secure. The trouble is, they're not going to retire this year. They plan to do it eight years from now. Using Jim Bly's Rule of 72, the $18,000 that would serve them well now, would have to be $36,000 eight years from now. This means you will need two dollars for every one dollar you need now.

Where are those two dollars for every one dollar going to come from? In their figuring, Joe and Jane were counting on $10,000 a year from a pension and a small annuity investment plus $8,000 a year from Social Security, giving them a total of $18,000 a year. The $10,000 pension and annuity amount was calculated to be what they will receive eight years from now. Social Security benefits will rise to an estimated $15,000 a year, based on projected increases coming from higher tax bases and rates. The $10,000 pension and annuity income added to the projected $15,000 Social Security income will give Joe and Jane $25,000 a year eight years from now. But, as we've seen, they'll be needing $36,000 to maintain their current $18,000 purchasing power. With only $25,000 coming from their pension and Social Security, this leaves them $11,000 short.

Being $11,000 short when Joe and Jane start out their retirement is bad enough. But, when you figure that their income from the pension and annuity will keep right on losing purchasing power after retirement, they're in real trouble. The Social Security benefits will be indexed to the inflation rate and will keep going up year after year. But this won't be enough to keep Joe and Jane anywhere near the standard of living they assumed they would be enjoying.

When people reach 65, insurance companies figure there's a good chance of living on to age 80. If you figure you'd need $36,000 a year when you retire in eight years, you'd need close to $133,000 a year to keep up your same standard of living when you reach 80. So, you see, it isn't just how much you'll be needing when you actually retire. It's how much extra you'll be needing every year you live *after* you retire. The longer you live, the more money you'll need. And, you won't be getting it from that pension, annuity or any other benefit that provides a fixed annual income. There's hardly a pension plan in the country that's indexed to cover inflation. Few employers outside the government can afford it. And, it seems, even the government can't afford it.

THE INVESTMENT MYTH

If you think you're going to fill in the gap with investments, forget it. According to Joseph J. Minarik, a research associate with the Brookings Institution, in Washington, people who rely on income-producing bonds and stock dividends are getting squeezed by inflation and the tax system.

A bond or savings certificate may stay even with or slightly ahead of the inflation rate because it pays relatively high interest. It falls behind eventually, however, because of taxes. Income from bonds, savings certificates and stock dividends are called "unearned" and they are hit with the highest possible tax rate. Don't count on these income-producing investments to protect your standard of living in retirement.

After your children are on their own, you may think you'll be able to set aside some extra money for investments. It's not easy. As you earn more money from your work, you're bumped up into higher and higher tax brackets and you pay more in taxes than you gain in pay raises. You can actually lose thousands of dollars in the upcoming years because of the workings of our tax system. This means you'll find it difficult, if not impossible, to save enough money to build up any significant investment capital.

On top of the tax gouge, people over 40 tend to get smaller pay increases than those under 40. Because employers incur higher costs to supply benefits to older employees—or so they say—they tend to give smaller raises. Employers usually want to give bigger raises to younger employees to keep attracting new talent. All the government wage charts show much smaller annual pay increases for older workers.

The reverse is true for the self-employed. People with their own businesses and professional people, says Bly, tend to pay themselves less in the earlier years as they build their capital base and pay themselves more in the later years when they can afford it. This is an important point. Think about it. People who are not dependent on some employer for their wages and pensions, tend to have more money and more desire to work in their later years. We'll talk some more about this in Chapter 10.

If you can't maintain your current standard of living with Social Security and a fixed-income pension, then where *will* the money come from? Investments, maybe? Unless you're a stand-in for a millionaire, at this stage of the game you'll never be able to pile up enough investment cash to effectively maintain your hoped-for standard of living when you retire—taxes and inflation make it hard to accumulate much capital.

THE INCREDIBLE
SHRINKING NEST EGG

You can get some mileage out of investments, as we'll see in Chapter 10, but not enough to keep pace with inflation. "No matter how you add it up," says Professor James H. Schulz, of the Program in the Economics and Politics of Aging at Brandeis University, "you need an enormous nest egg to cope with inflation." Hardly anybody, he says, has this kind of money. Even if you started right now, you probably couldn't pile up enough money to stave off inflation during a long retirement period.

To get an idea of the task you face, let's say you have a $100,000 house and your equity (what you own) is $70,000. You also have $20,000 in savings and other income-producing investments. This gives you a total of $90,000, which might seem like a tidy sum. On top of this, you also have a Social Security asset value of $140,000. This is an estimate of how much capital it might take to pay all your Social Security benefits after you retire. If you're lucky and work for a reasonably generous employer, you might be entitled to a pension that has an asset value of $180,000. At 9% inflation, your salary will increase and your pension amount as well.

When you add it all up, your house, your savings and investments, your Social Security and pension asset values, it comes to $390,000. It seems like a pretty hefty amount of money.

But, let's see how hefty it really is. If you want to maintain a standard of living in today's dollar purchasing power at, say, $20,000 a year, you'd need something like $110,000 a year twenty years from now when you figure you want to stop working.

To be able to produce that kind of income in twenty years, you'd need assets of $1,030,000 right now—today. This means your current assets of $390,000 which looked so hefty at first, are actually $640,000 short of the mark. And, believe me, this example I've given is not just for wealthy people. It's a lot more commonplace than you might think. You may need less. But, even so, over the years you still would need something in the hundreds of thousands of dollars. And, of course, you might need more. Start doing some figuring.

WORK: YOUR MOST VALUABLE ASSET

But, don't despair. Both Jim Bly and Jim Schulz, the experts in this business, say that most of us never consider our most valuable, potential asset. We add up the value of our homes, savings, stocks, pension plans and the like. But, we miss the really big one: *our own ability to work and make money*. "It's your most valuable asset when you think about it," says Bly. When you continue to work, part or full-time, instead of retiring, your pay tends to keep up with inflation. The purchasing power of a pension falls off fast as inflation eats it up.

On top of this, your ability to work longer keeps you from drawing on your savings and other investments. "You should work as long as you can," says Bly, "so you can stave off having to use your capital." By doing this, Bly explains, "you conserve your assets for the time when you really need them . . . when you simply can't work and may need to pay for extra help at home." All this, of course, contradicts dreamy expectations of a long life of leisure. Many of us have some sort of vague concept about taking it easy after a certain year, but we're not really aware of how much it will cost or where the money will come from.

"Most older people," says Jim Bly, "don't realize what a big price tag leisure has." If most of us don't know the whopper price tag that hangs on the life of leisure, we also don't know the value of our own workability. There are really few, if any, investments that can match your own potential ability to work and make money. The skills in your hands and your brain could be worth hundreds of thousands of dollars—enough money to offset any leisure deficit you might encounter in your later years.

Let's say you want to start taking it easy some time in your sixties. Now that you've read Jim Bly's horrible example of what happens to your so-called retirement income, you may be just a little bit scared. You start looking around for "quick investments," and you find the cupboard bare. There's nothing short of robbing a bank or winning the lottery that's going to make it for you that fast.

You can, however, work at something that makes money and doesn't require working flat-out, full-time at some dull job. While you still have some power and some security, based on your current work, you might be able to explore a sideline occupation or skill that could open the way to making some money after your official retirement date.

WORKING YOUR WAY THROUGH "RETIREMENT"

It doesn't need to be too big a job to have a significant impact on your retirement income package. Let's say you can find a way to make $10 an hour for 20 hours a week. Or, if you think $10 an hour is too high, then $5 an hour for 40 hours. This gives you $200 a week. Let's say you only want to work 40 weeks, leaving three months off during the year to travel, see your kids, or take a few courses. Working the 40 weeks would give you $8,000 a year to supplement your retirement income. If you were over 65 and earned this money now, you'd get little or no money from Social Security because you'd be over the earned income limit and wouldn't qualify for full retirement benefits. Starting in 1982, however, you'll be able to earn up to $6,000 a year after age 65 and still receive full Social Security benefits. And, this income "cap" will certainly be raised. Congress is considering raising the limit, and it will certainly be above $8,000 a year by the time you plan to cash in with your employer.

In our example of working on after your official retirement, then, you'll earn $8,000 your first year (40 weeks work). This can be added to your pension and Social Security benefits. But, unlike a fixed-income pension, your workability will almost surely keep up with and, very possibly, surpass the rate of inflation. Using a 7 percent inflation factor, you'll be making around $10,500 after five years, $15,000 your tenth year and nearly $21,000 in your fifteenth year.

To make $8,000 a year (at 7 percent interest) from some kind of investment, you'd have to have around $115,000. But, every year your investment would have to be larger to keep up with inflation. In 15 years, your income-producing investment would have to total $300,000 to provide $20,500 a year which is what you'd need to maintain the purchasing power of your original $8,000.

You see, your own workability is worth a lot more than you thought. If you were to work full-time, at higher wages than $5 to $10 an hour, your long-term workability could be worth half a million dollars in your later years, possibly more. When you realize how valuable you are as a wage earner, you might take better care of yourself. You'll get some detailed "preventive maintenance" tips on how to take care of your body-and-mind machine in Part II, Your Health.

If you continue working full-time at higher wages, you probably won't be getting much, if anything, from Social Security. And, pension plans usually require leaving the premises as a full-time worker in order to collect benefit checks. The trick is to get other work after "retiring" from your regular job, to try to arrange it so you don't make so much that you disqualify yourself for Social Security benefits. Staffers on key congressional committees say that it's entirely possible that the earnings cap for Social Security could be raised from $6,000 a year in 1982 on up to $15,000 a year or higher. There's a lot of pressure for it. You might be able to build a nice income package with your new work, your Social Security benefits and your pension checks—not to mention some investments and savings you might have kicking around.

INVESTING IN YOURSELF

Speaking of investments, don't forget that the number one consideration should be an investment in yourself and your spouse. It should be an investment in your long-term workability skills. Put it right there at the top of the list ahead of savings, stocks, bonds—the whole lineup. In later chapters, we'll look into various workability investments and strategies.

Of course, things would be a lot easier to plan if you knew exactly how long you were going to live. Like everybody else, you think you're going to live to a "ripe old age." But, who knows? The shorter your time, and your spouse's time, the less money you'll need. The longer your time, and your spouse's time, the more money you'll need. And older people are living longer and longer. Actuarial statistics show that the average American at age 65 can expect to live 15 to 20 years more. Older men have a good chance to reach 80. Older women have a good chance to reach 85 and beyond. This means that if you stopped working at age 65, you'd have to have enough money of your own plus money from Social Security and a pension, to cover the possibility of living another 15, 20, 25 years. You're caught in a bind: If you retire early to live it up while you're still young enough to enjoy it, you stand a good chance of outliving your capital—that is, ending up one step away from the poor house. On the other hand, if you live poorly now in order to build up a pile of money, you might not get a chance to enjoy it.

LIVE LONGER, WORK LONGER

When you were younger, you were worried about the possibility of dying too soon and leaving dependents without enough money. So, you bought insurance as a hedge. Now, you may be faced with the reverse situation. You might need some sort of insurance to protect yourself against living too long—living beyond your capital. You can buy insurance annuities that promise to pay a fixed amount of money per month for as long as you live past a specified date. But, as a rule, these annuities don't keep up with inflation and you end up with less and less purchasing power.

"We have to spread our income further by working longer," says Juanita Kreps, Secretary of Commerce in the Carter Administration, adding: "Ideally, if you could balance your desire for leisure with your need for earned income and continued participation on the job, you'd probably retire gradually rather than suddenly." Working longer, under the right circumstances, could be the insurance policy you need for protection against living too long and running out of capital. Not that the work would kill you. On the contrary, it would probably keep you in shape so you might live a little longer, and better.

There's no question about the fact that you'll have considerably more money and be able to do more if you continue working part-time or full-time. Take a look at these Labor Department statistics for Americans over age 65:

- The average working man has almost twice the income of the average retired man.

- The average working woman has almost three times the income of the average retired woman.

- Working people spend seven times more than retired people on eating out. They spend 4½ times more on automobiles, 3½ times more on major appliances and two times more on recreation.

Perhaps by now you're a believer. You want to have more money in your later years and you think working longer, hopefully at something you like doing, is the answer. But, wanting to work longer at something interesting is one thing; being able to do it is something else. Although the law now says nobody can force you to retire until age 70 (with a few exceptions), there are still plenty of employers who might try to get rid of you after you turn 60. They believe younger workers do a better job, even though one study after another says it's not necessarily so. Along with this vestige of "ageism," you might also be facing increased job competition from the famous baby-boom generation bulge working its way up in the ranks.

If you want to continue working with your current employer or with same future employer, you've got to know the age discrimination laws and your rights. Remember, hundreds of thousands of dollars, and the quality of life in your later years, could be riding on how well you defend yourself in the work place.

CHAPTER 2

YOUR AGE
AND YOUR RIGHTS

Let's say you like your job and the thought of retirement, at least early retirement, is a bit chilling. You like the social contacts at work and you like the image that your work gives you. You've also done a little checking, and you're not sure you can even afford to retire.

While you're thinking of working longer than you originally planned, your employer may be thinking in just the opposite direction. Rightly or wrongly, you may have been quietly classified as "dead wood," something to clear out to make way for younger "self-starters." If you are a man, your employer may think you're not current, not up on things. If you're a woman, you may have lost some of your "attractiveness." Translated, this means you've lost your edge in the unofficial beauty contest.

People who can't seem to crack into better jobs or, worse, are getting pressure from on high to move out and take early retirement, are more often than not victims of "ageism." For a tough definition of the word, listen to Tish Sommers, head of the Older Women's League:

"Ageism, like sexism, is a social disease. When we finally recognize that the main problem lies not with us, the older workers and housewives, but in the nature of the society that allocates persons in the prime of life to the junkheap. And, when we become angry enough to get together and perhaps throw a picket line around the junkheap, and say, 'I WILL NOT BE SCRAPPED, I HAVE A THIRD OF MY LIFE TO GO,' then we will be in good enough shape to change things around."

THE ABOLITION OF "AGEISM"

Indeed, things are already changing around. There is a picket line—albeit an invisible one—slowly forming around the workplace. The older generation is not as easy to push around as previous generations. They're pushing back and, in so doing, are turning things around for people who have the capacity to work and who want to continue working past some employer's idea of when they should retire.

"Remember," says Bernice Neugarten, University of Chicago expert on aging, "you're not over the hill at 40, 50, even 60. We're moving toward an age-irrelevant society. Age, like race and sex, is not a good predictor of what people can do."

Dr. Neugarten sees the abolition of age as an important factor in hiring, firing, retiring, and promotion as part of "the new struggle in our society for age rights. . . . It's going to be the civil rights movement of the 1980s."

This later expression of civil rights hinges on an important law, the Age Discrimination in Employment Act (ADEA). The ADEA, passed in 1967 and put into effect in 1969, filled in the gaps left by the Civil Rights Act of 1964. The

Civil Rights Act dealt with discrimination on the basis of race, sex, religion, and minority status, but it left out age. This oversight was tidied up in the ADEA, which decrees that it is unlawful for any employer to "fail or refuse to hire or to discharge any individual or otherwise discriminate against such individual with respect to compensation, terms, conditions, or privileges of employment because of such individual's age."

In other words you can't be fired, pressured into retirement, turned down, passed by for promotion, or denied training opportunities because of your age.

Initially, the ADEA protected workers from age 40 through 64. Mandatory retirement for most jobs could be imposed at age 65. This magic number, 65, was picked out of the air by Bismarck in the nineteenth century to signify the age at which German workers could start getting Social Security benefits. In the 1930s, when the U.S. got its Social Security law, the retirement age of 65 was adopted from the German model set up by Bismarck. There is absolutely no scientific backing for using age 65 to signify anything other than age 65.

In 1978 an amendment was passed which raised the mandatory retirement age to 70. The amendment was bitterly opposed by an array of employers with some notable exceptions (you'll hear about them later). Although many businesses grumbled, most grudgingly began to comply. Their lawyers told them "there must be no disparate treatment" for workers who are under age 70. In other words, you must be judged and treated just the same as the other employees—no matter what ages are involved.

There are some exceptions to the law, however. You can be fired for a good cause, and a few jobs may still have a "bona fide occupational qualification" based on age. These jobs usually include police work and other occupations where physical requirements are deemed important, but even these occupational qualifications are under attack as discriminatory. In addition, certain executives can be made to retire at age 65 instead of age 70 if they are going to receive pensions of $27,000 a year or more. Also, college professors with tenure can be retired at 65, though this is being phased out.

As you can see, it's a good, tough law, but it does not necessarily mean you're going to get automatic compliance. Since the law went into effect in 1969, more than 30,000 complaints have been filed and more than $100 million collected in monetary damages. A majority of the states have their own age discrimination statutes which tend to resemble the federal law. California and Connecticut have tougher laws. In these states, there is no mandatory retirement age. Civil Service employees also have no mandatory retirement age (as a result of the 1978 amendment to the ADEA). As a matter of fact, you will probably see age 70 eventually removed as a mandatory retirement deadline. Representative Claude Pepper (D.-Fla.), who was a major force pushing for raising the mandatory retirment age, said "it's just a matter of time before there will be no age limit for all but a handful of special jobs."

AGE DISCRIMINATION
DIES HARD

But, no matter what Congress says or does about mandatory retirement, there are still pockets of resistance among employers. Age discrimination dies hard. "One of the fears of businessmen," says Jeffrey Sonnenfeld in the *Harvard Business Review*, "is that they will no longer be able to ease out older workers.... Much of the initial reaction to the recognition of a graying work force has been to try to figure out new ways of 'weeding out the deadwood'.... Pension inducements, less generous performance appraisals and other rationalizations for eliminating older workers are being developed."

Sonnenfeld, a research assistant at Harvard Business School and lecturer on organizational behavior at Northeastern University, took a poll of business managers who were readers of the *Harvard Business Review* to see what attitudes they had about older workers. "Age stereotypes clearly influence managerial decisions," he said. The survey showed that managers thought older workers were more resistent to change and recommended transferring them or retiring them rather than helping them overcome a problem. These managers, Sonnenfeld said, "showed a tendency to withhold promotions from older workers compared with identically qualified younger workers."

Employers usually don't bring up the subject of age when they're talking to you about your "future" in the organization. They know better. They may have heard about those 30,000 cases and $100 million in damages paid out. But, they also count on the fact that many employees don't know much, if anything, about the inner workings of the age discrimination law. They push—gently at first—and then, if you don't push back, they push harder until they get you out.

In working on this book, I came across several people who, after years of good work, started to get "signals" that they were not wanted. The lure was early retirement pension benefits. Sometimes there wasn't even a lure. Some found that their employers used psychological warfare to try to force them out of their jobs. The pension and early retirement benefits (which are less than full pension benefits) were just a cover for what would otherwise be outright firing based on age discrimination.

One young man, a graduate student at a New England university, said his father, an engineer in his late fifties, was "sick with worry" about his job with an electronics company. Apparently, the management decided there were too many older engineers and started to slowly weed them out. In some cases the company threatened to bump older employees into some meaningless, humiliating jobs or transfer them to another area.

OLDER WORKERS: IMPROVING WITH AGE

All this, of course is the older employees' side of it. Many employers still contend that older workers are not productive. However, this point of view is not supported by the experts. According to labor economist Harold Sheppard, one of the nation's leading experts on aging and work, "If there is any slowing down (and not everybody agrees on this), the older workers' experience and dependability usually offsets it. Studies show that consistency of output may actually improve with age. Functional age is not identical with chronological age."

Dr. Sheppard's evaluation of older workers is backed up by many experts in the field, including J. Myron Johnson, professor of industrial psychology, Stevens Institute of Technology: "From a work capability viewpoint, the greatest physical decline occurs in the late thirties and forties with later physical decline not having a great deal of occupational significance." In his *Harvard Business Review* report, Sonnenfeld said employers can get much more out of older workers if they rethink job qualifications and training methods along the following lines:

"When time pressure is not a relevant factor, the performance of older people tends to be as good, often better, than that of younger people. In self-paced tests and in self-paced learning situations, older people do not have to make speed-versus-accuracy trade-offs and, consequently, their performance is higher. . . .

"Similarly, intelligence tests often have age biases built in with inherent speed-versus-accuracy trade-offs. Recently, researchers have tried to avoid such bias and have found problem solving, number facility, and verbal comprehension to be unaffected by age. . . . Education and training programs must reflect the special learning needs of older workers who can be taught new tricks, but need to be taught differently."

Unfortunately, some older workers are brainwashed into thinking something must be wrong with them because they're getting gray. They're the brunt of jokes about "being over the hill." In many respects, you're as old as you think you are. "Remember," says Alex Comfort in *A Good Age*, "aging is not a radical change. . . . You will not become a different person. . . . Your physical and social needs will not alter, your sources of value will not change. . . . But, you will have been assiduously trained by past indoctrination to think that aging is a change in yourself. . . . Except for limited physical alterations, it isn't."

It's these "limited physical alterations" that put fear in the hearts of some employees: "Watch out for the hair-dye and face-lift syndrome," says John Crystal, head of the John Crystal Institute and one of the best career counselors in the country. Crystal says that older employees should try to avoid "trying to look and act young, trying to compete head-on with the young." He offers this advice for older workers who want to continue playing the job game—and playing it well:

"It's a myth that competition is always rewarded. If you're over-eager, then others might want to get rid of you. Don't outshine other people. Develop teamwork. Become a vital cog, not a competitor. Spend a lot more energy on other people around you. Let them know what you're doing to help them. Keep them informed on the job you're doing. Don't become isolated just 'doing your job.' Don't assume everybody knows how good you are."

If you can build a solid base at the place where you work, you might be able to bring about some changes in your working conditions. "It may be possible to get together with other employees," says Richard Beckhard, head of Beckhard and Associates, a management consulting firm, and a professor at Sloane School of Management, M.I.T. "You have to know your rights under the law," Beckhard says, "and you have to get into a position where they can't force you out. . . . Then, you can negotiate an arrangement for continuing to work with more time off."

What you need then, is bargaining power. And, you won't get it sitting around wondering what might happen to you as you grow older. You should have some strategies for defending yourself where you work. Knowing how to defend yourself against ageism can do a lot for your self-confidence. To find out how to fight back if push comes to shove, I consulted Mike Batten, an expert on aging and author of *You and Age Discrimination*, a civil rights manual written for the Institute of Electrical and Electronics Engineers.

GOOD READING

For an excellent paperback dealing with the aging, their familes, and lawyers, with latest changes in the Social Security Act, tax laws, and the Pension Reform Law, I recommend Brown, Allo, Freeman and Netzorg, *The Rights of Older Persons,* available from Avon Books, 959 Eighth Avenue, New York, NY 10019.

CHAPTER 3

HOW TO
FIGHT BACK

When an employer wants to ease you out, says Mike Batten, you'll get some "signals." Learn how to spot them. Pay attention to what's happening to older employees where you work. How are they being treated? Keep count of who's leaving. Are they almost always older workers? When you talk to them, do you get any indication that pressure tactics were used?

"No law forbids layoffs," says Batten, "unless most of the people laid off just happen to be older workers." You have to get an idea of how many workers over age 40 are leaving under suspicious circumstances. If the reason for being laid off or retired is based on wages, job status, or proximity to full retirement, Batten warns, "it's suspect."

Is there any retirement policy or personnel action that attempts to pressure or lure employees into early retirement? If so, it's also suspect. Batten says you should look for such things as subtle threats to downgrade employees' wages or job functions. Another ploy is the threat of an onerous transfer to some organizational "Siberia." Be wary of any incentives or threats of negative action if they're aimed at making employees quietly leave through the back door retirement route.

THE PERFORMANCE APPRAISAL TRAP

The big thing to watch for in the 1980s, says Batten, is the "performance appraisal." A good number of employers already have legitimate performance appraisal methods, but others might introduce them as a means of getting older people out. When performance appraisals are designed to properly assess the competence of *every* employee and recognize the fact that someone can be burnt out at age 40 as well as age 60, you've got a fair and just personnel policy.

Watch out, however, for any sudden changes in the method of making performance appraisals. Are the appraisals really applied primarily to older workers? It's against the law for an employer to design a performance appraisal to weed out older employees.

If you have been the object of an appraisal, did you disagree with the rating? If it was a negative rating, did you have your job downgraded, your wages lowered, or a promotion denied? To build an age discrimination case, a lot depends on whether the downgrading hit people at all age levels. If there is any change in the appraisal system, make sure you are fully informed. Keep an eye out for any language or actions that appear to hit a greater percentage of older workers than younger workers.

Another signal of possible age discrimination by your employer is lack of employee training and education opportunities. This could seriously affect your longevity with the organization. Does it appear that the younger workers, or a preponderance of younger workers, seem to get most of the seminars, outside courses, and the like? Does your boss put you off when you inquire about keeping up with new training opportunities? Batten says this whole field of training and education opportunities could come under attack during the 1980s. The reason is clear. Many older workers are faced with a Catch-22 situation. They're put off by superiors when it comes to getting in on learning new technologies, new tricks of the trade. Yet when it comes time for a performance appraisal, they're labelled "out of touch."

KEEPING YOUR MIND
TUNED UP

In order to remain vital to your employer you've got to keep up with new knowledge in your field. Keep your mind going. It's too easy to become discouraged and accept the tenuous theory that younger people have more of a right to training than you do. Many employers these days have education programs which reimburse you for tuition and other expenses incurred in taking outside courses related to your job. You should take advantage of any tuition reimbursement program and, when you do take courses, be sure they're noted in your employment record. Don't be shy. If outside education programs are not offered by your employer, business association, technical society, or union, take some courses anyway and have them noted in your record.

"If you begin to see any evidence that the youngies and not the oldies are getting most of the education and training gravy," says Batten, "then you might have a good case of age discrimination." If so, you should try to get together with other older employees and consult with a lawyer. Or, forewarned, you might want to make quiet plans to shift to another employer who gives a better break to older employees. In some cases, if you can pull it off, it's better to switch than fight.

FOUR STEPS IN FIGHTING BACK

But, let's say you want to investigate the possibility of fighting back. Here are the steps Batten says you should take:

1. *Self Appraisal.* Make a hard-nosed appraisal of your situation at work. Is it really the employer's fault that you're being downgraded, put off or pushed out? Get some of your fellow employees to give their honest opinions. Don't just seek the opinions of your closest friends and family. Are you, in fact, just putting in time? If you don't measure up, you can either get cracking or investigate the possibility of switching to another job.

"You have to be honest with yourself," says Dr. Harry Levinson, head of Levinson Associates consulting firm and an industrial psychologist at Harvard Medical School. He offers this advice:

"Analyze your skills and capabilities as you grow older. Don't get yourself into a bind. You need to make a realistic appraisal of yourself. If you don't, you'll keep getting into trouble. Do what you do best. If you get into work you can't handle, you might blame the problems on other people. You think you're a victim of prejudice because you are old. You become irritable, hostile and lead an anxious life."

2. *Get a Lawyer.* If you have analyzed your situation and find that you are doing a good job, not just "hanging on," then you'll need legal help. Basically, you have two choices. You can go to a private attorney and explain why you think you're a

victim of age discrimination. Or, you can go to the nearest office of the Equal Economic Opportunity Commission (EEOC) and talk to a government lawyer. Consultation with government attorneys might be helpful in the preliminary stages without filing a complaint. When you file a complaint, the government has to start an investigation and this might tip off your employer that all is not well.

Whatever you do, you've got to do it within a certain deadline after your employer hits you with some form of age discrimination. In general, you must file a complaint within 180 days after the alleged violation. Technically, you might be able to file a complaint up to 300 days later, if your state has an age-discrimination statute. Your lawyer should be aware of the filing deadline for making a complaint to the government.

In a case where an employer is trying to force you to retire, you might be better off going to a private attorney who specializes in labor law. Because there are relatively few lawyers around who thoroughly understand the age-discrimination laws, it's important to shop carefully. Perhaps your local bar association can give names of labor-law or age-discrimination specialists. A university law school or a union office could also be of help.

In the process of filing a complaint, you may have to seek out other employees who have similar complaints to see if you can develop enough preliminary evidence to warrant a class action suit. Your attorney might be willing to take on this kind of a case, or even a good single-action case, on a contingency basis. If you win, your attorney gets a portion of the damage award. And, the damages can be considerable. According to Gilbert Drucker, a Labor Department attorney who has handled many age-discrimination cases for the government, one man in Milwaukee was awarded $240,000. Broken down, it came to: $160,000 double damages (two times his $80,000 back wages), $30,000 for "pain and suffering" and $50,000 for attorney's fees. If that had been a class action suit, Drucker says, the total award could have been up in the millions of dollars.

3. *Government Help.* If your case is not based on being forced to retire or if your employer is not some major corporation which is prepared to fight any and all age-discrimination cases at the onset, you might want to file a complaint with the EEOC. The government lawyers might have a better shot at a case where you were denied employment because of your age or were denied training and education opportunities. The government can subpoena an employer's files to determine if there are hiring and training patterns that show age discrimination. If only a small percentage of employees who are hired or get into training programs are above age 40, it could be a relatively easy case to prosecute or settle out of court.

The big advantage in going to the government for help, of course, is the fact that it's free. And, the government can use its clout to bring your employer in for conciliation hearings. More often than not, your employer may not understand the intricacies of the age-discrimination laws and might agree to taking you back, not forcing you to retire, giving you a promotion, giving you training opportunities, or whatever. You get what you want and you don't have to go through the anxiety and possible expense of a long court action.

After sixty days, if the government's efforts on your behalf come to naught, you can hire an attorney to take your own legal action. As a matter of fact, you might want to have your own attorney represent you at the hearing with your employer and ride herd on the government to hustle things along (government actions do tend to drag on).

These, then, are the steps you have to take to analyze your situation, gather evidence and seek help from an attorney—private or government. Of course, fighting back is not always necessary. Knowing your rights, you might be able to reason with your employer—especially if you have a group of other employees backing you up. You might be able to show how well older workers can solve problems, save money, make money, be dependable, and otherwise make your employer happy.

4.   *Prepare Examples for Your Boss.* In this respect, it might be worthwhile to take a look at how some employers have successfully used older workers and have, for all practical purposes, done away with ageism in employment. You might give your employer a copy of this book and put a paperclip on this page.

CHORES FOR OLDER WORKERS

One of the best examples to show your employer is the Polaroid Corporation's handling of older workers at its headquarters in Cambridge, Massachusetts. "In effect, we did away with any mandatory retirement age before the age-70 amendment even became law," says Joe Perkins, corporate retirement manager for Polaroid. Pitney Bowes in Stamford, Connecticut, TRW in Euclid, Ohio, and several other companies have done away with mandatory retirement age. Bankers Life and Casualty Company, in Chicago, for decades has had no mandatory retirement age.

But, Polaroid goes a lot further than the abolition of mandatory age retirement. The company has set up a wide variety of choices for older workers. They might work full-time, part-time, flex-time (flexible hours), share-time (pairing up with another worker) or even "rehearse" retirement with a firm promise of getting their old jobs back if they don't like the life of leisure.

On the theory that an older worker might want to keep on working, but take it a bit easier, Joe Perkins was asked about the popularity of working part-time past 65. "When some of our people started working part-time," Perkins says, "they found that they lost a lot of clout. Things were not the same, their influence was lost." He says some companies are having trouble selling part-time work to older employees for this very reason. However, some laboratory technicians and engineers at Polaroid, Perkins adds, "seem to like the part-time idea because they work on projects and retain their influence and clout. . . . Instead of working twelve projects a year, they work six or so and have plenty of extra time off for other ventures."

So, before you get into some sort of part-time deal with your employer, as a way of tapering off, think about the clout question. If it doesn't bother you, fine. If it does, then stick with full-time work and try to negotiate for longer vacations in lieu of pay raises.

In Polaroid's retirement "rehearsal" program, employees are offered a three-month leave of absence without pay. More often than not, they have accumulated some savings and in some cases can start receiving Social Security checks to help defray expenses. At the end of three months, the employees have the option of returning to their old job—no strings attached—or continuing on in retirement. How many come back? "It's about 50-50," says Perkins. "Some say retirement drives them crazy and others say they love it."

How do Polaroid's older workers stack up in comparison with younger workers? "We find that the people who want to continue working are almost always highly motivated, healthy workers," says Perkins, boasting that they have "an absentee-ism record that's twice as good as the record for younger workers." It's interesting to note, Perkins says, that "people who don't want to work or don't feel too well, take themselves out of the game. It's a self-selective process." So much for the "dead wood" theory at Polaroid. It doesn't happen. Bankers Life and Casualty reports the same thing. Apparently, you don't have to push people out. They tend to take themselves out when they don't feel like working anymore or don't feel up to the job. Employers take note.

At TRW's defense and space systems company on the west coast, some management and technical people are allowed to take more time off from work in their later years instead of getting pay increases. They can use the time to start their own businesses or take on other activities. As a rule, the older employee comes in two or three days a week as an in-house consultant. The company gets the employee at specific times to work on problem-solving, while the rest of the time is open for other things. One older engineer runs a golf driving range business and does consulting for other organizations that don't compete with TRW.

At Pitney Bowes, some older employees are kept on as teachers or "mentors" for younger workers. "We will assign a promising rookie to work with one of our wise older heads for a year or so," says a Pitney Bowes personnel officer. Apparently, some older employees have a knack for turning rookies into potential top management talent.

Pitney Bowes also has an educational assistance program that gives employees and their spouses financial aid to develop second careers or other interests when they eventually leave the company. At IBM, older employees can sign up for the Retirement Education Assistance Program (REAP) where you can take any series of courses you want in order to start your own business or sharpen second career skills. You get up to $500 a year.

In England, the Rubery Owen Company, which manufactures engineering equipment, set up a subsidiary called "Sons of Rest Workshop" which is restricted to workers who retire from the main plant and workers who just want to slow down. The subsidiary turns out protective clothing for industry and tubular steel furniture and does some sub-contracting work from the main plant. Many older employees continue to work in the subsidiary, at their own pace, on into their seventies. "The efficiency and motivation of the older workers," says a company official, "cuts costs and makes the project a profitable venture."

Inspired by the Rubery Owen project, the Philips Corporation in Holland helped start up a cooperative business for older employees. It's called *Sterk door Werk* ("Strength through Work"). Philips, a major manufacturer of electrical equipment and appliances, provided start-up loans and technical assistance to help get things going. The cooperative has done pioneer work in miniature machines and produces electronic equipment for teaching aids. Employees work three hours a day, five days a week. Morning and afternoon shifts handle a day's production. Absenteeism is almost nonexistent and the cooperative has paid off its debt to Philips—with interest. It's a moneymaker, and the older employees, who run the whole show, divide up the profits. The idea is catching on. These are just a few examples of what some European and American employers are doing to make better use of their older workers. How does your employer compare? Do older workers get fair and equal treatment? If not, you might have to consider looking elsewhere—a subject that will be covered in the next chapter.

CHAPTER 4

A NEW LEASE
ON WORK

You've heard the phrase: Getting a new lease on life. What about getting *a new lease on work*? For most of us, our work is what we are. Rightly or wrongly, in this country, people want to know what you *do* so they can decide *who you are*. But there's more to it than just snobbism. "A man's occupation," says Dr. Daniel J. Levinson in his book, *The Seasons of a Man's Life* (Knopf), is one of the primary factors determining his income, his prestige, and his place in society."

Work gives men and women some meaning to their lives, whether it's raising a family, climbing a career ladder, or practicing a trade. Finding some meaning in our work becomes even more important as we grow older. We want to achieve at least some of our youthful goals and we want to leave some mark—a ripple on the pond. "The striving to find meaning in one's life is the primary motivational force in man...This meaning is unique and specific in that it must, and can be, fulfilled by you alone...Only then does it achieve significance." So says Dr. Viktor Frankl, professor of psychiatry at the University of Vienna, in his classic book, *Man's Search for Meaning* (Pocket Books). After quoting Neitzsche, Dr. Frankl explains: "He who has a *why* to live can bear with almost any *how*." He explains that "man does not simply exist, but always decides what his existence will be, what he will become in the next moment."

You might not be feeling very good about the "next moment" because you're in a rut or are bored out of your skull. You know you have *something* to offer but what, where, how? As long as you're not spending extra time in front of the TV tube or making more trips to the bar, it's good to suffer some pangs of guilt and frustration about the direction of your life. "To become generative (getting out of a rut)," says Levinson, "you must know how it feels to stagnate, to have a sense of not growing, of being static, stuck, drying up, bogged down in a life full of obligations and devoid of self-fulfillment."

So it's okay to be in a rut and to anguish awhile, but it's not okay to stay there. You might get used to it and become glazed over by the drifting, the lack of tension. "I consider it a dangerous misconception of mental hygiene," says Dr. Frankl, "to assume that what man needs is equilibrium—a tensionless state. What man actually needs is *not* a tensionless state but rather the striving and struggling for some goal worthy of him."

CAREER SWITCHING

If you feel your striving and struggling at some paid job (or at home as an unpaid housewife) is not a worthy cause and not really what you want to do for the rest of your life, then investigate the possibility of switching careers—getting *a new lease on work*. Aside from being dull and unsatisfying, your current job might become increasingly dangerous as your primary means of financial and emotional support in any of the following three situations. First, as we have seen in Chapter 6, some employers are hell-bent on retiring you early, whether you like the idea or not. Or you may be a housewife whose children have moved on out into college or work and thus feel "retired" already as far as your community image is concerned. Or, your job may be in danger five or ten years from now because your employer is in a field that's becoming obsolete or a victim of increasing competition. RIF means Reduction In Force. Don't let it happen to you. Look down the road ahead and see what's waiting for you. If you don't like what you see, then start making plans to avoid it. Don't just sit back and wait for things to crash.

When you make your list of the kinds of jobs you'd like to have, jobs that could take you on into your later years, don't overlook your current place of employment. It's not always easy to switch around in the place where you work, but give it a try. "Most employers," says career counselor John C. Crystal, "simply can't understand that you might be able to do some other job and do it better. They find it easier to peg you at what you've always done." Generally, Crystal says, the larger the organization, the harder it is for older employees to move around inside. There are some exceptions, he says, mostly in the high technology industries (electronics, data processing, communications, and business machines).

The secret to switching jobs where you work, says Crystal, "is studying the situation and making a well-thought-out, written proposal to your boss." He cites the case of a woman in her fifties who was working in a hospital as a medical technician. After doing this job year after year—the same thing—she began to hate it. She didn't want to leave the hospital because she wasn't sure of what she could get elsewhere and, frankly, she loved the social network of colleagues and friends she'd built up over the years. After some counseling, Crystal says, the woman discovered what she really liked to do was work with numbers in the field of bookkeeping and accounting. She did all the bookkeeping for herself at home and got quite good at it. She persuaded the hospital management that she could become an excellent financial watchdog for their laboratory accounts. She knew the business and she knew the numbers. The hospital gave her a go at it, and now she has moved up the ladder in the accounting division and is much happier. She's making more money and feels she's really contributing.

GETTING THE BOSS'S ATTENTION

Crystal says "you've got to be willing to try anything to get the boss's attention." He smiles with satisfaction as he recalls the case of one of his "students" who, as an older man, felt he was definitely in a rut at the large, regional bank where he worked. Unlike the woman at the hospital, this man was fed up with numbers and wanted to work with people. Crystal suggested that the man make an appointment with the president of the bank. He advised the man to ask for just fifteen minutes and to say that he was interested in the bank's future, the future of the industry, and how he could be of help in solving any problems.

The president was taken aback (at least his secretary was) but an interview was scheduled for the third week of the next month ("he's a very busy man, you know"). A little nervous, the older employee entered the bank president's office at the appointed time and indicated his interest in knowing what was going on, what the problems were and what he might be able to do to help. Instead of giving him the fifteen minutes he asked for, the president gave him two hours. The chief executive was flattered and impressed that a lower-echelon employee was keenly interested in the bank's progress and problems.

"Guess what the man who didn't like working with figures is doing now?" Crystal asks, and answers the question quickly himself: "He's working at a new job at the bank, a job created by the president. He's working in employee relations where he can use his years of experience to help translate the boss's plans and problems to other employees." There's no talk of retirement now. The man has the job for as long as he wants it, or as long as he can get out the door and go to work. And, he feels he is really doing something meaningful with his life.

LOOKING FOR
UNMET NEEDS

In a situation where a housewife feels her "career" may be stagnating, Richard Bolles points to the famous case of the west coast woman who felt she had to be home every afternoon when her teenagers came home from high school. She had time on her hands and fell to watching the endless lineup of soap operas on television. She got to know all the characters, the plots, everything. When her friends missed a show or two because they were away from home, she would fill them in. More and more friends wanted fill-ins on what happened in the last episode of "One Life to Live," or "As The World Turns." Finally, she started writing down what happened. It occurred to her that she might just have a valuable commodity—soap opera happenings. Her husband staked her the money to buy three TV sets and recorders. She started reviewing all the soap operas and began selling her synopsis service to newspapers. The rest is history. Many papers now take her soap opera dope sheets so readers can fill themselves in on what they missed last week.

"You have to use this kind of discovery method," John Crystal says, explaining that housewives should look for unmet needs and things that bother them about their communities. If there's a need that's not being filled—then fill it. Crystal cites the case of a woman whose children were off in college and at work. She'd brought them up successfully through stormy times, involving problems with drugs, alcohol, and the police. But, as she read her daily paper, she would shake her head with concern at the confrontations between police and youths. Drawing on her experience with her own children and their many friends, the housewife drew up a plan, in writing, for a better way the police department could handle problems with young people. To her surprise, the chief called her in and asked her to elaborate. She ended up counseling the department—for pay—and other departments started signing her up for consulting work. Now, she's a "specialist" in police community relations work.

DEFINING YOUR GOALS

These cases are spectacular, and John Crystal is the first to admit they're not typical. More often than not, you have to look elsewhere—outside your place of work or your home—to find something more fulfilling to do with your life. You need a long-term plan. "You have to define your goals," Crystal explains, "up to the day you die." He suggests writing your own obituary, putting down all the things you would like to accomplish before you die. Start from the end and work back to the present. The main thing is to discover what you really want to do with the rest of your life. Once you've discovered what you really want to do—as opposed to what you think you ought to do—then aim yourself in that direction.

Naturally, John Crystal can reach into his case files and come up with a good example to illustrate what he means when he insists that you should do what you really want to do. "This man," says Crystal, "worked with an auto parts company and felt he had definitely peaked and wanted out. . . . But, he didn't know where to go or even how to get out." After analyzing how he spent his time on what he liked to do, the man discovered that he was an antique, art, chinaware, and tapestry buff. He spent most of his "free" time going to museums, art shows, and antique shops. He knew values, names, histories—the works. "So why is this guy spending most of his free time in the art business and not getting paid for it?" Crystal always likes to ask this type of question when people tell him what they really like to do. You guessed it. The art buff is now working for a major auction house, combining his "free time" passion for paintings with his past business experience.

ANALYZING YOUR SKILLS

In order to get paid for doing what you love to do in your free time, you have to analyze your skills and present them in such a way that a prospective employer will see that you can solve problems and save money. Self-analysis is crucial. You've got to reach into your head and come out with the things you do best and what you really like to do. A good way to start is to read a book on career self-analysis. One of the best, in my opinion, is Richard Bolles's book, *What Color Is Your Parachute?* (Ten Speed Press). Then, if you want to delve further into the inner workings of the science of career-changing, read Bolles' and Crystal's textbook called *Where Do*

I Go from Here with My Life? It's a "life planning manual" published by Ten Speed Press.

For the basics of getting an employer's attention and writing "qualifications briefs" (don't call them résumés), read Richard Lathrop's *Who's Hiring Who?* It, too, is published by Ten Speed Press, which seems to have cornered the market on career books. In case you can't find some of these books, the address for more information is: Ten Speed Press, Box 7123, Berkeley, CA 94704. Lathrop's book is good for career changers as well as housewives going back to work and children or grandchildren who may be looking for their first full-time job.

Another good book on self-analysis and career change is *Making Vocational Choices: a Theory of Careers* (Prentice-Hall), written by career counselor John L. Holland. Bolles recommends Holland's book in his own book. Others that I have found to be worthwhile are: *Go Hire Yourself an Employer*, by Richard Irish. (Doubleday), *Successful Midlife Career Changes*, by Paula Robbins (Amacom) and *The Hidden Job Market*, by Tom Jackson and Davidyne Mayleas (Times Books). Look them over. Some fit certain personalities better than others.

DOING WHAT YOU REALLY WANT TO DO

As for the art of analyzing one's self to discover what you really want to do, Dick Bolles sums it up this way:

"We need to look back and see when we were (and are) enjoying life—and precisely what activities we were doing at that moment, what skills or talents we were employing, what kinds of tasks we were dealing with, what kind of accomplishments were being done, and precisely what was turning us on."

To get started, Bolles suggests writing a very informal diary of your entire life. Include everything—your work, your spare time, your skills, what made you happy, unhappy. As we have seen, in the case of the man who was an art and culture buff in his spare time, your own spare time could be more revealing than all the job-work you've done. Strength of desire is what counts. *do what you really want to do.* It sounds so simple. But, all too many of us do not work—for pay—at what we really like doing. Make it a major goal for the rest of your life. *Work (for pay) at what you really like doing.*

FIVE STEPS TO A NEW JOB

Unfortunately, many people go about it the wrong way. They dust off a bio, résumé or curriculum vitae and mail it out to one and all. This, nine times out of ten, is a monumental waste of time. "Some companies," says Bolles, "receive as many as 250,000 resumes in a year. And the key word for personnel departments (and executive secretaries) is not selection, but *elimination.*" Bolles says there's no short cut. He lists these steps:

1. Decide exactly what you want to do (using the various above-mentioned books for self-analysis techniques).

2. Decide where you want to do it (within your own organization, in another organization, or even in another part of the country).

3. Research the organizations that interest you. Interview their top people—not for a job, but for information about their problems, where they think their business is going. (Remember the man who interviewed the bank president?)

4. Approach the one individual in each organization who has the power to hire you for the job you have decided you want. (They might even create a job for you.)

5. Present the prospective employers with a well-written proposal of what you can do for the organization, using your various skills, to solve problems, save money and make money.

All this takes time. It may take months, even a year or two. But, says Bolles, "a frantic hurry to get the whole job over with can be deadly." Do your homework. Make a job out of it. Consider it the most important research work you've ever done.

THE RETRAINING MYTH

There's no magic button you can push, no easy way out. So, beware of the "retraining trap." The great cry today is "retraining." Just go back to school and presto! You've got the key to a new job, a new career. Needless to say it usually doesn't work so easily.

Of course, once you get into another job or another field, you might find that you could use some specific course to move into a particular slot that requires it. If so, your new employer will probably pay for it.

The retraining myth is a knee-jerk reaction to technological change. "Get retrained and get a new job" is the slogan. It should be: "Get a new job and *then* get some training (if need be)." Housewives sometimes fall prey to the "get-a-course" trap. What most employers really want is not a list of courses, but hands-on, practical skills and experience presented in a way they can use to tackle specific problems. This doesn't mean you shouldn't take a course to polish an old skill or enrich your life. Not at all. You've got to keep your mind active, keep it challenged. Take courses, by all means, but don't suddenly decide you want to get into a certain career and think that just taking a course is the answer.

THE PENSION MYSTIQUE

Another myth about switching jobs is the "pension mystique." You hang onto a dull job because of the pension—the "golden handcuffs." You say: "Just a few more years." By the time you get the pension, you might have bored yourself to death. Naturally, if you just have one or two more years before you become eligible for a lot of money—no strings attached—then, by all means hang in there. While you're waiting, though, you might be getting your "next career" all lined up by working part-time in the field or doing some volunteer work that's related to it.

Be sure to check with your employer's personnel office or the person who understands the pension program. Perhaps you've already become "vested" for certain benefits. This means you've put in enough time to get at least a percentage of your pension, no matter what, by the time you reach a specific retirement age. You can be long gone from your employer and have your pension checks start coming in at, say, age 62, no matter what you're doing or where you're working.

The law requires that you be given full information on just how much of a pension you're entitled to and how many years, if any, you need for entitlement. It's quite possible that you could switch to another employer, retain some rights to your first pension, and be able to build up enough rights to a second pension.

In some instances, a working couple can build up two, three, even four pensions by the time both decide to call it quits. On top of their multi-pension package, they will be entitled to Social Security benefits. With the mandatory retirement age pushed back to age 70 (maybe even eliminated), you've got more time to build up a second pension.

Figure out how much you could make combining part of your first pension with a second. You might even want to accept a little less in wages on the new job if the work is more exciting and you have a chance to build up a second pension.

As you grow older, certain fields seem to offer more possibilities for second and third careers. One of the best, they say, is in sales. If you are good at selling or if you know a lot about a specific product or subject, you can keep on selling until you drop. What's more, you can often negotiate a work schedule to suit your own pace.

CAREER SWITCHING:
A CASE HISTORY

At age 69, Bill Svidlow was working for the Zale Corporation in Dallas. Bill was the general manager of one of Zale's department stores. When he got tired of running a big store (all the delivery and labor problems), he thought he'd have to retire. Instead, the company offered him a job as a part-time salesman in one of the company's jewelry stores. He comes in three or four days a week and takes plenty of time off, especially in the summer when business is slow. He and his wife like to travel and they do a lot of it in the summer. Zale gets to keep Bill Svidlow's great knowledge of sales and customer relations, and he gets to keep busy at his own pace. "This kind of arrangement suits me just fine," Bill says, adding "if you like your work and you can find ways to still get the job done, you should never quit."

A man who retired from the Postal Service got into sales through another route. All his life, he had been a stamp collector. He became an expert and knew the values of all kinds of stamps. He was hired as a salesman for a major stamp dealer and is now working at what was once his hobby. He had never been a salesman before, but his knowledge of stamps quickly turned him into "one of the best in the business," according to his boss.

A Word of Warning: Watch Out for Career Charlatans

People who want to change careers, especially men who feel they could be doing something bigger and better in some other organization, may fall prey to the promotion and promises of the career charlatans. These hucksters trade on the fact that you're vulnerable and have doubts about job hunting. You probably haven't had to sell yourself as a prospective employee for years and you're intimidated by all the stories about how difficult it is to get another job when you're in your forties or fifties.

You see an ad in the paper or a magazine that sounds like just the thing you need. The ad usually plays on the word "executive" or "professional" and insists that you can get a terrific new job if only you use the huckster's "proven system" for marketing your experience.

"I signed up with an agency that said it was looking for people who wanted to get into 'executive' jobs at good salaries. Eventually, I paid out more than $3,000 and never got a job...not even a nibble."

This lament comes from a middle-aged man who fell for an ad that said: "Our business is placement... We avoid false-hope promises in favor of reality." The only "reality" is all too clear. The man was taken. The more some company or agency promises to get you a high-sounding job, the more you should run, not walk, in the other direction.

"The legitimate placement agencies," says Richard Hill, executive director of the National Association of Personnel Consultants, "never charge the applicant a fee until a job has been found and accepted. Sometimes no fee is charged to the applicant—the employer pays."

As a rule, in the higher-paying jobs, the employer pays the fee. In true "executive search" organizations, says John Schleuter, director of the Association of Executive Recruiters, "the employer always pays—always."

Read the contract offered by a "search" company and compare it with the much looser language in the advertising (or the verbal promises). You'll no doubt find a disclaimer down somewhere in the fine print that says: "No placement is guaranteed." Many states and some cities have licensing laws for placement agencies. Ask about the agency's license. If there is a license and it does not say the agency is in the "placement" business, watch out.

Be sure you know who pays what fee under what circumstances. When an employer pays the fee in some instances, you may have to pay a portion of the amount if you leave the employer before a specific deadline. Usually, it's from three to six months.

Be aware that there are basically four types of employment or search agencies:

1. PLACEMENT. These are usually referred to as employment agencies. Except in Vermont, Mississippi, and Alabama, licensing is enforced. You never pay a fee except, perhaps, a small registration fee, until you get a job. Often the employer pays. Some employment agencies have branched out into "search" organizations that recruit for certain employers. Applicants are not charged for this kind of "search" matchup.

2. EXECUTIVE RECRUITING. These people are sometimes called "headhunters" and are paid by employers to find special employees, usually for management or professional jobs. Sometimes these recruiters work on a retainer, sometimes the employer pays the fee when someone is hired. In neither case do applicants pay a fee. Job seekers' résumés and interviews are welcomed, but no "placement" is ever promised.

3. EXECUTIVE COUNSELING. These organizations do not officially promise to get you a job (read the contract). Some help you prepare yourself for getting a job and mail out your résumés (which they offer to slick up). Some job seekers swear by them, others swear at them. You take your chances.

4. TEMPORARIES. You work for the agency, which "rents" you out temporarily to employers. They're great for housewives, students, and others who want to work part-time or want to explore other career possibilities on a part-time, sampler basis.

CHAPTER 5

HOUSEWIVES: AN ENDANGERED SPECIES

What you've read in the preceding chapter can, for the most part, be applied to men or women. Women who are working full-time outside the home pretty much face the same problems of retirement and switching careers as men face. You might argue that women, as a class, face tougher problems than men because they tend to have lower-paying jobs and less interesting jobs. But this situation is changing. There are many more women these days with good jobs who want to keep on working. There are also plenty of women today who want to switch to a second career, and there are more opportunities for such women than ever before.

But, there is one kind of woman, perhaps a dying breed, who does face different problems than those encountered by men. This is the full-fledged, full-time, battle-scarred house-wife. She has *worked* all right, but our society doesn't consider her a "worker," primarily because she doesn't get paid. If she were to be paid according to her contribution to society, she would be getting a handsome salary indeed, according to economist-author John Kenneth Galbraith in his book *Economic and Public Purpose* (Houghton Mifflin).

"The conversion of women into a crypto-servant class was an accomplishment of the first importance. Menially-employed servants were available only to a minority of the pre-industrial population; the servant-wife is available, democratically, to almost the entire present male population. Were the workers [housewives] so employed, subject to pecuniary compensation, they would be by far the largest single category in the labor force. The value of the services of housewives has been calculated, somewhat impressionistically, at roughly one-fourth the total Gross National Product. The average housewife has been estimated to do work, at wage rates for similar employments, worth about $13,364 a year [around $22,000 in today's dollars].... The servant role of women is critical for the expansion of consumption in the modern economy. That it is so generally approved, some recent modern dissent excepted, is a formidable tribute to the power of the convenient social virtue."

Since Galbraith wrote this stinging analysis of the value of a housewife, more and more women have left homemaker jobs for full-time work. They either needed the money or were fed up with being declared second-class citizens by a society that only values "paid" work.

Even though economist Galbraith says you're worth a mythical $22,000 a year as a housewife, that's all it is—mythical. You may have real money problems ahead if you're "just a housewife." If career men and women face the problem of a retirement squeeze-out, so do you, as Tish Sommers, president of the Older Women's League Educational Fund explains:

"Women who are predominantly homemakers face 'mandatory retirement' earlier than men, through widowhood, divorce, and the phenomenon described by that phrase 'the empty nest.' Since home-making is not considered work, this is not recognized as a lay-off. These middle years are the most vulnerable for a dependent woman because there are no cushions for her occupation. She is not yet entitled to Social Security and other benefits payments or services designed for the so-called elderly."

PLANNING FOR
YOUR FUTURE

The first step away from dangerous dependency on one's husband and one's home, is to get comfortable about planning for your future. Not *his* future, yours. "Somewhere along the line," Tish Sommers says, "you're going to move from dependency to self-sufficiency—the sooner, the better."

How do you go about lining up satisfying, paid work that can provide financial and emotional security? For the answer, Activist Sommers explains in detail:

"First you have to make a search. It seems like there's a big smorgasbord of opportunities. It's almost overwhelming. But, the options aren't really there. They just seem to be. For older women, this is a period very much like a second adolescence. Suddenly, a woman is trying to figure out what she wants to do with her life.

"This is a period in your life to start taking women's courses in confidence and assertiveness. If you can do this while you are still married and have a solid economic base, so much the better. You can try the volunteer route [more on this in Chapter 6] but do it differently than it's usually pictured. Work on a volunteer job as a stepping-stone toward a paid job in the field you've selected. It can build your confidence because it's less threatening than a job in the world of paid work.

"At this stage, many women have an unrealistic concept of what the world of work is like. You have to get out there and taste it. You have to be someplace on time and get a routine other than the household routine.

"If you know exactly what you want to do, you're lucky. Perhaps you had a skill or career in the past and now it's just a question of getting back up to speed. If, for example, you were a nurse, you can take some refresher courses and get right back into things. Your acquired homemaking skills can now be blended with your updated technical knowledge to qualify you for an even better job than you had before you were married.

"But many homemakers don't have any solid, premarital skills to polish up. Because they've had children and did pretty well with them, some women think they'd like to work at a paid job that deals with the management of children. They think that they can get into counseling. After all, they say, they've been giving advice to their own children. Then they find that counseling and working with children is an overcrowded field.

"There are ways, however, of breaking into this field. For example, you can get specialized training through a volunteer job in a crisis center or suicide prevention center. This is preferable to going back to some college or university and paying for courses in counseling kids. You take up some expensive line of study and you don't know what you're going to get at the end of it. You've got to experiment in the field that interests you and find out what you really want to do."

"I strongly believe in on-the-job training, either in a part-time job or in a volunteer, contract-job situation. There's a great deal of interest, and government money, now in vocational training for women in non-traditional skills. If a woman is interested in, say, appliance repairs (after all she's probably repaired many things around the house for years), she should contact a community college, local university, or department of education to see what kind of vocational training is available. The government is really looking for women to get into non-traditional skill jobs.

"Women should not overlook the potential for self-employment. Many homemakers have been terrific managers. These women have a lot of life experience and a lot of skills they may not recognize. They've had one career. The fact that they didn't get paid doesn't mean it wasn't work.

"Most of homemaking isn't technical. It's really comparable to business management. The development of service-oriented skills on a self-employment basis is a good way to go. If you have the knack of running your own little business, fine. If you don't, perhaps you can team up with another woman who does. The Small Business Administration, which can be found in the phone-book under U.S. Government, has some money set aside to help women (as a minority) start small businesses. The SBA is also a good source for information and pamphlets. Check with women's centers in community colleges and universities in your area. There's a big push on now, as part of the women's movement, to help women start up businesses or upgrade job skills."

At this point, I asked Tish Sommers about the problem with husbands who say they want their wives to work but who don't really mean it. How can husbands help their wives to become more economically self-sufficient? Tish Sommers replies:

"More and more husbands want to see their wives happy but, still, some of them hate to give up that nice maid and nurse they've had all these years. Most women have adapted themselves to their husbands' lifestyles. There's a lot of insecurity there, particularly for older women [Tish Sommers is in her mid-sixties]. These women need a lot of patience, support and positive reinforcement. But, not too much heavy advice. My advice to husbands is this: Helping your wife move from dependency to self-sufficiency is part of your job. It's helping her to become a self-sufficient widow if need be. Give enough help, but not so much as to smother her efforts. Don't take over.

"If a woman has trouble getting her husband to go along, she might try one of the many assertiveness courses that are being offered by universities, community colleges and local chapters of women's organizations. Some of these courses are good. Some aren't. In some, you can learn to be open and free and say what you really feel—diplomatically. There are many women who have repressed their own feelings and are afraid to say how they feel about a husband's lack of support or too much support. They don't know how to say 'bug off' in a nice way. You can actually learn how to help your husband help you. If you're not comfortable with the assertiveness training and find it too brash, drop it, or modify it to suit your own needs. There are books on the subject. Ask your librarian about it."

As a husband, I have some advice to offer other husbands—men who may not understand the value of having a wife who can earn her own money. First off, if you feel reluctant to spend money helping your wife develop job skills, consider lowering your own life insurance. When a wife can earn her own living, you just don't need as much life insurance. Investing in your wife's job skill development is one of the best investments you can make.

Once your wife is working, you might have a chance of building up double pensions. But, a word of warning: When a husband and wife are both making money, it's dangerous to live up to the combined incomes. If anything happens to either one of you, you're in trouble. Put a certain percentage of each partner's paycheck into savings. Chances are you might have to live off just one reduced pension someday and the drop in income (from the double paychecks) could be considerable.

Rosalind Barnett and Grace Baruch, psychologists at Brandeis University, are working on a National Science Foundation study of "Women In the Middle Years." In their research, the psychologists are finding that husbands often control their wives through the family purse strings. The husband feels the family money is *his* because he "earned" it. If the wife needs money to get some training for work, an assertiveness course or simply money for transportation and lunch to cover a stepping-stone volunteer job, she has trouble getting it. "We can't afford it," is the answer.

Even when husbands are supportive, some wives may find that all they can find on short notice are the typical dead-end jobs that bring in very little money. They don't have enough work experience to get the better jobs. Paying for training courses is not always the answer. Building up skills through carefully prescribed volunteer work can provide valuable on-the-job experience, and you don't have to pay to get it. How to use volunteer experience as a stepping-stone to a good-paying job is the subject of the next chapter.

CHAPTER 6

VOLUNTEER CONTRACTS

When you think of a volunteer job, you usually envision things like stuffing envelopes for a fund drive or driving some elderly person to the doctor or church. There are thousands of volunteer jobs, however, and an increasing number of them involve skilled work in a wide variety of career fields. Instead of just doing whatever volunteer work that comes along, you can design a career transition around a carefully selected volunteer contract job.

A volunteer work-contract can be a shrewd escape ploy if you know what you're doing. You don't just "give," you get something in return. You get experience in a field you're investigating, and, quite often, your volunteer job can be a stepping-stone into another career. In many instances, working at a volunteer job is actually better than getting a graduate degree. It's a lot easier to combine the volunteer work with your current job schedule—and it's free.

"When you go after a good volunteer job, one that has

lots of possibilities for career training," says Tom Quiesser, a management consultant who specializes in nonprofit organizations, "you have the ultimate in bargaining power." Because you're giving your time and your skills for free, you can demand a contract volunteer job that is spelled out to your liking and that has convenient hours.

FINDING A GOOD VOLUNTEER JOB

Where do you look for a good volunteer job? All around your community. Talk with friends to see what kind of volunteer work they're doing or know about. Check with people you do business with: your banker, insurance agent, accountant, lawyer, doctor or any friend who is involved in the type of work you enjoy. Pretty soon you'll hear of something that's exciting, something that's in the field you want to enter. Volunteer jobs are not restricted to charities. They can be found in all sorts of nonprofit organizations dealing with politics, the environment, housing, conservation, solar and alternative energy, better government, taxes—everything imaginable.

You might check with your Voluntary Action Center or whatever local organization that concerns itself with coordinating volunteer work. Los Angeles, for example, has a computerized system with thousands of volunteer jobs in the bank. It gives you the organizations, what they do, the neighborhoods they operate in and the types of jobs that are open. Boston has a unique organization called the Civic Center and Clearinghouse (CCCH) which matches personally-screened candidates with a wide array of volunteer jobs.

Herta Loeser, CCCH co-director, initiated "Project Re-Entry," a nine-month program for women who have been out of the labor market for some time and don't have much recent paid work experience. The women who come into the Clearinghouse eventually work as unpaid interns for six to eight months. They receive group and individual counseling and on-the-job training in their carefully structured internship placement. The main purpose of the Project is to take each woman carefully through the internship on out into a paid job in a field she has selected and which promises promotion and upward mobility.

VOLUNTEER INTERNSHIPS: A CASE STUDY

Herta Loeser points out how such a volunteer internship worked for a middle-aged, divorced woman named Annette. After raising a family, Annette found herself without a husband and with no job skills. She was frightened and depressed, with no idea of how she could find a decent job. Annette said that before she was married, she had been trained to work in biology. Project Re-Entry counselors arranged for her to work with newborn babies in a Boston hospital as a volunteer. She was able to apply her biology background to the volunteer job and did a lot of reading on the subject.

Annette worked up the ladder as a hospital volunteer. After six months or so, the hospital offered her a paying job with more responsibilities. The hospital is also paying for the extra training Annette needs in computer technology to go with her biology background.

Even though the initial placement is as a volunteer, Herta Loeser requires that each of the Project Re-Entry interns get a legal contract from the employing organization. In the contract, the work is spelled out and the training is carefully outlined by the supervisor designated. In addition, the intern gets a "transcript" showing what work was done and what skills were used. This kind of a job description and transcript is of great help in eventually landing a paid job. Employers can easily see the kind of work experience a candidate has gained through volunteer work.

Contract volunteer work is not just for housewives coming back into the job market. Tom Quiesser says "working men and women can also explore new career possibilities through volunteer work." Most organizations are pleased to have employees take on some sort of volunteer assignment. It performs a civic duty and is good public relations. You may even get a little extra time off. You keep your regular job (and pay) and build up experience in your new field through the volunteer connection. If you try going to graduate school to pick up "credentials," you might have to take time off work or even give up your job. This can be costly in actual income or foregone opportunities.

A properly selected volunteer job could give you more responsibility and management training than you're getting from your current job. You might end up managing thirty or forty people and have to handle as much as $1-million a year. It's possible in the volunteer world. It may not be possible in your current job world.

In some cases, a special volunteer job can be created to utilize your talents. If there's something you really want to do, you might be able to sell it to some volunteer organization. which will put you in charge of the new project.

Once you're doing something you really like as a volunteer, it's possible that someone on the board or someone you meet may spot you as a good candidate for some paid position. You've got the skills you brought in from your regular job, the motivation, and, the knowledge of the new field. You might get tapped to take over a job that's just right and pays more than you're currently getting. Or you might conduct your own job search through the volunteer connection. In this strategy you present your paid-work credentials and your new volunteer skills to potential employers you've met on the job. You're actually doing the work that they're interested in, not just talking about it or taking a course in it.

GETTING CREDIT
FOR VOLUNTEER WORK

Some states will even give you civil service credits for specific volunteer work, and a number of colleges and universities are now giving academic credits for volunteer work. To get academic credit, you write a paper on some aspect of your volunteer work and defend it before a panel of professors. If you pass, you get valuable credits toward a graduate degree. All you pay is a small fee for the testing.

To attempt volunteer work as a way into a new career, "you've got to have a positive strategy," says Jerry Kieffer, director of the National Committee on Careers for Older Americans. You have to make a self-analysis, using the techniques outlined in the previous chapter, to find out what you really want to do and then make a serious "job hunt" in the volunteer field. "Some people even advertise their skills for a good volunteer job," Kieffer says.

Another strategy to obtain a volunteer position is to make a deal with some organization that normally doesn't take on volunteers. You offer your skills, part-time, for six months— free. If you do the kind of job you think can be done, and they like you, then they agree to take you on full-time. During the six-month trial period, you work while they see how you can solve problems. Meanwhile, you don't have to leave your other job. You do your new work as a part-time volunteer, working evenings, weekends, or on occasional days off.

The key to all good volunteer jobs is to get into a line of work that really interests you. It could be working with the elderly, working with children, health and medicine, the environment, politics—whatever grabs your interest. If it's what you really like doing, chances are you'll be good at it. Somebody will see your light, spot you as a problem-solver and money-maker for their organization, and you're in.

GOOD SOURCES

For more information on volunteer contracts as stepping-stones to a new career, here are the addresses of two good organizations mentioned in this chapter:

• National Committee on Careers for Older Americans, 1414 22nd St., N.W., Washington, DC 20037. Ask for volunteer action or clearinghouse organizations in your area.

• Civic Center and Clearing House, 14 Beacon Street, Boston, MA 02108. Tel. (617) 227-1762. Ask for their list of books and other publications. They may also know of some volunteer organizations in your area. Please send a self-addressed stamped envelope.

CHAPTER 7

HIGH-DEMAND PORTABLE SKILLS

If a book can have a heart or soul, in this case it would include the concept of developing a high-demand, portable skill before it's too late. When you have a certain skill that brings in good money—anywhere, anytime—you've got financial independence. And, when you've got financial independence, you've got it made.

With a high-demand, portable skill, they can't fire you, retire you, or otherwise push you around. If it's a skill that doesn't require too much physical strength or other attributes that might diminish with age, you can continue practicing it for a long, long time.

Having such a skill gives you a great deal of confidence because it's a skill no one can take away from you. A high-demand, portable skill keeps money coming in as long as you feel like earning it, and, more importantly, it keeps you plugged into society. Because your skill is needed, you are needed. People keep reaffirming the fact that you're needed every time they pay for your skills. Discovering a potential skill, polishing it, and then marketing it is not for everybody. But before you cross it off as an impossible dream, follow me into the homes and shops of high-demand skill people who are making it, are happy, and show every sign of staying that way well on into their later years.

These people have learned a good lesson about financial security: Your most valuable asset is yourself and your workability. The more you invest time and money in developing a skill, the less you can become tyrannized by an employer's retirement policy or by age and sex discrimination. You've got what people want and they pay for it.

Building up such a skill should be considered by people who have a good job now but are not sure how long into their later years the job will last. Such a strategy should also be considered by housewives as an alternative to "just going back to work." If you've got what the market wants, then buyers don't care whether you're a housewife, retired employee, black, white, male, female, old, or young. You've got it. They want it. That's it.

THE GOLD MINE
IN YOUR HANDS

What kinds of skills are in high demand and are portable? "They're usually skills that require the use of your hands to repair things," says Dr. Harry Levinson, industrial psychologist at Harvard Medical School. "These skills," Dr. Levinson explains, "might have been shunned early on in your life because our society gave the repair business a lower status than office work or factory work."

Because of the low status initially given to repair jobs, those people who did enter the field are now a new elite. You have to go to them and you have to pay plenty. A person who is skilled in certain kinds of repairs can usually command enough money to stay ahead of the inflation rate. When retail prices go up, the cost of repairs usually goes up even faster. "If you can use your hands to specialize in some form of high-demand repair work," says Dr. Levinson, "you've got yourself a potential gold mine."

Having repair job skills is also a form of preventive medicine. Repair work brings you into contact with all sorts of people. It keeps your life lively. And, says Dr. Levinson, "using your hands seems to be excellent therapy for warding off depression." Skilled people seem to be happier, work longer and stay healthier than other workers.

Because you have a skill that keeps bringing clients or customers to you, Dr. Levinson says, "it's a form of insurance against the problem of friends and family drifting away from you, or dying, as you grow older." You keep creating a new circle of contacts. Dr. Levinson recalls the example of his own father: "For many years my father kept his tailor shop open even when he didn't make too much money. His shop was on the main street and people would drop in to have something fixed and they'd visit with him."

FINDING A HIGH-DEMAND SKILL

How do you find out what kind of skill you might be able to develop? "Think back to the days of your late adolescence or early childhood," Dr. Levinson says, "to something you could do before you got so well-off working you hired somebody else to do it." You are most likely to make good use of a skill you once had, a skill that may have lain dormant all these years.

When you think back, as Dr. Levinson suggests, try to

remember if you ever fixed your own bicycle, appliances, boats, or furniture. Chances are you were pretty good at something, or showed a tendency to be pretty good. Then, you let it slip away. But, Dr. Levinson says, "the potential talent is still there, tucked back somewhere in your brain."

Obviously, you don't want to devote a good part of your life to a skill that gets you into something you don't like. You don't just do it for the money; you work on a skill that gets you into something you love doing—something that brings you into contact with people in a field that has fascinated you for years. "The idea is to not get too grandiose," says Dr. Levinson. "You don't necessarily have to open up a shop, spend a lot of money and get fancy. The key is the fact that you can do this work yourself, control your own fate, keep in contact with people, and not be caught up trying to meet a series of obligations. You can make some supplemental retirement income (or primary income) and it doesn't require much capital investment."

If you have the capacity to use your hands well and are interested in some special field (sports, bicycles, art work, furniture, and the like), just look around your home and your community to see what needs fixing. See what breaks and what kind of trouble you have getting it repaired. Then, when you've selected one or two fields of interest, poke around and see who does the repair work, how much they're making, and how they got started. Don't worry about how much money you make at first. Look at it this way: You're going to graduate school and getting paid for it. Worm your way into the business or trade at hand and find out what's going on. You might learn that the repair work is not all that interesting—too little money for too much work. Or, more than likely, you'll learn that there's plenty of interesting work and there's a niche for you.

There are hundreds of skills you can investigate. You

might be standing right next to one and not recognize it. Some areas to consider are the following: Typewriter repair, report-writing (for businesses and government agencies), Swedish massage, physical therapy, tutoring, crafts, show dog handler, repairing old clocks, fine bookbinding, typing-editing-proofreading, variations on photography. Regarding the last option, one former amateur now makes good money photographing antique furniture and room designs. Look into whatever you're good at, or used to be good at, or whatever fascinates you.

To help stimulate your imagination, here's a sampler of what some successful older workers were able to do with some re-polished skills:

GOLF AND TENNIS

Steve Williams, who runs his own repair business, says "the demand for golf club repair is increasing everyday." As the purchase price becomes more expensive and as more golf courses open up, an increasing number of gold clubs have to be repaired, rebuilt, and cleaned. "You learn by doing," says Williams. You might buy some old, beat-up clubs and fix them, resell them, and get another set to fix. You can start by doing the easier repairs, such as fixing up nicks and scratches and wrapping the grips. For this you don't need expensive equipment, and you can do it in your basement, extra room, or garage. You can also work as an apprentice in a pro shop. "Because it's difficult to send clubs to the manufactures for repairs," says Williams, "the field is wide open."

A retired engineer from Peoria, Illinois, repairs and strings tennis rackets. "There's no formal way to learn," he says, "but you can get some training manuals." One of the best manuals, he says, is published by Associated Tennis Suppliers,

11111-A Flintkote Avenue, San Diego, CA 92121. It's called *Stringing Rackets for Profit* and it shows you how to set up a business, including details on every conceivable type of stringing job—racquetball, squash and badminton.

To be an independent tennis racquet stringer, this man says, you will need gear that costs from less than $200 (portable) to $1,000 (permanent), and you might need up to $200-worth of strings in inventory. You may not need this equipment when you start out, because you can apprentice at a pro shop or store. As a sideline, you can give lessons to beginners and sell all sorts of tennis equipment as a manufacturer's representative. "Best of all," says this ex-engineer, "you get to play on the best tennis courts around town and meet a bunch of great people." When you get good, you can do stringing work for big-name pros when they come through town for tournaments and exhibitions.

BICYCLES

Have you ever wondered who fixes all those ten-speed, multi-geared bicycles with caliper (even disc) brake systems and finicky wheels that need realignment? Bikes are getting to be as complicated as the early automobiles and they need master mechanics to keep them on the road.

"There's a terrific demand for top bike mechanics," says Fred Beachler of the National Bicycle Dealers Association. With gasoline prices on the rise, more and more people are turning to bicycles for commuting as well as for fun. Business is booming, and there aren't enough good repair people around to keep up with demand.

If you have a bike, or used to have one and had a knack for doing your own fixing, you might consider the possibility of becoming a master at repairs. If you do, you can go almost anywhere in the country and your services will be needed. The National Bicycle Dealers' Association is working on repair training programs to be run by regional and local associations. You can get into a training program or just sign on with a harassed bike dealer as a part-time apprentice. If you want more information on the bike repair business and training opportunities, write: National Bicycle Dealers Association, 435 North Michigan Avenue, Chicago, IL 60611.

RESTORATIONS

A lot of people think that someday they can retire and run a little antique shop. It's a nice dream, but the competition can be brutal and you often need quite a bit of capital to get started. Restoring and repairing fine furniture and other fine wares, however, is something else. If you can get good at it, you've got a high-demand, portable skill. A restorer doesn't need the capital required to start up or buy into an antique shop. Furthermore, the demand for service often brings in more money than you could ever make selling the stuff.

Robert Young, who does restoration work in Alexandria, Virginia, says you don't need to limit yourself to working on antiques. "We have a mobile society," he says, "and movers are forever scratching or breaking fine furniture." You can also build furniture to order, such as custom cabinets used for exhibiting china or collectibles. One husband-and-wife team does the full line of restoration and repair work. He does the structure and she does the upholstery.

In order to be a successful furniture restorer, you have to have a feel for working with wood and other materials. As in many other repair careers, there are two routes to success. You can teach yourself by getting books on the subject and help from hardware stores and wood shops. Once you get started you can take woodworking classes and keep moving up. Or you can work as an apprentice with a master restorer or cabinetmaker. While you're thinking about it, don't overlook restoring and repairing glassware, porcelain, and antique jewelry. The main thing is to enjoy what you're doing—and get paid for it.

BOATS AND SKIS

It's often hard to get good, speedy repairs for boats. The number of boats is increasing a lot faster than the people who can repair them. One couple in their early sixties began doing mechanical repairs, painting, and interior design work (custom curtains, bunks, tables, shelves). They have their own boat and now make money doing something they used to pay for.

Downhill and cross-country skiing are popular activities. Skis and the equipment that goes with them are in constant need of repairs. You can apprentice at a ski shop and eventually take courses offered by manufacturers. (You usually have to be sponsored by a ski shop.) Once you get good at it, you can set up your own repair business and follow the snow. Repair work also runs on into the summer and fall because of the backlog. The technology is changing rapidly and ski shops and resorts are on the lookout for first-rate repair hands.

HORSES

The horse business is booming, and more people are needed to instruct all those kids you see around stables and barns. The American Horse Council says there are millions of horses of all breeds trotting around trails and rings and even more millions of riders. There are also all kinds of riding styles—Eastern,

Western, and dressage. You can pick the style that appeals to you.

Were you once a rider? Are you now a rider? If so, you might qualify as an instructor. "Housewives coming back into paid work make excellent instructors," says Gegi Winslett, executive secretary of the American Horse Council's Horse Show Advisory Committee and top instructor, trainer, and horse show judge. Mrs. Winslett is also a housewife who went back to work and did what she wanted to do—be with riders and horses.

"You don't have to be a top rider to be a good instructor," she observes. "You do have to be able to teach—that is, have the ability to transfer your knowledge to another person, have an eye for the horse and rider and what can go wrong, plus relate to your students. Often a good teacher will turn out students that are better than he or she ever was."

Housewives, she feels, make excellent instructors "because they've been through the life-training business with their own children and are usually pretty good, sensitive teachers." Housewives can also relate to nervous mothers (and occasional fathers) who bring in young children for their first lessons. "When you've had your own," Mrs. Winslett says, "parents know you're not going to let their kids get into trouble." She notes that horseback riding is not like other sports such as tennis "because you're dealing with a powerful animal which has a mind of its own, and the situation can be dangerous if you don't know what you're doing."

The way to get started, Mrs. Winslett explains, "is to go back and take lessons from the best pro around. Refresh your riding skills and pick up the new things that have been developed since you used to ride a lot." Then, you contact the best stable you can find and put in your bid to help out with the regular instructors as an apprentice instructor. You eventually are trusted enough to take on a class of beginners and away you go.

One way to find the best stables and trainers is by going to horse shows to see what organizations have the best riders and have the most efficient, business-like operation. Start talking with the riders and introduce yourself to the instructors. "When you see one or two outfits picking up most of the ribbons, the ones that have the most discipline," Mrs. Winslett advises, "you head in that direction and get started with them."

By spending a relatively small amount of money, and perhaps a couple of years working your way up, you could become a good instructor. When you do, your services will be in demand wherever you go. Western riding is now big in the East and all types of English riding are big in the West. There are all sorts of style subdivisions. You can choose whatever style or breed suits your past experience and your present mood. Why pay for riding? They'll pay you.

GUITARS

Americans are buying guitars and other stringed instruments at a phenomenal rate. It's a booming business. The makers of acoustic guitars, electric guitars, mandolins, and banjos can hardly keep up with the demand.

"We're making guitars a heck of a lot faster than we're finding people to repair them," says Jim Bumgardner, a busy guitar repair specialist who lives in the Washington, D.C. area. "If you get good at repairs and know what you're doing," observes Bumgardner, "you can get all the business you care to handle." Bumgardner, who's in his fifties, limits his work to 4½ days a week. He and his wife take off two months out of the year for vacations and travel. "It's a nice life," he says.

Jim Bumgardner became interested in guitars, banjos,

fiddles and other such instruments as a boy "back in North Carolina," where his father had a woodworking shop. "When I was a boy," Bumgardner says, "I got pretty good at fixing up old guitars people threw out." Because he didn't have enough money to buy his own guitars, Bumgardner fixed up old instruments that were ready for the junk heap. He learned to play all sorts of instruments, and he's been playing them ever since.

"I never thought repairing guitars would ever be my life's work," Bumgardner explains as he recalls how he got into the repair business. "I thought you had to go to school and keep moving up into something," he says. He went on into electrical engineering. Eventually he became involved with an outfit that did a lot of government contract work. "I found out that I was working myself to death, up to ten, twelve hours a day on some contracts. I was very unhappy." One day, Bumgardner recalls, with a certain set to his chin, "I just upped and quit. I really didn't have anything in mind except that I knew I couldn't go on working like that." His wife was working for the government, so the Bumgardners did have an income while he looked for something to do with himself.

He remembered how much he enjoyed his life in North Carolina when he was a boy repairing and playing guitars. Bumgardner had kept his hand in over the years by keeping his own instruments in shape and repairing a few instruments for friends.

"I just started working on old guitars and took the samples around to some music stores and well-known guitar teachers, he recalls. They gave him test work and it wasn't long before he was into the repair business and loving every minute of it. He's making just about as much money as he made before, except now he's his own boss and has a skill he says will serve him for many years.

OTHER INSTRUMENTS

Guitars are not the only musical instruments that are in need of repair. Just look around town some Friday night or Saturday afternoon during the football season and see how many high school and university bands you can count. They all use musical instruments that are in constant need of repair, and some music shops might be willing to take on a handy person to learn the trade. You might have to work for minimum wages while you learn. If music is your passion, however, it could pay off. You might be able to repair instruments and later branch out into purchasing them for resale.

Piano tuning is an art and some tuners find old pianos they can refurbish and resell for a good profit. There are a few schools that teach piano tuning and local piano stores or university music departments should have some names.

If you have the capability to develop these types of high-demand portable skills, you can be a lot more independent because, more often than not, employers are looking for you instead of the other way around. The ultimate independence, of course, is not having to work for someone else. How is this possible? You'll find out in the next chapter.

CHAPTER 8

YOUR OWN
BUSINESS

Having a high-demand, portable skill is different from being in business for yourself—in two, sometimes three ways. First, as a rule you need little or no capital investment to build a high-demand, portable skill, whereas often you do need capital investment for a small business. Second, a high-demand portable skill is just that—portable—whereas your own business is usually tied to your home or someplace near your home. A third difference may be that with your own business, you're the entrepreneur, the organization. In a high-demand skill job, however, you may still be working for wages for other people. With hard work, and a little bit of luck, you can build your own little empire and tack your name on it.

TRAITS OF THE
SUCCESSFUL SELF-BOSSER

Not everybody has the motivation or the skill needed to start up and maintain a small business. You might have the traits, however, and not even realize it. According to a report in *Boardroom Newsletter*, Joseph R. Mancuso at the Center for Entrepreneurial Management in Worcester, Massachusetts, says a successful self-bosser often has at least some of these attributes:

1. Oldest child in the family, or the only child.
2. Started work young (ran a teenage or pre-teen business).
3. Has a desire not to work for someone else.
4. Is creative and sets realistic goals.
5. Calculates risks carefully and has difficulty in delegating authority.
6. Has a high ego-need for achievement which can often be traced to a relationship with a father who was probably self-employed.
7. An unusually supportive and understanding spouse or close friend.

This is an interesting list but it's just an indication of some of the important traits. There are lots of variables. Personally, I think having an unusually supportive and understanding friend or spouse is one of the most vital items on the list. It's hard enough trying to break out on your own. But, having a spouse against it, could doom the enterprise.

In my own case, I came close on some of the above items and struck out on the others. I was the third child. I started my own little business, Weaver Communications, Inc. when I was in my mid-forties. I had had a little business when I was a school kid (a neighborhood shoeshine and pick-up-and-delivery service) and my father had started his own business. I feel I'm fairly creative and have realistic goals (I want to keep writing until I burn a fuse or drop dead). I do have occasional problems delegating authority but I've been able to hire excellent assistant editors such as Martha Williams and China Jessup who have helped me greatly with my syndicated newspaper column, television reports, magazine stories, and with research for this book.

The most important person of all in this venture, however, is my wife Vida. Without her strong support, especially in the dark times when business was bad, I would never have made it. She has pitched in to help with reporting and research, and she has been bookkeeper and office manager. When I needed her she was there. Now she's exploring the possibility of developing her own small business, and I only hope I can give as much support as she has given me.

If it's worked right, a husband-and-wife team or a team of two close friends can do a lot to help each other start up a small business. While one is working full-time to keep the money coming in, the other can invest in building their own independent business. Then, when the business begins to bring in good money, the other partner can take more time off, quit, or "retire" and develop a second business or work in tandem with the colleague who already has something going.

Starting your own business is not easy and it's not for everybody. But, consider it. Investigate all the possibilities. If you and your partner can eventually become independent of the organizational world and have the ability to make money on your own, for as long as you want, you've got a powerful financial and psychological force working for you. Nobody can fire or retire you. You're your own boss and, within reason, you can set your own hours and vacation schedules.

STARTING YOUR OWN BUSINESS:
A CASE STUDY

Take the case of Marie (she wants her real name kept anonymous) and her husband. He worked for a management consulting firm. She was home raising a family. After awhile, she became restless. She didn't want to be tied 100 percent to the home and felt that being overly financially and psychologically dependent on her husband could be dangerous someday. She started analyzing her current skills and past passions. She had always liked art in school but was never an artist.

She decided to try pottery because it was a form of art but depended more on mechanical skills. She took courses at a nearby community college. "I didn't go into it necessarily to earn money," she says. "I just wanted to do something creative with my hands." She was impressed by the quality of the community college instruction. The courses cost very little so her initial investment was quite small.

As she began to make her own pottery, she discovered that there weren't any reliable suppliers for professionals. There were the hobby shops, but they didn't have the kind of equipment and materials that professionals need, and the hobby shops were too expensive. Marie began to get in touch with suppliers of kilns, colors, glazes, and other materials to set up her own supplies.

It occurred to her that she might save considerable money buying in bulk and selling to other potters in the area. She eventually made deals with various manufacturers around the country and set up her own supply shop. At this stage, her husband helped with some investment money and technical business advice (accounting, pricing, inventory control, and the like).

Now Marie has three pottery outlets around the country and her husband is working with her. They have something going which will provide financial independence. Other people have been hired to help run the business so she and her husband can vacation when they like. About the future, Marie says "we might continue with the pottery supply business or we might sell it and try something else. We have the options now."

In looking for ideas, you can see how Marie followed her artistic instincts and got into business because she discovered a need that was not being adequately filled. Maybe there's some business that interests you and you can discover a way either to make some component better than a major manufacturer or to supply some service that a bigger organization might not be able to handle as well. "You can often beat the big boys," says management consultant Dick Beckhard, "because you have more flexibility and you don't have the overhead."

GETTING BUSINESS ADVICE

When you start your own business, you may need the help of some professionals such as a lawyer, an accountant and possibly a banker. A good accountant is especially important, because he or she can tell you about all the tax-deduction possibilities a small business presents. You might be able to invest some money in such things as a greenhouse (if you're interested in the possibility of plant sales) or tennis or golf repair equipment. You can write off these expenditures now when you're in a higher income tax bracket and the investment will pay you back when you're older and are in a lower bracket. In a sense, the tax system can finance your initial small business investment. A good accountant who specializes in taxes or a good tax lawyer can explain it further.

These two professionals—accountant and lawyer—can also help you spot some warning flags in a small business investment. Watch out for a business that requires plunking down a considerable amount of money to "get in." Many of these deals are franchises. Some work fine—usually for people who are quite familiar with the field—but others can eat up a lifetime of savings and leave you with nothing to show for it. Never sign any business contract or agreement unless your lawyer and accountant have gone over the whole deal with you, explaining all the possible dangers.

Inventors—real or armchair types—should stay away from the "idea hucksters." These companies promise to evaluate your idea or invention and help you sell it. Somehow every idea seems "great." The Federal Trade Commission investigated several "idea" companies and found that out of 7,000 hopeful inventor applicants, not one made any money. They just kept paying and paying.

There is one notable exception. Actually, it's not a company, but a nonprofit cooperative. If you have an idea for a product or service that might be patented or saleable, you might want to get in touch with Inventors Workshop International, 121 N. Fir Street, Ventura, CA 93001. You pay modest membership dues and you get one free invention evaluation each year. You also get the organization's magazine, *Lightbulb*, which gives details of members' latest ideas and new laws pertaining to inventions. You can also get group legal services for a relatively small annual fee. The organization even has an Inventors Licensing and Marketing Agency as well.

GOOD READING

There are several books on starting up your own business. I have written one, *You, Inc.* (Dolphin) which goes into a lot more detail on how I got started and the psychological and financial problems we all have to face when we go out on our own. The use of "creative moonlighting" is explored as a way of investigating various small business possibilities without making too much of a commitment. As a matter of fact, you get paid while you do the exploring.

A helpful book for prospective self-bossers is called *How*

to Start Your Own Business—and Succeed (McGraw-Hill). It's written by Arthur H. Kuriloff, a specialist in small business management, and John M. Hemphill, Jr., Associate Dean of the School of Business Management, University of California in Los Angeles. Once you've definitely decided on what kind of small business venture you want to plow into, this book can make an excellent "graduate course." You're given step-by-step details on start-up decisions, market testing, production, employees, management skills, financial planning—the works.

You might also be interested in another book, *How to Form Your Own Corporation without a Lawyer for under $50.* Written by Ted Nicholas, a business consultant, it shows how to set up your own corporation and the variety of income tax breaks you get (pension plan, profit sharing, medical plan for yourself and employees). Personally, I think you ought to pay the piper (a lawyer) and get a legal lesson or two on how to stay out of trouble, but the book is valuable as an idea stimulator. For more information, write Enterprise Publishing Co., 501 Beneficial Building, Wilmington, DE 19801.

CHAPTER 9

YOUR HOME IS
YOUR TAX SHELTER

The majority of those over age 45 who are heads of households own their own homes, according to the Census Bureau. No matter whether you're married or single, your home has been your castle (sometimes your dungeon). It has probably been the best investment you've ever made.

You may have lived in your home for some time now, just taking things for granted. Meanwhile, the value of the average home has been going up around 10 percent a year. In some places, like San Francisco, it has even gone up as much as 20 percent a year. In other places, St. Louis for example, home values have increased at a moderate 5 percent a year.

So far, you've probably looked at your home as a money-eater—not a moneymaker. You've been paying the mortgage, the insurance, the taxes, and all those repair and remodeling bills. Money out—no money in. Yet, all the while, your home has been working like a quietly efficient Money Machine. You've been building enormous capital without even realizing it. And, as we've seen earlier in the book, you're going to need all the capital you can get from here on in. If you're not a homeowner, you've got problems. You're not letting the Money Machine work for you. Congress has fixed it so that homeowners get all the tax breaks while renters get worse than zero. Someday in your late-late years you might want to rent for the convenience of it and live off the money your previous home(s) piled up. But don't rent now, or if you do rent, at least talk to a good, tax accountant and get a rundown on how much you might be losing as a renter. You just might be persuaded to buy a condominium or a cottage.

YOUR HOME— HOW SWEET IT IS

Congress, you see, passed a tax law in 1978 which decreed that any homeowner who has reached age 55 is entitled to a one-shot, tax-free profit of up to $100,000 when the home is sold. Money you put into the home as a down payment and money you spent on a whole series of remodelings and additions (not regular maintenance) plus all the sales costs are deducted from the final sales price and are not included in the profit for tax purposes. And, even if your profit, after all the deductions, is more than $100,000, you will probably pay very little tax. This is because under the new law you only have to pay on the first 40 percent of any taxable long-term profit. So, if you made, say, a net profit of $150,000 on your home (not so hard the way prices are going), you'd only have to pay a tax on $20,000. And, because it is a long-term capital gain, you get taxed at the lowest possible rate—lower than the tax you have to pay on interest and dividends, even lower than what you pay on your wages. In other words, you get the best possible tax treatment at the best possible rate. On top of all this, Congress has said that the $100,000 tax-free bonanza will eventually be indexed to the inflation rate, which means it will keep growing. You won't lose any purchasing power. To make $100,000 tax-free these days, says one accountant, you'd have to earn $20,000 a year for seven years ($140,000 minus $40,000 in taxes equals $100,000). It's almost impossible to make this kind of money from stocks, bonds, and savings. After your own moneymaking capabilities and your Social Security and pension benefits, home ownership is your biggest potential source of money to cover your needs in the second half of life.

THE CATCH IN HOME OWNERSHIP

But, there's one big catch, of course. Unless you sell your house, or refinance it at higher interest rates, you can't get your hands on all that money. And, if you sell your home, you've got to move somewhere else. Moving out of a big, "empty nest" is no problem for some older people, but for others it can be an emotionally wrenching experience. After living in one place for some time, you have memories, and roots which shouldn't be downplayed. They can be extremely important.

REMODELLING YOUR HOME FOR PROFIT

For those who want to stay with their old home, Michael Sumichrast, chief economist of the National Association of Home Builders, suggests the possibility of remodeling your home so that part of it can be used as a rental apartment. It depends on whether your neighborhood is zoned for sub-rental properties. Some are, and some aren't. A quick call to your local government zoning office will set you straight.

You might be able to develop an "English basement" with a separate entrance and separate address. At first, one of your children might live in it. Later, you could rent the apartment and get a tax break as well. Even later, when you're older, you might want to move into the easy-to-operate apartment and rent out the main part of the home to a young family or to one of your children. Either way, you get three important pluses: income, tax breaks, and security (someone is more apt to be at home to help guard against burglary, vandalism and fires). For some older people, it's nice having other people nearby. For others, it can be annoying.

If you have a truly large home with at least three floors, you might toy with the idea of converting it into a mini-condominium ("tri minium" or "quadro minium"). This is a major project and needs plenty of advice from an architect-remodeler, a lawyer, an accountant, and a lender or two. Once remodeled to make an apartment on each floor (with separate entrances), your condominium units could be sold for a tidy sum. You select the one you want to keep and put the others on the market. This kind of a deal is usually restricted to larger houses in town or close to town. The zoning has to be right and the market has to be right.

REFINANCING YOUR MORTGAGE

But suppose you reject the remodeling scheme. You may want to get at the money that's already tied up in your house. How do you go about it? You could refinance your mortgage and, because it's probably at a much lower interest rate than the current rates, your lender will welcome you with open arms. Before you sign on the dotted line, however, consider that refinancing can be very risky, even though it does produce thousands upon thousands of dollars of instant cash. "Refinancing your home is a bad idea when mortgage rates are very high," says financial counselor Jim Bly, "especially if you plan to live in your home for quite awhile. If you can't get a solid investment that makes nearly as much money as the current mortgage rate, don't do it."

Bly and others do point out some exceptions to the "don't do it" rule. If you are in a fairly high tax bracket and plan to sell your home within five or six years anyway, it might not be a bad idea to refinance now, get the tax breaks, and invest the cash in another home as a rental property (perhaps even the smaller home you eventually plan to move into). You'll be paying a much bigger monthly mortgage bill, but you'll be ahead of the game on the tax deductions.

Another advantage to refinancing your mortgage is that it's quite possible you were getting little or no interest deductions on your old mortgage. Interest is heavily assessed early in the life of a mortgage and dwindles to near nothing as the mortgage grows older. Also, if you bought a house or a condominium unit to rent out (more on this in Chapter 10), you get an even bigger tax break than you would as a homeowner on the mythical "depreciation" of your rental property (another blessing from Congress).

If, by chance, mortgage rates ever drop to the point where they're near the rates you can get from quality investments, you might also consider refinancing. Have an accountant show how much money you might make through the tax savings. You might want to do this even if you plan to stay in your home for some time. Be sure to compare the various ways of borrowing on your home. Refinancing through the mortgage is just one way and is not necessarily the best for your money needs. Ask the accountant and others about "wraparound" mortgages and second trusts that let you keep your old, low-interest rate but unlocks cash to be used for buying a rental property or for a son or daughter's down payment on a home.

OTHER WAYS OF MAKING MONEY ON A HOME

Getting money for a down payment on a child's first home is not a bad idea for some parents. Here's how Sumichrast of the National Association of Home Builders describes the process:

"If you're in your forties or fifties, you provide the down payment on a home for your son or daughter and, at first, you rent the home (condominium or small house) to either of them until he or she learns how to run a property and learns how the insurance, property taxes, repairs, and tax deductions work. You get a tax break and the child learns a lot. Eventually, the child can buy the home from you or you can sell it when the child moves and use some of the profit as a down payment gift on a home the child owns outright."

Or, you might try the reverse. Depending on ages and tax brackets, one or more of your children can buy your current home. They can form a corporation or partnership to pay the mortgage and other major expenses. You pay a fair rent and get a big wad of money from the sale which can be used for other investments to live on when you want to take it slower. The children save money on their taxes and have a valuable property to cash in when you die or decide to move. An important caveat: Have a lawyer supervise the transaction so you will be protected with a long-term lease. If one of your children has a divorce problem or a change of heart, you don't want to be in a position where you could be pressured to move out.

Maybe your children are not ready for a deal like this or are just not interested. Consider, then, your own parent or parents. (See also Part IV on parents.) It's possible that you could do them a favor and save money on your own taxes by purchasing their home. It's worth looking into. Have your accountant come up with some figures to see how each of you might benefit. Remember, when it comes to homes and taxes, you've got three generations to consider—your own, your children's, and your parent's. Arrangements with any of them might not work, but consider all the possibilities before you make an important housing decision.

CASHING IN ON YOUR HOME

Let's say you've weighed the advantages and disadvantages of staying versus selling and moving to a smaller place. You figure the old homestead is not designed for two people (even less so for one). It's too hard to keep up and, of course, there's all that piled up profit to unlock. You're 55 or older and you want to cash in. Housing economist Sumichrast, who is the co-author of *The Complete Book on Home Buying* (Dow-Jones), says a growing number of older people are developing a philosophy of life that goes like this:

"They want to do things now. They want to cash in and live a little. They figure if they wait much longer before taking that trip abroad or starting some new venture, they might drop dead first. They want a property that's smaller, easier to take care of. They also see the energy crunch coming and realize it will cost a fortune to heat and air-condition the big home. They also want to move in closer where there's little or no driving to do. They don't want to become slaves to home fuels and gasoline."

BUYING A CONDOMINIUM

Dr. Sumichrast believes that the condominium can make an ideal home if it's carefully chosen. There's a lot less maintenance and, as a rule, when you want to take off on a trip, you can just lock up, knowing that your place is not nearly as vulnerable to burglaries and fires as the old house with a yard. Many condos have all sorts of amenities such as year-round swimming, tennis, shops, even medical offices nearby. Others are right in town within walking or public transportation distance from work and off-work activities.

If you decide to consider buying a condominium, study the contract, the bylaws and all the information condominium developers must provide by law. If possible, get a lawyer who has worked on condominium purchases and sales. Ask a lot of questions. How does the owners' association work? When do unit owners get complete control of the building? What are the restrictions? Remember, you're buying into a business—not just a home. Be prepared to serve on owners' association committees. Find out how much the monthly service assessment will be (on top of your mortgage, insurance and taxes). Is there a reasonable amount being charged for future repairs and contingencies? Sometimes a condominium developer will artificially set the monthly assessments low to lure you in. Then, a year or two after every unit has been committed, monthly payments are suddenly hiked 50 percent or more to cover the true costs. There are a number of books on condo buying. Look them up in your library. You'll find out, for example, that buildings which have development financing backed by the government provide more consumer protection than most buildings without this backing.

There are advantages and disadvantages in buying and owning a condominium. As a general rule, condominium units do not appreciate in value as fast as individual houses, though there are exceptions, depending on where you want to live. On the other hand, it might be easier to get financing for a condominium than it is for an individual house, and the down payment is usually much smaller. Because you don't have too much money tied up, you can use the proceeds from selling your old home for investments, living it up—or both.

MOBILE AND "MANUFACTURED" HOMES

If there aren't any attractively priced condominiums in the area where you want to live, how about considering a mobile home? Wait a minute—don't flip the page. There are mobile homes, and then there are mobile homes. Sometimes, as we'll see below, they're even called "manufactured" homes, with nothing mobile about them.

A lot of mobile homes are located in "parks" on rented land. Many parks have swimming pools, club houses, and all sorts of amenities, while other parks are quite drab. You can find out a lot about what's going on by talking to residents. They're usually quite chatty. As a matter of fact, one of the main reasons for living in a mobile home park is the communal spirit you find. For an older couple or for a single person, this can be an instant antidote for loneliness. For others who like to be more independent, a mobile home park can be too intrusive on one's privacy.

The "manufactured" home is quite a different breed. It's made in a factory from a developer's specifications and is shipped to the building site in two or three big pieces (with all the rooms completed inside). At the building site it's quickly put on a waiting foundation and is plugged into the utilities. When you see it, you don't see a "mobile" home (with tie-downs and "skirts")—you see a home that resembles one that was built on a lot in the traditional manner.

With these "manufactured" homes, you own the land and get a mortgage, just as with any other house. The difference is that you pay about one-third less than what you'd pay for a similar quality house constructed on the site in the old way. In addition, you get moved in much faster. You can order all sorts of custom combinations when you pick your building site. Then, in six weeks or so, the home is built, shipped and installed, ready to go. Engineers say these manufactured homes are as good, or better, than traditionally built homes.

There are two main advantages to owning your land as well as your home. First, you get more appreciation in value. Because good park sites are scarce in some areas (California for example), a mobile home in a good park on rented land appreciates in value. But a manufactured home on your own lands tends to appreciate a lot faster. Second, when you own the land you can get a regular, long-term mortgage. When you rent the land, on the other hand, you get a shorter-term loan and a higher interest rate.

For more information on where to find manufactured homes in landowner housing developments, write: Manufactured Housing Institute, 1745 Jefferson Davis Highway, Arlington, VA 22202. You can also get information on mobile homes from this association and from the Better Business Bureau, Department of Housing and Urban Development, county (agricultural) extension offices and county and state consumer protection offices.

EVALUATING YOUR HOME

Finally, you ought to do some figuring on how much you'll make on your current home if you sell now, ten years from now, or later. You'll want to know how much money you'll have to buy a condo, manufactured home, or some other type of dwelling.

First, check with your local government or local realtors to see at what rate homes like yours have been increasing in value over the past five years.

As a national average, homes have been going up 10 percent a year in value. For argument's sake, then, let's use the 10 percent average. As a guide through the complexities of this financial planning woods, I asked the help of Dr. Thomas Harter, chief economist for the Mortgage Bankers Association.

Dr. Harter uses an $80,000 home as an example (because it's on or near the national average). He looked up the 10 percent inflation rate (or interest rate) over ten years and got a figure of 2.594 from the chart. By multiplying the figure by $80,000, he came up with $207,526. That's what your $80,000 home will be worth ten years from now. It's assumed you've lived in your house long enough so that your mortgage will be paid off or almost paid off.

Suppose you sell your home and net $193,000. At this point you have essentially three options. One, you can buy a smaller home and pay around $100,000—half the sales price of your old home. Suppose you put down $30,000 on the new home plus closing costs of $3,000, which comes to $33,000. Rounding off the numbers, you end up with around $160,000 cash and a $70,000 mortgage. You can invest the $160,000 and get around $12,800 a year at 8 percent interest. Inflation will eat away at it making it necessary to come up with more money over the next ten years to maintain your original purchasing power.

The second option is to buy your new home with cash. In this case you won't have any monthly payments to make and you'll have $93,000 to invest. This would bring in around

$7,500 a year at 8 percent. And, of course, it too will be diluted by inflation. But, you'll always have your new home as a capital reserve, whether it's all paid up or partly paid up. The new home should keep increasing in value. With this kind of a backup, you might want to dip into the principal of your investment from the profit on the first home. With a paid-up new home, you could invest the $93,000 and get around $9,000 a year, drawing on both interest and principal. But, your $93,000 investment would run out in twenty years. By that time you might be dead or you might be able to refinance your smaller home.

Your third option is to cash in on the whole home ownership business and rent a small apartment. You could then invest the money from the sale of the home and string it out until you died.

These are just three scripts. There are infinite variations. In each you can get an idea of how to figure the value of a home for the future and how to get money out when you need it. Use this information as an idea stimulator and guide for counseling sessions with an accountant or financial officer at some bank, credit union, or savings and loan association.

"The trick," according to Dr. Harter, "is to have a home that suits your needs and have extra income long enough so you die before the money runs out." This is the same exhortation we got from Jim Bly, the financial consultant, earlier in the book when we looked at inflation and wondered where the money was going to come from.

SETTLING YOUR ACCOUNTS— THE IDEAL

To sum up, the ideal that people like Jim Bly and Tom Harter dream about goes like this:

1. You give your children enough money now, or over the years, for a down payment on a home and/or a cash nest egg. This is their "inheritance."
2. You sell your profit-bloated old home and buy a smaller, less expensive one.
3. You work as long as you can and live off the invested profit from the first home as long as you can.
4. When you run low on money, you finally sell your smaller home and move into some apartment that's convenient to all vital services.
5. When they add up your estate, they'll find a perfect score—zero. All debts paid. No expenses except the final rites and these are covered by a special savings account.

It is, indeed, a financial counselor's dream. You and your capital go out at the same time. Of course, you can't do this unless you have some sort of direct pipeline to God. "If we only knew exactly when we were going to die," sighs Dr. Harter, "it would make financial planning a much tidier business."

CHAPTER 10

INVESTMENTS
AND TAXES

When it comes to money for investments, most of us plan on using what's left after all our spending. "It should be the other way around," says financial planner Jim Bly. "You should only spend what's left over from your investment plan. You make your investment and then curtail spending to what's left."

Bly admits that "most people don't want to do this. They want to spend now and worry later." You may have a vague notion that by investing in something such as stocks, bonds, or savings, you'll somehow be fairly well off in your later years. The three foundation blocks for retirement, you're told, are Social Security benefits, pension benefits, and "investments."

You probably think Jim Bly's investment philosophy of "invest now, play later," is too harsh. And, you may be right. But, there are some investment practices Bly and others say you should be aware of that could help you build more capital than you thought was ever possible. If you can't—or won't—cut your monthly spending to scrape up enough money for investments, then start looking at what's being taken from you in federal and state income taxes. You probably just pay the taxes without realizing that there are some ways of greatly reducing the bite.

INVESTING IN RENTAL PROPERTY

"Why not let the IRS help pay for your retirement assets?" This question is posed by my tax consultant, Paul Offenbacher, who always likes to investigate the possibility of investing in rental properties or other properties that offer a whole series of tax breaks. If you're careful, Offenbacher, says, "investing in a rental property is one of the quickest ways to make extra money for your later years." He reviews the tax breaks we touched on in the last chapter:

1. You get a deduction for the interest you pay on the new mortgage. You can also deduct other landlord business expenses (insurance, maintenance, and the like).

2. You get really big reductions in your tax bill because of depreciation allowances for the first five years or so. You can consider that your rental property "depreciates" in value even though everybody knows it actually "appreciates."

3. When you sell your property, usually after five or six years, the profit you make is considered a long-term capital gain and is taxed relatively lightly. You only pay on 40 percent of the gain, and you pay at the lowest rate.

"The biggest tax bite," says Jim Bly, "is on *unearned* income from savings and bond interest and stock dividends." Therefore, Bly says, it pays to find losses (such as the depreciation allowance in rental properties) and other write-offs to greatly reduce your tax bills in your high-income years. "You squeeze your tax payments," he explains, "to find investment money." If you unload your dividend and interest-paying investments and put the money into a long-term capital gain investment with early write-offs, you can, indeed, squeeze your tax bill for extra investment cash. By the time you get ready to work a little less after age sixty-five, you might have bought and sold enough rental properties to make a pretty good pile. After age sixty-five, you get double standard deductions and exemptions on your tax return. Then, you can convert your rental properties into investments that provide more immediate, spendable income. With your official "senior" tax status, you'll pay a lot less to Uncle Sam than you did before your sixty-fifth birthday.

It's nice if you can earn a little income, after all expenses, on your rental property—but it's not necessary. In fact, if you are in a high enough tax bracket, a "negative cash flow" (which is the jargon for monthly losses) could be turned into a net gain because you'll be paying less income tax.

THE RISKS OF INVESTING
IN RENTAL HOUSES

So far, a rental home, like your own home, might seem like an unstoppable Money Machine. It's not. There are two basic risks to be aware of:

1. *A bad location.* The rental property must be selected with utmost care. You've got to get a home that fits your local rental market. If your monthly costs are too high, you might have to charge a rent that's out of reach for the majority of prospective tenants. Further, if the home doesn't appreciate in value at least at the national average (10 percent a year), it might not be worth it. Talk with several people in rental real estate, including an accountant and a lawyer who have done a lot of rental-property business. Talk with various lenders. In short, do your homework and ask a lot of questions.

2. *A bad tenant.* Screen prospective tenants thoroughly. A good friend rented a home she inherited from her parents. A neophyte real estate agent thought the man and wife (and two kids) who wanted to rent the place looked like "nice people." They may have been nice, but they sure didn't have enough money to keep up the rent payments. Much money was lost in unpaid rent and lawyer's fees. Even if the rent is paid on time, a sloppy, destructive tenant can wipe out your profits with refurbishing and repair bills. Learn from a lawyer or others in the business how to screen tenants. Better yet, get a well-recommended real estate management company to do it for you.

One final warning that should go without saying: If you can't afford to have your money tied up for at least four years, don't get into rental properties. It's a relatively long-term investment. If you have to sell out within a year or two because you need the cash, the sales costs could wipe out all your profits and then some. And, be sure to stick to an area you know—your own home town and environs. Be wary of investing in out-of-town or "resort" rental properties.

Knowing what you're investing in is vital. "Frequently it's not so much the investment that's risky," says Jim Bly, "it's the investor." He warns against "giving your money over to someone who's going to make money for you." If they're so smart, why aren't they millionaires? Study whatever you go into. Know the market, and, especially important, know how long your money will be tied up. Get opinions from several sources, especially sources that aren't directly in the business of selling whatever you're buying. Understand the tax laws and how they fit into your investment picture. Become friendly with a good tax accountant, one who has experience in the field you're interested in.

EQUIPMENT LEASING

With all these caveats and questions, you might initially look at the next type of tax-saving investment—equipment leasing—with considerable skepticism. But, it's not as far out as it sounds. Remember, the idea is to find some investment that gives you loss write-offs so you can reduce your current high income tax bill. Like home rental properties, equipment leasing also provides depreciation allowances and deductions on the interest you pay for the purchase loan. But the tax savings you get are bigger and show up sooner.

With the money you don't spend on taxes, you can invest in a home rental property and have a combination of tax-avoidance powers working for you. This is a better move than simply putting the money into savings. Equipment leasing is not for everyone, but it should be investigated and talked over with people who know the business. According to tax specialist Paul Offenbacher, here's how it works:

"You pick out the type of equipment that you can purchase with a down payment you can afford. A number of people are purchasing a dental chair, an X-ray machine, or other types of health-care equipment. By talking to your dentist or doctor about the machine, you find out how it works and whether it might become obsolete too soon.

"You then check with accountants, bankers, and leasing companies that have machines that are within your reach. Get three or four deals and select the best. Let them know you're shopping so they'll be competitive. Make them spell out just how much money you have to put down, the loan, and the tax break (first year, second year, right on through to the year when it's best to sell the equipment). You should know just how much you'll make on your investment. Aim for 20 percent or better.

"Let's say you've selected a dentist's chair because it's in demand for young dentists starting out and it doesn't become obsolete too fast. Let's also say that you and your spouse have a joint income of $24,000 a year, and that this puts you in the 33 percent tax bracket. (Your kids are on their own and you have no other dependents.)

"You buy a chair and the equipment that goes with it for $50,000. You put $10,000 down, taking the money from savings, stocks, and other high-tax investments. You borrow $40,000 on an equipment loan. Right off the bat, you get a $5,000 investment tax credit, which for your 33 percent tax bracket is like a $15,000 tax deduction. The $5,000 credit is tripled for the deduction because you're in the 33 percent (one-third) bracket.

"By purchasing your equipment at the end of December, you get a tax break for the whole past year. You get a bonus $2,000 depreciation allowance for the entire year, even though you didn't own the equipment until December. This gives you $48,000 to depreciate over a maximum of seven years, making it around $7,000 a year. But, under fast depreciation rules, you get double depreciation, or $14,000 in deductions.

"Let's assume, with your income and the fact that you have no extra dependent, you pay around $5,000 a year in taxes. With the investment tax credit you get by purchasing the equipment in December, you could have your entire $5,000 tax bill wiped out. Other tax savings you get are carried back for a refund. This would be the depreciation bonus of $2,000 (at one-third your tax bracket, equals $667). Suddenly, you've squeezed $5,667 out of your tax bills.

"In the second year, you get a $14,000 depreciation

deduction plus a $4,000 interest deduction on the loan. This totals $18,000, but you get income from the leased equipment equal to your note payment. You paid out $8,000 on the loan ($4,000 interest and $4,000 principal), so you subtract $8,000 income from the $18,000 (depreciation plus interest) and you get a loss of $10,000. By being in the 33 percent tax bracket, you get one-third off your current tax bill (which includes the extra income). This comes to around $3,333 and, when you add it to the $8,000 you got from the lease income, you end up with $11,333 cash coming in. Cash going out was $8,000 on the loan, so you net around $3,333 after taxes which can be added to the $5,667 you made the year before. You can invest this $9,000 as a down payment on a home rental property.

"By the fifth year, you have a problem. Your $8,000 loan payment now only involves $1,000 in interest and $7,000 in principal. The depreciation allowance only comes to $1,000. So, out of $8,000 income, you only get to take off $2,000 and must pay tax on the $6,000 remainder. If you sell out earlier, you avoid this tax on the income, but you have to pay back some of your investment tax credit. Selling in the third year would require giving back $3,333. Selling in the fifth year would require giving back $1,667.

"This is why leasing can be attractive for people who need a tax break in their high-income years (with no dependent children). They can get the tax break now and build up enough capital to provide income later when they'll face a lighter tax."

As you can see, the explanation is complicated. It's sort of like following a bouncing pinball until it hits the right combination of electronic contacts and the board lights up—and you win. But, the equipment leasing litany does have a fascinating logic to it. Congress has piled up bonuses for certain types of business investments, and, as you can see, they're not restricted to tycoons and other fat cats. After all, Paul Offenbacher's equipment-leasing heroes are a couple, both working, who make $24,000 a year. This couple had been hit by higher taxes because of their double income and the fact that their children could no longer be counted as dependents.

THE PROBLEMS WITH
STOCKS AND BONDS

Apparently, for people in the second half of life, neither Paul Offenbacher nor Jim Bly puts too much faith in old, standby investments like stocks and bonds. When you're starting pretty much from scratch and want to build up considerable capital before you reach your middle sixties, the traditional investments are vulnerable to heavy taxation.

If you already have stocks that have appreciated considerably in value or inherited some that have appreciated since the initial purchase, you may find yourself in a bind. The stocks may not be paying out much income in dividends, and the income that is paid out is taxed at the highest rate. If you sell part or all of the stocks, you'll be hit by a huge tax on the capital gain (because they've appreciated so much in value). In a sense, your money is locked up in the stocks because of the heavy tax you'd have to pay.

Let's say you need the money now for other investments or you need higher income because you plan to slow down with your work and expect lower income from wages. Some tax accountants and lawyers say there are wily ways of converting long-term capital gain stocks that pay little in dividends to investments that pay out much higher dividends. Unfortunately, these sly people won't tell me their secrets. They say if I blab about it in this book, the Internal Revenue Service might clamp down on their offbeat, but supposedly legal, tax-avoidance devices. You might be able to find some tax expert who knows a method of unlocking money which is tied up in stocks with big capital gains, but be careful. If IRS calls you on it, you could face a sizeable bill for back taxes.

WIPING OUT TAXES
THROUGH DEFERRED GIVING

There is a way to convert low-income, highly-appreciated stocks into bigger dividend payers without incurring a capital gains tax. As a matter of fact you even get a sizeable tax *deduction* when you make the move. Of course, there's a catch—a big one. You have to officially transfer ownership of the stocks to some qualified nonprofit institution such as your college, university, religious organization, hospital, or one of the major medical research associations. You give the institution, say, $20,000 in low-yield stocks that have appreciated in value over the years. It would cost you plenty to sell these stocks because of the capital gains tax.

Now the institution can sell the stocks (without paying any capital gains tax) and agree to invest the money in much higher yielding bonds or securities. You (and your spouse, if you choose) get this higher income from the new investment until you die. And, in the year that you make the "deferred" gift, you get a sizable income tax deduction. When both you and your spouse die, the income stops and the nonprofit institution gets the $20,000 and all future income.

Example
Mr. Chase is 55 years old, and Mrs. Chase is 52. They have some stock that they bought for $5,000 way back when, and it's now worth $20,000. It is a

solid investment but the earnings only amount to 3.2%, and with the current inflation rate that's just not enough earning power. If they sell the stock they will have a capital gain of $15,000. But they are subject to tax on 40% of the $15,000, or $6,000. Assuming they are in the 50% tax bracket, this means a $3,000 tax bill. Thus, only $17,000 is left to put into higher-earning investments.

But by using the stock to fund a charitable unitrust at Old Siwash U. the Chases avoid any capital gains tax liability. The Chases chose an 8% payout rate. Thus, on the same assets that used to pay them $640 a year, they now earn $1,600. Quite a boost. In addition, they are entitled to a current charitable contribution deduction of $2,274.

Finally, the Chases are relieved of the burden of investment decisions. By creating a charitable trust they have the additional protection of professional money management. Worry over the investment is left to others.

According to Douglas Givens, Director of Development at Kenyon College, in Gambier, Ohio, there are three basic types of tax-avoiding, deferred-giving arrangements:

1. *Charitable annuities*. These pay you a fixed income for life (and the life of your spouse or other person if you want) and are vulnerable to the ravages of inflation.

2. *Pooled income funds.* You get dividends according to what the pooled donors fund earns. If the pooled money is invested well, you could get increasing amounts.

3. *Charitable Life-income Trusts.* This is a popular form of deferred giving, especially for people who kick in $20,000 or more. With it, you get your own, private investment fund, tailored to your specific needs. You may select fixed income for life or a variable income based on the annual value of the trust. The latter can be a great hedge against inflation. You usually need a deferred gift of $20,000 or more because less than that would make it too expensive to set up a single trust fund.

"When you go in to talk to an institution that encourages deferred giving," says Givens, "you can get a lot of free tax planning advice on your will, marital trusts and trusts for your children. You can investigate all these options at no charge." If you are interested in making a rather hefty donation to some worthy cause, by all means look into the tax-saving possibilities of deferred giving.

SINGLE-PAYMENT
DEFERRED ANNUITIES

One way to defer taxes is single-payment, deferred annuity, which has nothing to do with non-profit organizations. It's sold—rather aggressively—by insurance agents and stock brokers. Be careful here. Some of these annuities involve big sales charges and pay out relatively small amounts in dividends and interest. The main attraction is the tax gimmick. You defer taxes on money the annuity earns until your later years when, as a rule, you're in a lower bracket and won't be hurt so much by taxes when you start getting the income. *Changing Times* cites this example of how the deferred annuity works:

A couple with $22,000 yearly income invests $10,000 in a deferred annuity that pays 7 percent interest. Normally, this would produce a net value to the couple of $16,134 after ten years. If, however, taxes are deferred and the amounts saved are added to the investment, the net value would be $19,672. No tax would be payable on isolated, partial withdrawals of principal during the deferred income period (IRS says it's a return of capital).

The only reason I mention the single-payment, deferred annuity is because it's being pushed a lot these days by insurance and investment sales people. Before you sign anything, it would be a good idea to have your attorney or tax accountant go over the deal to make sure you're getting enough of a tax saving and enough appreciation to make it worthwhile.

ADVICE FOR
HOUSEWIVES AND WIDOWS

What would happen if your husband died? Would you know what to do with the insurance money or the various stocks, savings accounts, and other investments that have accumulated? Or, if you already are a widow, do you know how to manage the money that was left to you?

Many middle-aged and older women don't have the foggiest notion of what to do with investments. I'm not a chauvinist. It's the truth. There are women, of course, who are shrewd investors and know all about how to avoid heavy taxes, but the average housewife or widow is mystified by money matters. The husband usually has been in charge of the investments, for better or for worse. "There are a lot of women," says University of Maryland's Marilyn Block, "who don't even know what their husband's salary was when he died. They were handed X-dollars every week to do the shopping, and that was it." Older women, Dr. Block says, "must get to know the stockbroker, the tax specialist, the banker—everybody in the money world—*before* their husbands die or divorce them."

Widows and divorced women who suddenly find themselves managing some money, should sit tight at first. Don't make any sudden moves unless there's some sort of crisis. Don't sell the house. Don't sell the stocks. Don't invest in anything. Let things ride until the full grieving period, which can be a very confused time, has passed. A lot of advice may be offered by your children, relatives, in-laws, and well-meaning friends. Ignore it, politely. Seek advice, when necessary, from professionals in the field—an accountant who specializes in taxes, a recommended lawyer, banker, or officer at your credit union or savings and loan association.

As a rule, the first type of financial advisor a new widow might confront is an insurance agent—the one who helps you get your benefit check. By all means, lean on this insurance agent and ask for advice about money matters, but don't buy anything. If after a year of settling down, the insurance agent has something interesting to offer in the way of insurance or annuities, let him (or her) sell it on the merits. Check it with other experts. Don't just do what someone says you ought to do.

Start working out a personal plan which should include financial goals, budgets, tax moves. After one year, you might want to sell your home. By then, you'll be emotionally calm enough to make a rational decision. Widows and housewives should take the time to learn about taxes and investments. It could mean the difference of thousands of dollars gained or lost over the next decade. You can take tax and investment courses offered by community colleges and university continuing-education programs. Finding a good tax accountant and paying the going rate for one hour is not a bad idea (two hours might even be better). Come in with a tape recorder or big, legal note pad and take it all down. You have your questions organized. You bring in all your past income tax returns and an outline of your financial situation (income, debts, assets, insurance, investments, home value, etc.). Your questions will probably be a lot sharper if you've taken some basic course in personal finance. Maybe your course professor can offer some names of good tax accountants who are willing to take on family accounts.

JOINING A STOCK CLUB

You can learn a lot about the stock market (if you have some stocks) by joining a stock club. Brokers often have the names of stock club members in your area. You can also learn—and make some money—by investing a little at a time, say $20 a month, through fractional-share investment plans. You "dollar average" by putting in the same amount of money every month like a savings plan. This way, your losses and gains are "averaged out." If you buy a fraction of a stock share one month and it goes up in price the next month, you've gained money on the initial investment, but you'll have to pay more for the next investment. If you buy a fraction of a share one month and it goes *down* in value the next month, you have a loss on the initial investment, but you get to buy the next fraction at a lower price. It usually works out quite well and is, perhaps, the only "safe" way to dabble in the stock market while you learn. Don't be sidetracked by some broker who wants to talk you out of this slow, but sure, purchase method (because it brings in very little commission money). No matter how much of an "inside deal" the broker claims to have, stick to your "dollar-averaging" plan. Select stocks that are household names—ones that you've known and respected over the years because the companies involved sell quality products or services that are always in demand.

Unfortunately, most brokerage firms do not offer these sensible "dollar-averaging," fractional-share purchase plans. At last count, however, at least two companies do offer the plans as a promotion to attract the small investor. They're Merrill Lynch and Bache, Halsey Stuart. Both have offices in most urban areas around the country.

A final suggestion: See if you can find a woman stockbroker, insurance agent, accountant, lawyer or banker when you're doing your homework on the major money decisions in your life. Naturally, there are many men in these fields because, until recently, the money world was a "man's world." But, more and more women are entering this hitherto male sanctuary and they're doing very well indeed. They have to because of the competition and the "old boy" prejudice against women.

It makes a lot of sense for women to become pros in such areas as insurance, investing, and other elements of financial planning. It's usually a woman who is the beneficiary of some man's insurance policy. Why should a man sell insurance to another man when it's the woman's financial life that's at stake? Aside from talking with women in the financial world for advice on money matters, you might consider joining them some day. Once you've started your financial education—which you must, to survive—you might become fascinated by the whole subject and begin to get really good at it. If so, it could be a possible new career for you. As a widow, housewife or divorced person, you might be able to use your life experience to help other women. You could be off and running as a professional money manager.

CHAPTER 11

PENSIONS: EMPLOYER PLANS/ SOCIAL SECURITY

So you have a pension plan. You assume automatically that it's going to provide money for your retirement. It just might not provide one cent. A lot of qualifying clauses are neatly woven into most pension plans and you'd better know exactly what they mean. If you don't know how much money you're going to get and when you're going to get it, then start asking some pointed questions.

Under the Employee Retirement Income Security Act (ERISA), your employer must give you all the basic information about your pension plan in plain English. Remember that employee benefits booklet they sent to everybody awhile back? You probably just glanced at it and filed it someplace. Get it out and read it: There's lots of money in there. Once you get a good idea of how your pension plan works, make an appointment with the person (or department) that deals with employee pension questions. Specifically, you want to know how much money you "own" in the plan. If they say you have X-dollars "accrued," that doesn't necessarily mean you "own" it. Find out how much you have "vested." This means you have put in enough qualified work time to be entitled to a specific amount of your pension at some future retirement date. You may be "partially" vested, or "fully" vested. If you're not fully vested or even partially vested, you should find out how long it will take before you are vested. Sometimes it takes five years, sometimes ten.

It's important to know these facts because, with vested rights in a pension, you can leave your employer for a better job (or to start your own business) and know that at a certain age in the future (usually sixty-five), you'll be entitled to regular pension money. Note, however that you have to write to your old employer and apply for your pension checks, because they usually won't do anything until they hear from you. Also, if you leave an employer who owes you a future pension, be sure to get a statement to that effect—in writing.

> *Under ERISA, the Social Security Administration is required to notify people of any deferred, vested pension benefits to which they are entitled, at their request or when they apply for Social Security benefits. SSA will provide people with a statement as to the nature, form, and amount of any pension to which they had a vested right at the time they ceased being covered by a pension plan.*
>
> *SSA has no responsibility for updating this information to the point in time when the individual applies for Social Security benefits and the pension information is transmitted. The Social Security Administration merely acts as a conduit and also has no responsibility for the accuracy of the information in the statement. The information is furnished to SSA by the*

Internal Revenue Service which receives it from pension plan administrators.

Another point to find out is whether your pension has a Social Security "offset" clause. If there is a clause, you might not get much of a pension and might consider switching to another employer with a better plan. With an "offset" clause, an employer can promise a certain percentage of your wages as retirement income, but to make up this percentage, the employer can "offset" or take away a portion of the pension to make up for what you get from Social Security.

Ask your employer to spell out exactly what Social Security will provide and what the pension will provide at your future retirement age. You might be shocked to learn that Social Security provides most of the retirement income and your pension provides peanuts.

TYPES OF
RETIREMENT PLANS

There are basically two types of retirement plans. One is called a "defined contribution" plan, the other the "defined benefit" plan. With the latter type, you are guaranteed a certain amount of money every month during retirement until you die. With the "defined contribution" plan, you're not given any guarantee of what you're going to get. The employer defines how much will be contributed toward a retirement fund and under what circumstances contributions will be made. A profit-sharing plan is a form of defined contribution arrangement. The employer agrees to put in money if there's a profit. There's no requirement that a specific amount (or any amount) must be contributed. When you retire, you get your share of the pot plus interest in the form of an annuity, which provides monthly income for as long as you live, or in a lump sum.

The defined contribution plan is becoming popular for two reasons. First, an increasing number of employers do not want to be tied down to putting money into pension plans that require specific amounts whether business is good or bad. Second, employers have to contribute much more into employees' Social Security accounts these days because of the increased payroll withholding taxes designed to keep the system afloat. The more employers have to pay into the Social Security system, the less they want to put into pension funds.

For these reasons, you shouldn't count too heavily on getting much more money out of a pension plan. At best your plan might hold the line at present levels. And remember, whatever you do get from your pension, inflation will cut its purchasing power in half within eight years—maybe even sooner.

THE FUTURE OF SOCIAL SECURITY

Unlike the vast majority of private pension plans, Social Security benefits are indexed to the inflation rate. This means, as the Consumer Price Index (CPI) moves up, your monthly Social Security checks are adjusted upward to offset the loss of purchasing power.

Social Security, however, was never designed to be the main provider of retirement income. It was just supposed to be a minimum "base" on which you built the bulk of your income from savings and pension plans. Now, for many people, Social Security provides most of their retirement income.

Because of the inflation-protection feature and the fact

that people have been living longer and retiring earlier, Social Security benefits are becoming too costly to expand any further. As a matter of fact, over the next few years, you might see more attempts by Congress to "prune" Social Security benefits to save money. One effective way to cut back is to discourage early retirement. Congress has already raised the mandatory retirement age from sixty-five to seventy, and has provided Social Security benefit incentives for people who continue working past sixty-five. People who are eligible for retirement with Social Security benefits can get 3 percent a year extra for each year they continue working up to age seventy. Because the incentive additions are compounded, you can get as much as 16 percent added to your benefit checks when you retire. Compare this with the 20 percent reduction in benefits you get if you retire early at age sixty-two. A person who would normally get $10,000 a year at age sixty-five, gets $8,000 if retirement is at sixty-two and $11,000 at age seventy. Beginning January 1982, if this person is able to continue working at age seventy (it's age seventy-two until 1982), he or she will start getting a full $11,600 a year from Social Security on top of full employment wages.

As for early retirement, you might see Congress pushing the current age sixty-two back up toward sixty-five (where it used to be). Just pushing the early retirement age up a few months could produce a saving of billions of dollars.

It looks like we just cannot afford to support a growing population of people who retire earlier and live longer. And, we're not the only ones. You can see the pressure building for later retirement in other countries.

By the year 2000, according to the United Nations, the world population of people over sixty will be 585 million—a 100 percent increase in less than 30 years. In Japan, where many workers are forced to retire at age fifty-five, there's pressure to keep them on to age sixty and beyond. Japanese men actually have a greater life expectancy than American men (seventy-one years compared to sixty-eight), yet they have what amounts to a mandatory retirement age (an age at which you can be forced to retire) set at fifty-five. We now have it set at seventy. It's becoming much more difficult to support a rapidly growing Japanese "retired" population.

In Russia, the retirement age is sixty for men and fifty-five for women, as it is in Italy, Hungary, and Yugoslavia. In West Germany, on the other hand, because of a labor shortage older workers are encouraged to stay on. Some older workers are even allowed to receive pension benefits on top of their wages. In Norway, Sweden, and France as well, older workers can have considerable extra money added to their public pension benefits if they continue working past the official retirement age. You might see the same sort of thing in this country later on in the decade as fewer young workers enter the labor market.

Apparently, the industrialized countries are finding that it's a lot less expensive to encourage people to work longer than it is to try to take care of them for long periods of retirement. And, as inflation takes its toll, individuals are a lot better off working than they are trying to make it on the dwindling purchasing power of private pensions.

WOMEN AND RETIREMENT

While other countries struggle with the problem of raising the mandatory retirement age, the big issue now in the United States is women's rights in retirement. Of special interest to American housewives is the whole question of widow's benefits. In the past, a wife got nothing if her husband died, but things are changing.

The ERISA provisions, which went into effect in 1976,

spelled out some new rights for widows of pensioners. If, for example, a man dies after he retires, the law says his widow will automatically get half of his pension. But to qualify for this provision, the man's pension may be reduced at retirement to cover the added expense. The husband can elect to waive the widow benefits, in order to get more money during his lifetime, if he signs an official waiver form.

Unfortunately, all too many men are signing this form, leaving their wives uncovered. This is a dangerous gamble, because women statistically live around seven years longer than men, and men tend to marry women who are younger. In short, the average housewife's chance of being a widow in this case—without her husband's pension—is almost a sure bet.

To correct this situation, some employers are now sending notices to employees' homes advising *both* partners of the widow's benefit option. Some companies are even requiring the spouse to sign a statement indicating that she understands the implications of the widow's rights waiver.

Similar complications exist around the whole question of a husband dying on the job, before he retires. If this happens, the wife very often gets nothing even if the husband intended her to have widow's benefits after he retired. For a widow to get a share of her husband's benefits after he dies several conditions must be met:

- His retirement plan must have a provision allowing him to take early retirement;

- He must reach a specified age (usually 55).

- He must also have signed a paper that says he's willing to take a reduced early retirement benefit in order to have his wife covered while he's working.

Here's how a typical widow's benefit might work:

Let's say the husband will get $10,000 a year for his pension. He meets the three conditions just outlined, so his wife is covered for widow's benefits. Some time after age 55, he dies (either while working or after early retirement). His initial $10,000 a year pension was reduced to $8,000 a year because of the widow's benefit provision. She therefore gets half of her husband's benefit, or $4,000 a year. This is $6,000 a year less than the original pension called for, but it's a way lot better than nothing. This benefit money will make it easier for the widow to develop a high-demand, portable skill or build her own business.

THE PENSION RIGHTS OF DIVORCÉES

If the proper action is taken by the husband, as we've seen, a widow can benefit from a pension plan. The pension rights of divorced women, however, are now being battled in the courts. According to Sara Kaltenborn, an attorney with the Justice Department's Civil Rights Division, "the Supreme Court will have to decide whether homemakers have a right to a percentage of their husband's pensions after divorce." She refers to the case of *Stone* v. *Stone* in which a divorced woman sued her husband's pension fund to get money the court decreed she should have as part of her award. Her husband wasn't paying up, so she went right to his pension fund. She won in the district court but the decision is being appealed.

There's already a precedent for divorced women having rights to their husband's pension benefits. Congress passed a law which orders the Civil Service Commission pension fund to make direct payments to divorced retirees' wives if a court orders it or if state law requires it as part of community property entitlement. (Under community property entitlement, each partner gets half of the wealth accumulated since the marriage began).

Divorced women can qualify for a wife's benefit equal to half of their ex-husband's Social Security benefits if they were married at least ten years. They can't be married at the time they make the claim and they have to be at least sixty-two. If their ex-husbands die, these divorced women can, at age sixty-five, claim 100 percent of his pension benefits like any other widow.

There's one exception. Divorced women who work for the government (federal, state, local), and were not covered by Social Security, must have been married at least twenty years for reasons that are too complicated to elaborate.

To summarize, you can see that housewives, whether married, widowed, or divorced, have to know their rights under the pension and Social Security laws. "Most women," says Kaltenborn, "tend not to give much thought to their retirement income until they reach the age when they need it and discover that it isn't there. However much lip service society pays to the value and importance of wives and mothers, it generally reserves its rewards for those who engage in a long life of income-producing work." What she means is: Husbands are usually entitled to full pension benefits—housewives are not. The Social Security system is definitely slanted toward husbands who get paid for their work and away from housewives and homemakers who don't get paid. For every year a mother takes off from work, she gets a zero on the Social Security account sheets. Ten to fifteen years of zeros means she'll probably never earn enough Social Security credits to be entitled to her own benefits. Unless her accumulated Social Security benefits add up to more than one-half her husband's benefits (which would constitute a wife's benefits), she gets nothing on her own. Congress is toying with the idea of giving women Social Security credits for the time they spend raising a family (or, at least not penalizing them for it). If you're interested in this issue, write to your senators and representatives.

IRAs AND "KEOGH PLANS"

A final note about a special form of pension. It's called an IRA (Individual Retirement Account) and is a tax-free investment opportunity reserved for people who are not covered by an employer pension plan. You can put 15 percent of your annual wages or $1,500, whichever is less, into a government-approved investment such as a savings certificate or mutual fund. There are also "Keogh Plans" for self-employed people which are similar to IRAs except you're allowed to put in up to $7,500 a year or 15 percent of wages, whichever is less. You can get more information on IRAs and Keogh Plans from your nearest bank or Internal Revenue Service office. The advantages of both IRA and Keogh Plans are:

1. The money you contribute reduces your taxable wages.

2. The money that's earned in the accounts over the years is not taxed. Taxes are deferred until you start taking the money out in later years when, supposedly, you are in a lower bracket and have more exemptions and deductions. You have to leave your contributions in IRA and Keogh accounts until age 59½. If you withdraw money before that age, you get hit with a stiff tax penalty.

As you can see, IRA and Keogh accounts can provide tax breaks for people in their higher income years. They are especially interesting for people in their forties and fifties who start their own mini-businesses while they're still holding down full-time jobs. Look at this case in point:

The husband has a full-time job with a pension plan. He also has a little sideline business as a consultant. He sets up a Keogh plan (IRA, if he's incorporated) to reduce his taxable income and put money aside for the future.

The wife also has a full-time job with a pension. She, too, has a small, sideline business as a riding instructor. She sets up a Keogh or IRA to reduce her taxable income and set money aside.

When you add it all up, they both will get two, sizeable employers' pensions and two mini-pensions plus Social Security benefits—five different benefit checks. This case is unusual, but not impossible. It's worth investigating.

GOOD READING

For more information on pensions, the following are helpful.

• *Pension Facts # 1* and *Pension Facts # 2* (for wives). You can get copies of these must-read reports by sending a self-addressed, stamped envelope (business size) with 25 cents to: Pension Rights Center, 1346 Connecticut Avenue, N.W., Washington, DC 20036.

• *Everything You Should Know about Pension Plans.* This book is written and published by Fay and Leo Young, pension consultants. Write: Liberty Publishing Co., 50 Scott Adam Road, Cockeyesville, MD 21030

CHAPTER 12

LIFE INSURANCE

The whole question of having enough life insurance or the reverse, having too *much* life insurance, depends a lot on your circumstances and, of course, the intensity and sales skills of the insurance agent who originally sold you your policies. I'm not going to try to explain all the brambles and thickets in the life insurance woods—only the main paths. Many books have been written trying to explain the concepts and the jargon.

But, here you are in the second half of your life with your children off on their own or nearly so. Or, perhaps you're a single person who is concerned about your money making powers being threatened some day by disability. For the most part, your financial needs in your forties and fifties are different from those in your twenties and thirties. As a married person, you are primarily concerned about "protecting the children" in case the breadwinner(s) die. As a single person, you were probably more concerned about your ability to continue working in your career.

My own definition of the purpose of life insurance, after reporting on it over the years, is this:

• The primary function of insuring one's self is to provide enough money for a spouse and heavily dependent children to survive the transition after the death of the major breadwinner. This is what insurance was originally invented to do.

• The secondary function of insurance is to provide some tide-over money for a surviving spouse later in life, especially if that spouse does not have a paid job and might have difficulty obtaining one.

• The third, traditional function of insurance is to provide enough cash after one's death to handle special burial requests and unpaid, unreimbursable medical bills. "Don't be a burden on your family" is the theme here.

Because we dislike dwelling on the thought of our eventual demise, insurance has been "packaged" to make it appear as if it were a fascinating investment whereby we can "protect" our loved ones and make a lot of money in the process. Nonsense. Unless you're in some stratopheric tax bracket and your tax accountant (who doesn't sell insurance) can convince you to buy a policy as some sort of tax dodge, don't buy insurance as an "investment." You can make more money with super-safe government securities.

To help explain the possible insurance needs (or lack of them) for people over forty, I dropped by to see Ben Lipson, a Bostonian who specializes in getting policies for people who have been turned down or have been burdened with "high-risk" surcharges. This specialty sometimes puts Lipson in an adversary role with insurance companies. He occasionally looms as a sort of Ralph Nader heavy at industry conventions.

Because Ben Lipson knows the business cold and because he is so objective about it, I asked him to address his comments and observations directly to you. Consider it a free consultation as he sits at his desk, leans back, and starts talking:

"When people get married, they buy life insurance. It's for a growing family. Then, the kids grow up and move out. Maybe the wife starts to work. But, the entire family situation has changed. If you recall, you probably bought your first insurance from some friend or golf or tennis companion. You really didn't *buy* it. Some young man probably *sold* you the insurance, and you may not have gotten the best advice on what kind and how much to buy.

"The original reasons for owning insurance may no longer apply. The wife and children at one time were heavily dependent. But now the children are supporting themselves and the wife is working. There are two incomes. A husband may need less insurance and a wife may need some insurance of her own to help her husband adjust to his single income if she were to die first.

"In the case where you have both husband and wife working, try to get as much as you can out of employers' group benefit plans. Some employers will give you life insurance as a *guaranteed issue*. This means you get it even though you may have had a heart attack, cancer, or whatever. If all employees get the insurance, you can get it as long as you are fit to work. Your employer's plan may even allow the purchase of extra, low-cost group insurance and, in a few instances, coverage for your spouse. Husbands and wives should investigate all the various possibilities of getting in on group life insurance and group disability insurance. This kind of insurance can be a real bargain for people in their forties, fifties, and sixties because the younger people in the group subsidize you. Some jobs are almost worth it for the free or low-cost life, health, and disability insurance you can get."

(A point to note here as the Insurability Specialist Lipson takes a phone call. With the age for mandatory retirement raised from 65 to 70, employers will probably have to provide life insurance and other insurance coverage to older workers if younger workers get it. Otherwise, unless higher costs can be proved, it would be a case of age discrimination. And, in the not too distant future, there probably won't be any mandatory retirement age at all, which means older workers could be covered for as long as they are able to work—conceivably, into their seventies and eighties. Actually, companies that have no mandatory retirement age report that relatively few older workers die on the job. That's why they really aren't that much of a risk).

DIVORCE AND
LIFE INSURANCE

The call that Lipson took during this brief pause was from a man who was contemplating divorce. He wanted to know what happens to his insurance during separation and after the divorce. The beneficiary is his current wife. Lipson sets a date for an appointment, puts down the phone, and continues:

"Divorces and separations present a number of problems. What happens to the life insurance? Are there legal obligations? If a wife owns the policy (for tax reasons) and pays for it with her own money, all the proceeds flow to her tax-free if and when her husband dies. But now there's a divorce. She remarries and still owns the insurance policy on her first husband. If he dies, she and, presumably, her second husband get the money.

"During a separation, if the husband owns the insurance policy (and most husbands do), the wife might remain as the beneficiary. But, at some stage, the husband may want to change the beneficiary benefits over to his children or someone else. This is why you need professional advice (both legal and insurance) in working out insurance plans for the Second Half. You may want answers to questions concerning the possibility of separation, divorce, changing beneficiaries, coverage for both working partners—all the contingencies."

CHECKING OUT YOUR OLD LIFE INSURANCE POLICIES

Planning for contingencies is certainly a good idea, but what about all those old, presumably outdated, insurance policies we may have purchased years ago? What do we do with those? You check them out and, says Lipson, here's how you handle it:

"If you don't have an agent or broker nearby, write to the company policyholders' service department. Ask for a 'current inventory statement' of all your policies. They'll need to know the numbers. You want to know the current values and, even more important, what options are available. They must give you all the options in writing. Demand it.

"If an agent contacts you in person, which sometimes happens after you write in, be careful. Insist on all the options in writing so you can study them. Don't be sold something new over the kitchen table. Beware of any proposals to put your available cash or dividends into other insurance products, services, or investments such as mutual funds, stocks, tax shelters, or annuities. They love to swoop in and get you nailed down with something else. Don't get me wrong. The agent's advice may be valid. But, you want to check it out through some more objective source such as your banker, tax accountant, or lawyer.

"For example, an agent's line might go like this: 'We can double your insurance at little extra cost.' They take a loan out of your old policy and buy more insurance. It may or may not be a good idea. If you really need more insurance, it's okay, but if you don't, it's a loser. In general, these are the major options you'll be faced with:

"You can surrender a policy or policies. If it's whole life insurance (as opposed to term insurance), you get the net cash value (after any loans) plus any dividends. You have to ask yourself if there's still a need for this amount of insurance. Your children may no longer be dependent, your spouse may be dead or you're divorced. Maybe the difference between the cash value and the actual death benefit doesn't justify continued protection with all those premium payments.

"As an example, take a $25,000 policy with $17,000 accumulated cash value. You're paying, in effect, for only $8,000 worth of insurance, assuming there are no dividends. You can take out the $17,000 and put it to work in a savings certificate or bonds or something else that earns more money than the insurance company pays (which is a relatively low interest rate). Or, you could get $20,000 paid-up insurance, which means you pay no more premiums and your beneficiary gets $20,000 when you die. Of course, if you die tomorrow, it's a bad bet. But if you don't, it's a good bet. But remember, when you cash in an insurance policy, don't just blow the money on some iffy investments or round-the-world splurges. Put your money into something that earns top interest (or invest in a well-chosen rental property).

"As a variation on cashing in completely, you might want to consider reducing the amount of your insurance. You can cut your original $25,000 policy in half. You get one-half of the $17,000 cash value to invest ($8,500) and keep one-half the $25,000 face value ($12,500) as death benefits. You split the difference. You get less to invest, but more death benefit coverage (which may be just enough to fit your current needs).

"Instead of cashing in, you might want to take out a policy loan. On the older policies (which you may well have), you can borrow money for as little as 5 or 6 percent and you can borrow up to 95 percent of the cash value (in our example, 95 percent of $17,000 is $16,150). You put the borrowed money into a solid investment that pays 8 or 9 percent interest (or, home rental property). This reduces your coverage, but your money is in a safe place and is earning more than you were getting. If you have a high-interest mortgage on your home (9 to 10 percent), you can reduce the impact by paying some of it off with your low-interest insurance loan.

"Remember, there are two types of insurance companies. One is called a stock company where you pay the same premium during the life of the policy with all values guaranteed. The other is called a mutual company where you may get dividends (because policyholders are part owners). If you own both types of policies from two or more companies, it's better to cash in a stock company policy rather than an older mutual company policy if the dividends of the latter have been assigned to pay the premiums. If you just have policies with a stock company, then it's usually better to cash in the newest one (assuming the face values are the same) because it will carry the highest premium rate."

As a final comment on reviewing old insurance policies, Lipson offered the following checklist:

1. Who owns the policy? Who is the beneficiary? Do you want to change them? Do you need to update the addresses?

2. What's the method of payment to the beneficiary? It's usually a lump sum and this may not be suitable. A financially inexperienced beneficiary may be better off with monthly payments until a sound investment program can be drawn up, or a trust set up.

3. Are there any riders or restrictions on the policies? You might be paying too high a premium because you've changed jobs (to a lower risk occupation) or your medical record has improved.

4. Is there any clause that reduces the face value at a certain age? Any restrictions that come or go because of your age? If the policy is part of an employee benefit plan, it may now be illegal to apply the previous age restrictions under the amended age discrimination law.

Lipson's advice is honest and objective but it was given by one man to another man. The woman's point of view, especially the single woman's point of view, is missing. To fill it in, I talked with Jean Strong, who does research for Time-Life Books and who previously sold life and health insurance. Jean feels single women have much different insurance needs. She explains:

"Many women in their forties and fifties either never married and devoted their lives to careers or were married and are now divorced or widowed. We have our careers, we may or may not have children, and we have no spouse to take care of us should we get sick for an extended period.

"A big worry for many single women is protecting our workability. We, perhaps are more concerned with having income protection insurance than most men because until recently it wasn't available to us on the same liberal basis as for men.

"We should always get whatever disability insurance our employers offer, but, in addition, we should consider getting our own portable plan. Its expensive, but the expense can be cut down by arranging the time periods required before the benefit payments begin. I have some disability insurance that starts paying after two months off work and pays for as long as two years. Then I have additional coverage for a smaller benefit that starts after six months and pays as long as I am disabled. If a disability lasts more than a year I might become eligible for permanent disability insurance (at no additional cost) through Social Security. You should figure out how much you'd need to cover minimum living expenses in case you're unable to work for various lengths of time. Don't try to come too close to your full wages—it would be too expensive and usually only 60 percent is insurable anyway. (Be sure to get non-cancellable, guaranteed renewable coverage).

"With a rider on your life insurance policies, you can arrange it so your premiums will be paid if you're disabled. I think everyone should have this feature. It doesn't cost much.

"As to how much life insurance a single woman should have, that depends. Usually, you need enough to cover any unreimbursed medical and hospital bills, your burial expenses, and other outstanding debts. Nobody wants to be a burden on her family and friends. A $5,000 or $10,000 policy should do it. You can get a $10,000 term policy and reduce it as you grow older (and it becomes more expensive). Or, you can get a more expensive whole life policy (which keeps the same premium, year in and year out. If you prefer whole life over term, you should *opt* for a lower cash outlay, lower cash value plan. If you are buying a home with a friend, you might consider getting a decreasing-term, mortgage-payment insurance in case one of the partners dies or becomes disabled (but shop for it, don't just take what the lender offers).

"Women, and men too, should consider seeking advice from women insurance agents. The insurance business is still primarily a men's club. But more women are coming in. Because many women feel they have to work harder to line up loyal clients for referrals, they might be more sympathetic listeners. You may get more service, more questions answered, more ideas that fit your special needs. As for married women, in many cases, the husbands handle all the insurance purchases, but wives are usually the beneficiaries and they should know what's going on."

GOOD READING

One of the best books on insurance, written in plain English, is *How To Pay Lots Less For Life Insurance* by Dr. Max Fogiel, insurance consultant. For more information and the current postpaid price, write: Research and Education Association, 342 Madison Avenue, New York, NY 10017.

CHAPTER 13

FOUND MONEY

It would be misleading if I didn't end this money section of the book with some comments on appraising your needs or requirements for money. Your economic situation is a classic case of supply and demand. You work, save, and invest to *supply* money for your needs and desires—your *demand*. Up to now in Part II, the focus has been on the supply side: building up a high-demand, portable skill, starting your own business, playing the organizational game, changing career tracks, and making money on home rental properties and other investments.

But what about your *demand* for money? Is it cast in concrete? Must you have X number of cars, boats, stereos, and other badges of affluence? How about your home? Could you be just as comfortable, perhaps more comfortable, in a smaller home that's a lot less expensive to maintain? What about your great expectations? Do you feel that a major goal in your forties, fifties, and sixties is to travel, travel, travel? Are there ways to travel that might be more satisfying and a lot less expensive than a tinsel-tan cruise or a checklist tour?

SAVING MONEY BY SETTING PRIORITIES

What's necessary at this stage in your life is a priority list. What are the things that you really feel down deep you need or want. What's important to you? What can you cut out that costs money? What must remain inviolate because it's part of your personality, part of your commitment to yourself or to others?

It might be interesting, if you can muster the discipline, to put an artificial "firing" or "retiring" restriction on your personal finances. Sometimes getting fired or forcefully retired is the best thing that can happen to a person. There's an emergency. Money must be cut. It can be humiliating, or it can be like going on a crash diet. You cut out a lot of fat and realize you never needed it in the first place.

In a sense, I imposed an artificial firing situation on myself and my family. When I was in my forties, I felt stifled in the organizational world. I was working for a national business magazine as Washington bureau chief and felt frustrated. Too many people were telling me what to do with my life—when to come to work, when to go home, when to go on vacation, how much money I could have. My suggestions and ideas were being "processed" by other people and, I thought at the time, they weren't getting a fair hearing.

So, with some savings and one contract from a syndicate, I quit the good job I had and started my own business. This meant that my income dropped to almost one-third of what I had been getting. I had a home to pay for and education costs for our two boys. Still, I thought: Better to fire myself with some foreknowledge and preparation, rather than have someone else do it without any warning.

My wife Vida and I had a real problem. We had to cut our living costs at least in half. We couldn't use a surgical knife. We had to use a meat axe. We got together in the evenings to prepare our lists of "What Has To Go." While we were making these decisions, Vida fought to keep things that seemed part of our personalities. "When a plane's in trouble," she said, "you might throw out some seats and some baggage to lighten the load. But, you don't throw out the pilot and the co-pilot." She meant you don't throw out your own personality needs—or your partner's.

CUTTING COSTS—
HOME, CAR, TRAVEL,
ENTERTAINMENT

We found that a major cost-cutting item was our home. We built it. We loved it. But it fostered a way of life that was, perhaps, too costly. We looked at other homes and realized we could cut thousands of dollars in mortgage, maintenance and transportation costs. (In the final analysis, we didn't do it. We stuck with our home. But we knew the money was there if things got really bad.)

Next, we found that our two cars were costing a fortune. We got rid of one car. I used the public transportation system and Vida used the car for the boys' transportation, shopping, and all that goes with maintaining a home. Selling that car for a good price saved us at least $2,000 a year. Now the saving would be more like $4,000 a year. To figure out how much your car is really costing you, tote up these amounts: depreciation, interest (if you have a loan), gasoline (add extra here for next year's gouge), insurance, repairs, maintenance, parking—everything. You might be able to get a booklet on this from the nearest chapter of the American Automobile Association. In general, you'll find you're paying close to 40 cents a mile and at an average of 10,000 miles, that's $4,000 a year.

Can you get along with one less car? Can you pool rides? Can you use public transportation? Can you use taxicabs or rental cars when need be? When you buy your next car, consider the possibilities of a "clunker." Buy an old car for $800 or so. Have a mechanic go over it carefully (before you pay) and have it fixed up. For less than $1,000 you can get a "good-transportation" car that will dramatically cut your costs. The advantages are several. There's little or no depreciation—that's already happened. You don't need any collision insurance at all, just liability. You don't need anymore body repair work. Just let the fender dings stay as they are. (This is a great way to save money on car purchases but my wife won't go along with it. We have a relatively new car, but plan to keep it for five years.)

After the home and the car, comes travel and entertainment. One person can travel to some place in the United States or abroad and spend $500. Another person can take the same itinerary and spend $5,000. How much importance do you put on the trimmings? Is the place you're going to visit interesting enough on its own, or are the accommodations and the "style" of travel the important thing? You can get to a fairly distant spot and spend very little on the luxuries. Or you can go to some nearby place (even a fancy motel on the edge of town) and live it up. Both have their therapeutic advantages.

When we were cutting our cash outlay by one half, we chopped out travel to resort places. We used to go to Florida in the winter. The air fare, hotels, restaurants—all cost plenty. The August after I "fired" myself, I took a tent trip to the Catoctin Mountains in Maryland with our two boys, Paul and Michael. Vida was not into camping and begged to stay home and "just relax with all the peace and quiet around me." The boys and I spent a grand total of $67 on the whole trip. We put up a tent on a state-park camp site (at $2 a night), cooked our own food, went hiking and fishing, swapped stories, listened to the radio at night (Washington Redskins' pre-season game) and endured a raging thunderstorm. Vida was serene, sleeping late, swimming at a neighborhood pool, "puttering," and studying.

We cut out fancy restaurants and rarely ate out except at an occasional tiny restaurant that was "cheap and charming." We didn't give any more big parties and relied, instead, on doing things together with friends—talking, an occasional movie, potluck dinners. Thousands of dollars were saved and we didn't seem to miss anything very much.

If you're creative and have other resources, other interests, you can do many things that don't require a lot of money. Art Norris, an official with the National Institute on Aging's Gerontological Research Center (GRC) in Baltimore, says "We've seen people take a cut in income after retiring and be able to adjust quite well." Norris is referring to the GRC longitudinal study of some 650 men's lives over the past twenty years. These men have been observed as they were aging. Many of them have been professional people who had been accustomed to living well. GRC's Norris explains their philosophy of shifting priorities: "When they had less income, some of the men developed a network of friends and family ties. They visited a lot. They did things together. It's the European coffee house idea. You don't spend so much money on things as you spend time with friends. When you do travel, you travel together for companionship and cutting costs. Instead of an ocean liner or a transatlantic jet, use a station wagon or a camper."

CUTTING COSTS:
A CASE HISTORY

Still, others can manage to do a lot of traveling because they like the globetrotting life. To make ends meet, they have to cut elsewhere. Take the case of a California doctor, J.R. (Pete) Morden and his wife Alice. They wanted to spend much more time traveling to places they dreamed about and spend a lot less time working. They were able to make drastic cuts in their spending, according to a detailed personal finance profile in *Medical Economics* magazine. Because of the de-emphasis on work, the Mordens' income was cut to around $20,000 a year. But, their regular living expenditures (not including travel projects) were cut down to around $15,000 a year.

How did they do it? According to the *Medical Economics* profile, they moved to a mobile home in an area where some other doctors and retired professional people had moved. This cut their housing costs to a fraction of what they had been spending. They entertained each other in the mobile home park. By cutting their living expenses way down, the Mordens were able to spend much more money on their annual travel jaunts abroad and around the United States.

As for the splurging on their travel dreams, Dr. Morden says: "The way I see it, Alice and I can look at each other and know we've done some things. We'd rather see the world now and think about it later, than wait until we're in our seventies and then wish we'd acted when we could. When that time comes, we'd rather have memories than money." Because the

Mordens have drastically cut their living costs, it looks like they'll be able to have some memories *and* some money.

When you're working on your own balance sheet and cast an anxious eye on the money supply, don't forget to do some sharp pencil work on the demand side of the ledger. Any fat you can cut out of your "demands," is found money—tax-free income. But when you cut out the fat, don't hit bone. Don't cut out items that are a part of your being. When my wife and I did our chopping, we realized that her studies at a nearby university and my horse, Little John, were part of our personality structures. Cut them out and we might have to spend money on psychiatrists to put us back together again. The Mordens kept their dream travels, and we kept our university connection and our horse. Saving your money is one thing—saving your sanity is something else.

This brings us to the next section on health. If you have money and health, you're two-thirds the way toward having a high-scoring second half of life. The missing third, so far, is love, which we'll investigate in the section on happiness. It's all summed up in this old Spanish toast: "*Salud, pesetas y amor, y tiempo para gozarlo.*" Translated, it means: Health, money, and love and time to enjoy them.

Part II
Your Health: Time for a Tune-up

CHAPTER 14

A VULNERABLE AGE

"Somewhere between the ages of fifty-five and sixty-five, the number of people who have one or more chronic disease conditions skyrockets." So says Dr. Ernest M. Gruenberg, Chairman of the Department of Mental Hygiene, Johns Hopkins University School of Public Health. It's a vulnerable age. "If you can get through your fifties without much of a mishap," according to Mike Batten, a specialist on aging, "you probably have a good chance of leading a healthy, active life on into your old age."

The reason the years past 45 can be crucial as far as our health is concerned, is that we have accumulated a number of bad habits and our bodies are less able to take the abuse. While we were rushing through our twenties and thirties, climbing career ladders, raising families, moving from place to place, we might not have given proper attention to our bodies. Like machines, they need a maintenance review every so often. Now we're at the 50,000-mile tune-up stage. There's some wear there, but there could be a lot more mileage left if we start doing something about preventive maintenance and repairs now.

Of course, there's a big difference between our bodies and machines. With the exception of the occasional heart transplant or other transplant or prosthesis, we cannot yank out old parts and put in new ones. We have to work the repairs from within by changing our habits and tuning our body functions. We are linked to our families' health histories with inherent strengths and weaknesses, but, by and large, our future is in our own hands. We can take care of our body machine or we can let it rust and wear out.

The failings older people are likely to encounter, says Dr. Gruenberg, "are consequences of changes in the body brought on by slow, progressive conditions. It's not because people are old that they get sick. It's because the disease process has had time to go on for so long."

Gerontologists are in agreement that the human body naturally declines in strength and disease resistence as we grow older. With men, the decline starts some time in the early twenties. With women, it probably starts eight or ten years later. It's not that we all face a decline but the *rate* of decline that's important. People who drink a lot, smoke a lot, eat a lot, and don't exercise will, on the average, have a steep rate of decline noted on the charts. People who don't smoke, eat carefully, limit their drinks, and exercise vigorously three times a week will have a line on the charts that declines slowly—like a glide, not a power dive.

Although some of the damage you do to yourself is cumulative, a lot of it isn't. You're at a crucial point in your life. You can continue taking your body for granted, or you can start making some long-term maintenance commitments. There's still time. The decision is yours.

TAKING CARE OF YOURSELF

Maintenance, by the way, doesn't mean visiting the doctor more often, or taking more pills, or cranking up for some form of surgery. Maintenance means *taking care of yourself.* All too many older people rely on other people to take care of their ills. In a national survey on *The American Family*, conducted by Yankelovich, Skelly and White for General Mills, these responses were elicited from prominent leaders in the health field:

People labor under the fantasy that the doctor can cure anything. Also, they depend on their doctor to be knowledgeable—and don't think they, themselves have to be.
—Dr. Roy M. Menninger, president of
the Menninger Foundation

People know that certain behavior is not conducive to good health but they persist in this behavior nonetheless. They live for the moment and don't have adequate self-discipline.
—Dr. Ernst Wynder, president of
the American Health Foundation.

The General Mills survey concluded that sedentary jobs were just part of the problem. Women working outside the home and increased leisure-time alternatives have placed limits on how much time we have to exercise and otherwise take care of ourselves. Too many of us, the report concluded, "are more interested in relaxing, watching television or going out to a restaurant, bar, or movie than regular exercise."

But things are changing. People past 45 or 50 are now better educated and better informed than previous generations. Health is the subject of growing interest and concern. People are more apt to re-assess their values as they move into middle age. You see many more older people jogging, playing active sports, walking long distances, eating more sensibly. And, this is paying off. The heart attack rate has declined 20 percent in ten years. People are living longer, especially women.

Dr. Alex Comfort, the gerontologist and sex educator, insists that society often psychs us into "feeling old" as we move along in years. He calls this sociogenic aging and believes the prejudice and misconception it breeds causes as much as 75 percent of the damage we attribute to "aging." He says it's "imaginary or imposed aging."

In a sense, we talk ourselves into it. We hear all sorts of horror stories about older people in institutions, older people in feeble condition, and we assume that it might hit us some time before we retire. Yet much of what happens or will happen is in our heads—in our attitude. "Among our urgent needs," says Merrell M. Clark, president of the Edna McConnell Clark Foundation, "is the need to curtail the infernal, self-destructive, bad news about American aging."

THE 50,000 MILE TUNE-UP

One way to curtail the bad news, of course, is to avoid becoming a part of it. Start now to review what you can do to put your body and mind machinery in good working order. To help you prepare a "tune-up" list, I interviewed scores of the best health educators, physicians, physiologists, nutritionists, and other body scientists. I also went for a checkup myself. I have the readings and notations on my condition before the tune-up and one year later. Therefore, I'm not just reporting what the people in the white coats or gym shorts say, but also what is happening to me and to lots of others who face similar health conditions as they grow older.

There are certain basic things we can do with our lives that could substantially better the odds for a much happier, healthier life in our later years, but the investment has to be made now. It may come as a shock to you, but *exercise* is one of the most important items in your Second Half health tune-up. You may scoff at this, pointing to some parent or other older person who lived to a ripe old age and never ran one block, never lifted anything heavier than a teacup or a martini glass. The insurance companies and health statisticians, however, can point to thousands of others in the same age group who did not exercise and who are now in miserable condition (or dead).

We've seen that one's work or portable skill can be extremely important for one's mental and physical health. Exercise ranks with what you do as a major element in prolonging active living. Diet comes in as a close third (some say it should be higher). The second half of your life is a crucial stage when you have to analyze what's going into your system in the form of food, alcohol, and smoke.

Some smokers, drinkers, over-eaters and non-exercisers feel strongly about maintaining their habits. Don't worry, they say. They don't seem to care what happens "down the line." So be it. This section of the book on health, at least, will examine the choices and let you make up your own mind.

First on the list of choices, an in my opinion the most important, is exercise.

CHAPTER 15

Rx: EXERCISE

"Remaining active is the key to staying alive," says Dr. Theodore Klumpp, medical consultant to the President's Council on Physical Fitness and Sports. By "remaining active," Dr. Klumpp means regular, vigorous exercise. You "take" exercise, he says, like a maintenance drug—for the rest of your life. Backing up Dr. Klumpp with a series of studies on the effects of exercise, Dr. A. H. Ismail, a physical fitness expert at Purdue University says: "People who exercise regularly deserve lower insurance premiums because they spend less on medical care." After four years of studying non-accidental medical insurance claims, Dr. Ismail found that one group of policyholders (men from age twenty-three to fifty-five), who exercised regularly, spent a total of $3,963 on medical claims while an otherwise similar group of non-exercisers spent $7,698.

"At least one aspect of aging," says Dr. Raymond Harris of the Center for the Study of Aging, Albany, New York, "is decline of efficiency, and it can be inhibited by fifteen years or more—provided there is systematic and lasting application of suitable physical training." We weren't designed to be sedentary, he says. "A trained sixty-five-year-old," says Dr. Harris, "may have a better physical work capacity than an untrained thirty-five-year-old." Changes in physical work capacity are not inevitably a result of aging. They are, Dr. Harris maintains, "the result of physical disuse and lack of activity which exercise and training can improve."

THE BENEFITS OF EXERCISE

For men, exercise can help make the heart, lungs, and circulatory system stronger. As a man grows older, the weakest link in his physical well-being is, perhaps, his heart. Exercise may help stave off heart attacks, and, if a heart attack does come, exercise helps limit the damage and speed up the recovery.

For women, exercise is vital in maintaining bone strength through the later years. While men's genetic background make them more susceptible to cardiovascular disease, women's background makes them susceptible to bone loss called "osteoporosis," discussed in more detail in Chapter 20.

Besides making you better able to resist heart attacks and bone loss, exercise has all sorts of other benefits. After a few months, you begin to look much better. You're better able to keep your weight down. In many cases, your blood pressure will drop to better levels. Your resting heartbeat is lower, which means your heart is more efficient, and you have the capacity to work longer, play harder, and endure stress better.

Exercise can also do a lot for your mood. Frankly, I never relished the thought of getting up early for my alternate morning jogs around the neighborhood. Some say it's "exhilarating." Not me. After I have jogged, showered, and eaten breakfast, however, I feel ready for a full day's work. The day goes much better, because regular exercise can act as a powerful anti-depressant. According to biologists, our brain produces a chemical called norepinephrine which seems to stimulate the production of endorphins. These endorphins can work as an anti-depressant to make us feel bright and optimistic. Exercise apparently stimulates the production of norepinephrine, which in turn stimulates endorphins.

As you feel better and look better, you're encouraged to keep on with your exercises until they become a regular habit. The trouble is, many of us want a quick fix when it comes to feeling good or losing weight. We take pills or we try one phony diet after another. Pills and diets by themselves, however, never work for any length of time. Appetite and hunger have been programmed into our brains at an early age and we simply cannot fight them all our lives. Human beings don't like to starve themselves. If you build up your exercises, however, your weight will come down, slowly but surely. More important than the actual weight loss is the type of weight you'll be getting. It will be a lot more muscle and a lot less fat.

Changing fat to muscle takes time. You're not going to see "magic" results in ten days, or your money back, as some of the more ridiculous diets claim. I went from 185 to 170 pounds, but it took more than a year. Actually, my waistline and other noticeable areas of flab slimmed down before much weight loss was noticed on the scales. This is because muscle takes up a lot less space than fat. Some exercise physiologists say you should check your weight at the beginning of your program, as a baseline, and don't keep looking at it. Check it every two or three months. Just because the scales don't show a dramatic drop, you might not think you're getting anywhere. This is misleading. Your body muscles may have become marbleized like the deluxe steaks you see on the meat counters. It takes months to work this ingrained fat out of your muscles.

HOW EXERCISE WORKS

Covert Bailey, a nutrition consultant, has become an expert on fat metabolism and muscle structure. He was asked by Liz Elliott, editor of *Jogger* magazine, to explain how exercise knocks down fat and builds muscle. His response:

"Fat enzymes inside muscle cells decrease when you are sedentary. So the ability to metabolize fats lessens as you sit around more. Also, when you become sedentary, you lose lean

Activity	Calories/hour	Time needed to burn 2,000 calories
Good		
skating (moderate)	345	5 hrs. 48 min.
walking (4½ mph)	401	5 hrs.
tennis (moderate)	419	4 hrs. 45 min.
canoeing (4 mph)	426	4 hrs. 41 min.
Better		
swimming (crawl, 45 yards/min)	529	3 hrs. 47 min.
skating (vigorous)	531	3 hrs. 45 min.
downhill skiing	585	3 hrs. 25 min.
handball	591	3 hrs. 23 min.
tennis (vigorous)	591	3 hrs. 23 min.
squash	630	3 hrs. 10 min.
running (5.5 mph)	651	3 hrs. 4 min.
bicycling (13 mph)	651	3 hrs. 4 min.
Best		
cross-country skiing (5 mph)	709	2 hrs. 50 min.
karate	778	2 hrs. 34 min.
running (7 mph)	847	2 hrs. 22 min.

(These figures are for a 152–lb. person. If you weigh more, you'll burn up more calories in the same time; if you weigh less, you'll burn fewer.)

Source: The *Executive Fitness Newsletter* Jan. 14, 1978. Published bi-weekly by the *Rodale* Press, Inc., 33 East Minor St., Emmaus, Pa. *Reprinted by permission.*

body mass. The lean mass you lose is muscle and muscle burns up about 90 percent of what you eat. So, if you lose a little bit of this muscle that burns up around 90 percent of what you eat, a small loss ends up to be a rather significant calorie-burning decrease. This is why you shouldn't consider weight to be any index of your health (unless there's a sudden, unexplained change). It's the body fat content that's important."

The trouble is, measuring body fat requires a complicated weight-displacement measuring routine that involves being submerged in a large vat of water. However, you can still get a good indication that fat is disappearing by your waist measurements, loss of flab between the hip bone and lower rib cage and the flab under your upper arm. If you are exercising regularly and your slacks are a little slacker, then the fat is melting. Keep it up.

When you get rid of fat that has collected on your frame and in your muscles, lots of other things start happening in your body chemistry. One of the most important is the buildup of HDL in the blood stream. HDL sounds like some sort of detergent for oil or gasoline products. In fact, it does work rather like a detergent in your blood. HDL stands for *high density lipoprotein*. It's part of the cholesterol group in your blood. As you may already know, too much cholesterol in the blood is believed to cause clogging of arteries which, in turn, can cause heart attacks. Lowering one's cholesterol, especially for men, has become a national health and nutrition goal.

Actually, the lowering of one's cholesterol count is just part of the answer, and perhaps not the most important part. Raising the HDL level in cholesterol may be even more important. Studies have shown that people with high HDL levels, no matter what their cholesterol count, are far less likely to suffer a heart attack. The HDL does, indeed, seem to work like an arterial detergent.

"We are finding that exercise is one of the most important factors in raising HDL levels," says my doctor, Oscar Mann, an internist-cardiologist. Because my cholesterol level was high (293) and I was sitting in an office much of the time working as a writer, Dr. Mann "prescribed" exercise, saying it was the most important preventive "medicine" I would be taking for the rest of my life.

THE STRESS TEST:
KEY TO YOUR
EXERCISE PROGRAM

He gave me a complete physical, including arranging for a rigorous stress test on a treadmill machine. Anyone over forty who has done little exercise should have a stress test. The price ranges between $100 and $175, but the tests can be next to worthless, depending on who does them and how they're done. Dr. Mann recommends a testing routine designed by the famous Dr. Sam Fox III, who runs Georgetown's cardiac rehabilitation center. Dr. Fox says "you've got to be really pushed. They have to take you up to your limits, or the test won't do much good."

Unfortunately, all too many doctors are fearful of pushing patients very hard with stress tests. They're afraid of something going wrong, something that could trigger a malpractice suit. A well-monitored test, however, can be quite safe. Any abnormalities that show up on the instruments can alert the monitor so the test can be quickly terminated.

During the test, you walk fairly briskly on a mechanized treadmill which is slowly raised in elevation. Your heart and pulse and breathing are monitored on instruments. You keep up a conversation with the doctor in charge to report any discomfort or distress. Your heart is checked before and after the test and your recovery period is carefully watched.

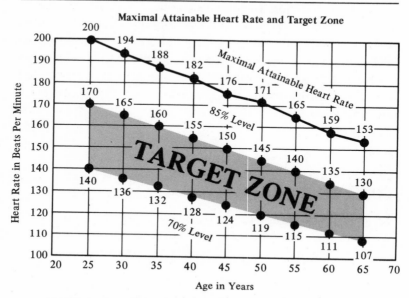

Maximal Attainable Heart Rate and Target Zone

This figure shows that as we grow older, the highest heart rate which can be reached during all-out effort falls. These numerical values are "average" values for age. Note that one-third of the population may differ from these values. It is quite possible that a normal 50-year-old man may have a maximum heart rate of 195 or that a 30-year-old man might have a maximum of only 168. The same limitations apply to the 70 per cent and 85 per cent of maximum lines.

Reprinted with permission from *Beyond Diet: Exercise Your Way to Fitness and Heart Health,* by Lenore R. Zohman, M. D., CPC International, Inc., Englewood Cliffs, N. J. 07632.

My test showed that I had a "capacity for more exercise" and had a metabolic rate of 12 to 13. The test was administered by Dr. Mary Restifo, a heart specialist, who gave me a book of instructions on how to build up my exercise program, take my pulse, and select the proper exercise heartbeat levels. (The booklet she gave me, *Beyond Diet: Exercise Your Way to Fitness and Heart Health,* is available through doctors' offices or through local chapters of the American Heart Association.

According to the booklet, a person my age (55) has to build their heartbeat to at least 120 per minute during exercise without pushing it up much over 140. The instructions for taking the pulse suggested using the carotid artery on the neck with a light touch of the finger (so as not to impede the blood flow). The second you stop exercising, you take a ten second count and multiply it by six to get beats per minute. I quickly learned that 20 beats in 10 seconds was 120 bpm and 25 was 150 bpm—my outer limit. From 22 to 23 bpm was my ideal ten-second pulse for exercise.

A look at the charts on pages 150 and 151 will show you

How to Use the Target Zone
The crucial part of a workout is the duration one stays at the target zone, the 70 to 85 per cent of maximal heart rate zone.

The Exercise Training Pattern

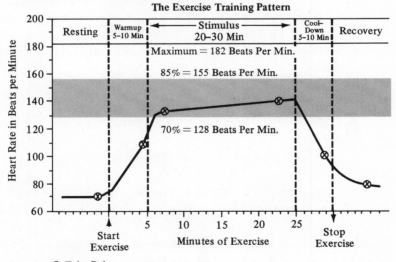

⊗ Take Pulse

Reprinted with permission from *Beyond Diet: Exercise Your Way to Fitness and Heart Health*, by Lenore R. Zohman, M. D., CPC International, Inc., Englewood Cliffs, N. J. 07632.

what your bpm range should be during exercise. Generally, you figure 220 minus your age as the base point. Then, multiply your base by 85 percent to get your upper limit. I took 220, minus my age (55) to get an absolute limit of 165. My safe limit—with reserve—would be 165 times 85 percent which is 140 beats per minute. I go over 140 occasionally but try to keep the rate at something around 130 to 135.

THE EFFECTS OF EXERCISE

In the next chapter, "Running and Dancing," I'll go into more detail on how to work into the proper exercise routine. For now, let's look at the effects that my exercise program had on my body and its inner workings. A year later, I returned to Dr. Mann for a checkup and another stress test by Dr. Restifo. Here are the results:

- My weight had dropped from 185 to 170 (on my scales).
- Cholesterol had dropped from 293 to 264.
- HDL had risen from 39 to 45.
- Triglycerides (related to diabetes) dropped from 169 to 159.
- Metabolic rate on the stress test improved from 12 to 15.
- As dividends, I was much slimmer, muscles were hard and my mood was cheerful and optimistic.

On top of this, my doctor says that, by continuing on my exercise program, I can expect my HDL level to rise, which could provide protection against a heart attack.

When you select an exercise program, you need some form of activity that will raise your pulse to the minimum beats per minute. This minimum must be sustained for steady periods ranging up to thirty minutes. Exercises that can lift your heart beat to this level are called "aerobic." Exercises like weight lifting that do not raise the heart beat to the minimum rate, but which do tone muscle and build strength, are called "anaerobic." Aerobic heart-development exercises include, running (jogging), aerobic dancing, cross-country skiing, skipping rope, running in place, swimming, cycling (outdoors or stationary indoors), and rowing. Brisk walking for several miles can also be aerobic.

Swimming, rowing, and cycling are good exercises but are not as efficient in working the heart in a reasonably short period of time as are exercises where you carry your own weight such as running and dancing. Such sports as handball, racquetball, squash, tennis, football, soccer, and downhill skiing are vigorous enough but are usually too intermittent to get the proper aerobic effect. Horseback riding can be an excellent exercise if it is done at a vigorous pace and is sustained for an hour or more.

Weightlifting, calisthenics, golf, gardening, Swedish massage, and social dancing are good for muscle tone, relaxation of the mind, and coordination but do not produce the necessary training effect for heart development and preservation.

To test your fitness, you can try walking or jogging for one-half mile. If you can't make one-half mile in 12 minutes, according to Dr. Harold Elrick, formerly of Harvard Medical School, you are definitely in "poor" condition. Dr. Elrick, who is co-author of the book *Living Longer and Better* (World Publications), says you are in "fair" condition if you can do one mile in 12 minutes. You are in "good" shape if you can do 1½ miles in 12 minutes. I do 1½ miles in 15 minutes with a couple of hills along the way.

If you haven't done any strenuous exercise for some time, you should have a physical checkup (with a stress-to-your-limits treadmill test). Ask your nearest medical school where a proper stress test can be obtained. Remember, you really have to be pushed to make it count. Once you have been tested, your doctor or an exercise physiologist can prescribe a course of action. The key is not to push too fast at first. Keep your heartbeat at or around the appropriate level. When you stop exercising, the pulse should drop to 115 or below within 2 minutes and below 100 in 4 minutes. The faster the pulse drops after exercise, the more efficient your heart has become. As a general rule, after five minutes of walking and relaxing after you've run, your pulse rate should be within twenty beats of your pre-exercise resting pulse rate.

CHAPTER 16

RUNNING
AND DANCING

When my doctor told me I had to do some exercise to make my heart work at a certain rate, the question was: What kind of exercise? I looked over the field. Swimming I liked, but I couldn't get to a pool in the off season. Riding an exercise bicycle was certainly convenient but seemed awfully boring. Ditto for rowing machines. I could skip rope or run in place, but that also had a sort of mindlessness to it. I finally chose jogging as the most convenient, least costly, and least boring activity available.

Having done some reading on the subject, I learned that jogging or running can be quite cost-effective as far as time and money are concerned. Because I am carrying my own weight, I can get my heartbeat up to my minimum 120 bpm fairly easily and can keep it there for the prescribed period of time. I don't need any expensive equipment (except proper shoes) and I can run around my neighborhood or at some nearby field.

My doctor and others told me that my exercise had to be something convenient and not too loathsome—something I would keep on doing. Although I didn't particularly like running, it seemed like the least loathsome and the most convenient. I could set my own hours to suit my daily schedule.

I was warned about the Great American Hangup: Anything worth doing is worth doing to excess. All too many novice runners just lace up their shoes and run right out the door. It's little wonder a Minnesota clinic reported that runner injuries tripled in one year. Thirty-five percent of the injuries were serious, affecting the knees.

Because I am in business for myself, I could ill-afford being knocked off work for any length of time. So I read several books on the proper preparation for running and the proper pace for beginners.

PREPARATION IS
HALF THE BATTLE

It's important to buy appropriate shoes for jogging. The shoes should have wide, cushioned heels to absorb the contact with pavement or hard ground surfaces. There are all sorts of sleek-looking running shoes with fancy names and fancy designs. Stick to shoes that are for "training," not "competition." The competition shoes are for a different stride.

Before starting out the door, you have to take at least ten minutes to warm up. You can use a series of exercises recommended by the National Jogging Association (NJA) or design your own set. You can get more information on warm-up techniques and other runner's lore from James E. Fixx, *The Complete Book of Running* (Random House). This is one of the best books on running, but there are many others in the library.

As the books point out, you have to stretch your back and leg muscles carefully—not with sudden pulls or jerks. The books outline the main stretching exercises needed to get your legs and the rest of your body ready for jogging. I also do 20 to 25 sit-ups (with my feet tucked under a bedroom dresser) and the same number of push-ups. This helps get the juices jangling in the morning and, more importantly, helps tighten up the muscles around my belly and chest (which had fallen into flab).

A brief note here on the feet—the point of contact with the road or ground. I had a cyst on the ball of my right foot that had nothing to do with jogging. It had been there, like a little knot, for a couple of years. I thought it would bother my running so I had a podiatrist (recommended by the NJA) take it out with minor surgery. The podiatrist took X rays of my feet and explained why I would probably need "orthotics," leather or plastic inserts for the arch area.

They're made by taking a plaster cast of the foot so they'll fit perfectly. You take out the sponge rubber pad that most running shoes have in the arch and insert the orthotics. When you lace up your shoes firmly, the inserts are held in place. I also like to use fairly thick socks to help absorb some of the pounding. The shoes you get should be fitted over your socks and orthotics (if you need them).

Anyone who begins to have sore feet, ankles, shins, or knees, should stop running and hike themselves to a recommended podiatrist or orthopedist (the NJA can supply names for your area). Since I started running more than a year ago, I have never had a single minute's soreness in my feet or legs. Occasionally I get a little stiff, but it's only temporary.

PLUSES AND PITFALLS— START SLOWLY

After I started running, I modified my routine to fit a schedule suggested by Dr. Gabe Mirkin, assistant professor of sports medicine at the University of Maryland. Mirkin, the author of

The Sports Medicine Book (Little, Brown), says the most effective aerobic routine requires 30 minutes on alternate days, three days a week. You may not be able to run 30 minutes at first, but you should walk as briskly as you can for that period of time. Then, step up the pace until you're slow-jogging and eventually running. The trick is to get your pulse up to a safe point above 120 bpm and hold it there for 30 minutes.

Don't worry about your speed, or about how many miles you go. These things are meaningless by themselves. Some novice runners, especially those in their middle years, like to brag about how many miles they run and how little time it takes them. Ignore it. Just set your goal on doing 30 minutes, three times a week, with a heart beat of 120-plus. As your heart, lungs, and muscles begin to get into shape, you'll find that you'll have to add an extra block or two in order to put in the required 30 minutes. And you'll have to move at a slightly faster pace to keep the heart beat up.

There are two major items that can alter your heartbeat while you're running: *hills* and *heat*. If you have no hills, fine. You can run at a steady pace. If you do have fairly steep hills, take it easy on the incline and lean a little forward as you run. Test your pulse on a hill to make sure you're not exceeding your safe limits. In general, if you're puffing so hard you can't carry on a conversation with somebody, you're overdoing it. Slow down.

As for heat—watch out. It can be the most dangerous thing you encounter as far as your heart is concerned. A truly hot day can race your heart something awful when you're running. Either avoid the hot part of the day or jog a lot more slowly. Stop to take a couple of pulse readings just to make sure you're not pushing the beats per minute up too high. And to be safe, don't run right in and take a hot shower. Heat from a shower can speed up the heartbeat to dangerous levels if you haven't properly cooled down. Let 5 or 10 minutes elapse after exercise, and then take a cool or tepid shower.

This brings us to the importance of cooling down. After your 30 minutes of exercise, you've got to keep moving around slowly for 5 minutes or so to let your heartbeat come down and allow your muscles to adjust. Your pulse should be down to something under 100 bpm before you stroll in for a shower. As you become fit, your pulse should drop quickly to the 100-minus bpm level. This means that your heart is now more efficient and doesn't need to work so hard for so long. Also, when you wake up in the morning, before getting out of bed, your resting pulse could eventually get down to 60 bpm or so.

When your heart can get the job done with a lot less pumping action, you're really in good shape. And when you've accomplished this, the odds for living a longer, active life tilt much more in your favor.

On the days that you are not doing a 30-minute strenuous routine, don't just stay in bed a little longer. You should do something easy such as a brisk 20-minute walk, or a 10-minute run. The reason you work on a hard-easy schedule, according to University of Maryland's Dr. Mirkin, is to build muscle. This combination, he says, is the best way to do it.

THE IMPORTANCE OF
A REGULAR SCHEDULE

My schedule goes like this: I run Monday, Wednesday, and Friday mornings—30 minutes each. Before running, I do 10 minutes of warm-up and stretching exercises. After running, I take 5 minutes to "walk down." On Tuesday, Thursday, and Saturday mornings, I take a walk or use my wife's exercise cycle for 15 minutes while watching the TV news. On Sunday I go horseback riding with a friend. The riding is exercise, but it's main value is relaxation—sort of a mini-vacation.

Your own schedule will probably take all sorts of other directions. But just remember, the 30-minute "hard " exercise should be in there somewhere—three times a week. Tennis and other recreational sports can count for your alternate or off-day exercises. Don't overdo it—and don't underdo it. Your body will tell you when you're overdoing it, so listen to what it says and peel back on the alternate-day work. If you become really fatigued and feel out of sorts, give yourself a week off and just take a few walks in order to stay loose.

Dr. Mirkin says you should do your strenuous exercise every other day, three times a week, because "the exercise at first breaks down muscle and the off-period allows for a bigger buildup." He says various physiology studies have shown that the 30-minute period is just about right. If you exercise less, you don't get the best training effect. If you exercise more, you don't gain that much in extra training. Unless you're involved in some sort of competitive racing, the 30-minute every other day routine seems the best.

COMPETITION—
IS IT FOR YOU?

As for competition, some books recommend it as a great way to keep up your interest in exercise. I wouldn't touch it with a 10-foot vaulter's pole. Competition in the form of distance racing can be especially dangerous for older men. If you're competing against yourself, or some friend, in sticking to your schedule or reaching your goals prescribed by some doctor—okay. But timed distance running, that combines speed and endurance, should be avoided. If you do it, you should know all the risks. The least you can do is take a strenuous stress test and get proper training from a professional coach or exercise physiologist.

"Competition, although healthy in many respects, can lead to dangerous overexertion and health risk for some highly competitive males," says Mr. Graham Ward, Chief of Health Education at the National Heart, Lung and Blood Institute. Mr. Ward warns: "Don't let some 30-year-old down the street keep challenging you to push past your prescribed, safe exertion levels."

A dear friend of mine, in his late forties, just had to prove that "there's some fire in the old boiler yet." He had been a top-ranked college athlete and wanted to get back into shape, so he ran a lot and trained a lot. His aim, after several lesser races, was the New York Marathon. The day of the race was one of the hottest on record. After running about 7 miles of the 26-mile race, my friend collapsed with a heart attack. He was lucky. It was a warning. Now he's sticking to regular, moderate exercise prescribed by his doctor.

ASPECTS OF EXERCISE

So far, the emphasis has been on running or jogging (I've never been able to determine which is which). This type of exercise can do wonders for your heart, lungs, bones, weight, overall appearance, and well-being. But jogging or running is not the only activity that can do the job. As a matter of fact, jogging and running lack the kind of variety of movement that requires balance, timing, and coordination. Running is too simple for this. You just plod along the same way every time.

"You should maintain your nimbleness and balance," says Dr. Robert N. Butler, Director of the National Institute on Aging and author of the Pulitzer prize book *Why Survive?*

Being Old in America (Harper and Row). Dr. Butler says there are two, equally important aspects of exercise: *strengthening the heart* and *balance and coordination*. You can't do just one and ignore the other. "If you let yourself slide into inactivity," Dr. Butler says, "you may face the risk of falling and breaking a hip in your later years." And, as you probably know, a broken hip can seriously handicap or lead to fatal complications for a person in their sixties or seventies.

If jogging doesn't do much for one's nimbleness and overall body coordination, then what does? Dr. Butler recommends dancing or other activities that require rhythmic coordination. Some types of karate training require precision and coordination. So does ballroom dancing, disco dancing, and square dancing. "By keeping in shape, keeping nimble," Dr. Butler says, "you tend to look better and feel better about yourself. Even your sexual activities seem to be more enjoyable."

AEROBIC DANCING

As noted, dancing can be a good activity for tuning up your coordination. But there's one form of dancing that can also work your heart into much better shape. It's called "aerobic dancing" and, as University of Maryland's Dr. Mirkin says, "it's probably just about as good as running because of all the body movement."

With aerobic dancing, you go through a series of musical warm-ups and then move into a vigorous set of steps for 30 minutes to get your heart beat up over the 120 bpm minimum level. At the end of the session, you slow down and cool off with some quiet, relaxing rhythms.

"Some women like aerobic dancing better than jogging," says Betsy Jacobs, Associate Director for the Bethesda-Chevy

Chase (Maryland) YMCA. Ms. Jacobs was one of the pioneers in recognizing aerobic dancing as a civilized alternative to just plain jogging. She and Dr. Mirkin both agree that aerobic dancing can do more for you than jogging. You get the heartbeat up, you work more muscles in the arms, back, and neck (not just your legs), and there is much more emphasis on coordination and graceful movement. Ms. Jacobs says, "We don't get many men coming in for training . . . I guess they have trouble with the concept of dancing as something a male can do." But, some men do come in, she says, and they "get very good at it."

Aerobic dancing is a lot like disco dancing, with a dash of Dallas Cowboys' cheerleader bounce thrown in. If you think this is kid stuff as far as exercise is concerned, just try it some time. You'll be puffing and ready to sit down, after just a few minutes of whirling, stretching, jumping, and waving. This is why you've got to get some training. Learn the steps. Learn how to work up slowly. Remember, you're just as likely to collapse from too much aerobic dancing as from too much jogging.

Like jogging, aerobic dancing doesn't require much in the way of equipment. "Just a good pair of well-made tennis shoes," says Betsy Jacobs. The shoes are important because your feet take quite a pounding. You need the better-made tennis shoes because they give side support (unlike running shoes which concentrate on support for forward motion). And, your shoes must have a sole surface that slides (as do all good tennis shoes). Your clothing can be shorts and a T-shirt, leotards, or whatever is convenient for the room or outdoor temperature.

After you take some aerobic dance lessons at your nearest YMCA, community college or other adult education center, you can select your own records or tapes for doing the dance sets at home. You don't have to keep going to a class. Your time and schedule can be your own. You can do the dancing before breakfast, before lunch, or before dinner. Don't do any exercise right after a meal.

Once you get into aerobic dancing, you'll find that it will improve your looks and your entire attitude about yourself. You won't have to diet as severely to keep your weight under control, and you should begin to move with a special gracefulness. People will remark on how well you're looking.

Here's a case in point. Tish Sommers, the activist for older women's rights we heard from earlier in the book, starts each day off with a vigorous set of dance routines. She used to be a dancer and has kept up the stretching, motion, and timing routines. When I first met Tish Sommers to talk about this book, I couldn't believe what I saw. She had told me she was 64 years old in a previous telephone conversation. What I saw, however, was a stand-in for a handsome woman in her forties. Tish Sommers looked 15 years younger then her age—bright, graceful, slim, marvelous posture, the works. She has combined a life of challenging, active work with regular dance exercise and the combination appears to be unbeatable.

WALKING

There is another exercise almost all of us do—but we don't do it enough. It's walking. For some people, long brisk walks are just about as good as jogging, and probably more entertaining. The only trouble with walking is the fact that it takes more time to get your heartbeat up to the required level and keep it there. Nevertheless, walking can be a marvelous off-day routine for runners and dancers. It can also be a major routine for people who should not run or dance because of some medical problem.

There's a good book on walking written by Aaron Sussman and Ruth Goode, *The Magic of Walking* (Simon and Schuster). This book shows you how to put a lot more walking into your life. Like running, brisk walking makes the heart shape up. The best pace for walking is around 3 miles per hour. This takes you 1 mile in 20 minutes and is the pace the U.S. Army uses for long marches. You can use running shoes, but comfortable, thick-soled walking shoes are probably better. Don't walk in thin-soled shoes.

As you build more walking into your life, don't forget stairs. If you can climb the stairs where you work or use stairs instead of escalators in stores and other buildings, you'll be getting exercise dividends. When you walk, you should also begin lengthening your stride. This loosens up tense muscles and puts other, little used muscles to work.

CROSS-COUNTRY SKIING

In the winter, if you live in an area that has snow, or visit a snowy area for vacation, you might consider cross-country skiing. It is every bit as strenuous as jogging and aerobic dancing—perhaps more so. Don't take it lightly. If you're not in shape, go slowly at first and test your pulse.

In Finland, the sport is called ski hiking and almost everyone does it. Dr. Ilkka M. Yvori of the Rehabilitation Research Center in Helsinki, says "Hard ski hiking is potentially dangerous for an untrained person. . . . You must observe the same kind of caution as you do when you start running or any other vigorous exercise." The best way to benefit from ski hiking, Dr. Yvori says, is to go for distance, not speed.

Outfits for ski hiking cost considerably less than those needed for downhill skiing, and the trails are also a lot less expensive to use than the ski lifts required for downhill skiing. You rarely encounter big crowds or long lines when you ski hike, and the exercise you get can make an excellent winter alternative to jogging or aerobic dancing.

INDOOR EXERCISING

What about rainy, stormy days? Some mad, glazey-eyed joggers still go out, but I don't. I use my wife's exercise cycle and watch the early morning news-talk shows on TV while I pedal. Other people skip rope or run in place.

When I'm on a trip and don't feel like going up and down in a hotel elevator in my jogging shorts, I just run in place in my room, hoping the person in the room below is reasonably tolerant. I watch the TV news features while I jog in place and it works fairly well.

So far we've concentrated on exercise and its beneficial effects on the heart. Since heart disease is primarily one that worries men, women tend to think that exercise, for them, is not all that important. But it is. And there's a special reason for this which we'll discuss in the next chapter.

GOOD READING

Guidelines For Successful Jogging, published by the National Jogging Association, 919 18th Street, N.W., Washington, DC 20006. For a moderate membership fee, you get the book and a subscription to *Jogger* magazine. The association also sells shoes and other equipment to members at a discount.

CHAPTER 17

OSTEOPOROSIS: WOMEN BEWARE

If you are a white woman over age 50, you probably have osteoporosis. You don't know you have it, and your doctor probably doesn't know it either. Osteoporosis is called the "silent disease" because it eats away your skeletal bone mass—very slowly. Osteo, in Greek, means bone; porosis means overly porous. Put it all together and it means, weakened bones.

We all lose a little bone as we grow older. But, because of their genetic background, white women tend to lose much more. It all has to do with the endocrine system, loss of hormone production, and loss of ability to absorb enough calcium from your food. It's a complicated and little understood part of the body's chemistry.

Women are five times more likely to get severe osteoporosis than men, and for some reason, white women are more susceptible than black women. It usually starts in the mid-to-late thirties and continues slowly to erode the inner bone material. By the time a woman is in her fifties, she may have lost as much as 15 to 20 percent of her inner bone. By the time she reaches her seventies, the loss might be as much as 33 percent.

When you lose bone like this, all sorts of things can happen—and they're all bad. Women in their fifties are more vulnerable to wrist and arm fractures because of creeping osteoporosis. Studies of women aged 40 to 55 have shown a sevenfold increase in the annual incidence of forearm and wrist fractures. Moving up into the seventies, as many as one-fourth of the women have compression fractures of the spine caused by osteoporosis. This can cause the deformity know as "dowager's hump."

Have you ever wondered why you hear so much about older women suffering broken hips from falls? It's osteoporosis at work. Their bones become so brittle from the lack of support inside, they can shatter like china. Hospitals report up to a quarter of a million hip fracture cases every year, and the vast majority of these patients are older women. One study showed that nearly 15 percent of the aged patients admitted for hip fractures died in the hospital, from such things as pneumonia because of their weakened condition. About 50 percent of the women patients died within a year after they were released, probably because their resistence and will to live were broken down by depression.

It's estimated that at least 6 million women have osteoporosis, although they may not realize it. Women over 50 should move very carefully. If they are lucky enough to avoid a fall, the bones in their spinal columns may gradually collapse anyway, resulting in progressive deformity and nerve damage.

That's the bad news. Now, here's the good news.

OSTEOPOROSIS
CAN BE AVOIDED

Osteoporosis can be controlled fairly easily, and it may not be inevitable. Up until recently, most doctors thought osteoporosis was part of the aging process–unavoidable for older women. "This is not so," says Dr. Everett L. Smith, exercise physiologist at the University of Wisconsin Department of Preventive Medicine. Dr. Smith, director of the University's BioGerontology Laboratory, says, "Prescribed physical activity can produce an increased bone mineral content (rebuilding) in the young and old." This is an amazing statement.

Many physicians around the country still think that bone loss is, for the most part, inevitable and unstoppable. But here comes Everett Smith to say you don't have to lose bone. And, more important, if you have lost bone, you might be able to get some of it back. Dr. Smith has found that "increased metabolic demands of working muscles result in increased blood flow and blood pressure . . . and this increased strain placed on the living bone tissue produces bone accretion."

Dr. Smith came to this conclusion after a three-year clinical study of two groups of women in a Missouri nursing home. The women, all in their eighties, were divided into two groups. One group performed a series of prescribed exercises everyday, and the other group continued a regular, sedentary schedule with no exercise. By using a photon absorption device, which works like a single X-ray beam, Dr. Smith and his colleagues were able to measure the extent of bone change which had occurred.

The group of women who were not exercising showed a measured bone loss of 3.28 percent a year. The women who were exercising regularly showed a bone *gain* that averaged 2.3

percent a year. That's an overall turnaround of 5.1 percent a year. Dr. Smith's studies are backed up by studies in Knoxville, Tennessee, measuring bone mass in the arms of male tennis players. The tennis players, aged 55 to 75, had at least 10 percent more bone mass in their serving arms than they had in their other arms. Another study showed that runners aged 50 to 59 had 20 percent more bone in their legs than the nonrunning control group.

In his nursing home experiment, Dr. Smith found that exercise every other day, three times a week, was just right. Less time showed a slide back toward bone loss. The nursing home women weren't doing much when Dr. Smith came on the scene. They were just sitting around, or ambling back and forth to meals and bed. Once the program was underway, exercise activities were tripled. The women moved their arms and legs at safe levels to stimulate their hearts. They did various forms of aerobic dancing, walking, calisthenics, and other activities.

Besides gaining bone back, these women in their eighties "had a great time," Dr. Smith says. They looked better, they felt better, and their medications were reduced or eliminated. After four months, one arthritic woman could dress herself for the first time in several years. Dr. Smith explains, "Some women with inflammation in the joints are limited in their regular exercises during the period of their inflammation, but may benefit from swimming where there's less stress placed on the joints due to water support."

If men must exercise to lessen the threat of heart attacks, women must exercise to lessen the threat of developing "chinaware" bones. In his official report, Dr. Smith wrote: "This study demonstrated that physical activity plays an important role in maintaining and *increasing* [emphasis mine] bone material content." This means that bone in older people, unlike muscle, can be built. As we age, we're always losing some muscle. According to the National Institute on Aging's Gerontological Research Center, we might be able to slow down muscle loss significantly with exercise, but we can't gain back the amount that's lost by normal aging.

CALCIUM SUPPLEMENTS

While exercise is the most important element in preventing dangerous bone loss, it's not the only one. Calcium intake and the female hormone, estrogen, are also important. "Bone is like a calcium bank," Dr. Smith says, explaining that "if you're not putting enough in, your body will draw it out of the bone to maintain constant blood levels." Exercise, he says, seems to help retain calcium and even build it up in bone. Nobody knows exactly why.

To help keep the balance, Dr. Smith says, "The average woman over age 50 should be taking some calcium–one-half to one gram a day (500 to 1,000 milligrams) if her dietary calcium is lower than 400 grams per day. When calcium was given to a test group in a nursing home, a 1.6 percent average bone gain was noted in one year. A combination of exercise *and* calcium supplements is what Dr. Smith now recommends.

In a state-wide study, Wisconsin nutritionists discovered that the average woman was taking in around 500 milligrams (half a gram) of calcium a day. The government's Recommended Daily Allowance (RDA) for calcium intake is 800 milligrams. But many nutritionists believe this amount is too low, especially for older women. Dr. Smith says that some researchers have indicated that 1,250 to 1,500 milligrams may be a more appropriate daily calcium intake for a woman over 50. To maintain calcium balance from the fifties on, if you are already getting the average 500 milligrams a day through your diet, you need another 500 to 1,000 milligrams supplement.

One glass of skim milk or a cup of low-fat yogurt a day equals 250 milligrams of calcium. Adding another 500 milligrams of calcium supplement to a couple of glasses of milk or yogurt should be just about right for the average woman.

You might have trouble reading the dosages on calcium supplement labels. They're often quite confusing. You want 500 milligrams of calcium, not 500 milligrams of some mixture. Ask a pharmacist for help. The more skim milk or low-fat yogurt you take during the day, the less calcium supplement you'll need. If you can't stand milk or yogurt, then you'll have to take more calcium.

Marianne Ivey, clinical pharmacist at the University of Washington Hospital in Seattle, offers this note of caution: Calcium supplements are usually recommended for postmenopausal women. Lesser amounts are suggested for younger women. Anyone with a history of kidney disease should check with a physician before taking calcium. This is because calcium metabolism is closely related to kidney function. A blood test can reveal high uric acid or high phosphate levels. But for a normal woman, 500 to 1,000 milligrams of calcium a day should present no problems.

ESTROGEN THERAPY

You can prevent excessive bone loss with estrogen as well as calcium, because postmenopausal loss of estrogen makes bone more susceptible to calcium loss. But hormone therapy with estrogen has been linked with cancer. Some researchers believe taking estrogen might raise the risk of breast cancer. Cancer of the womb has definitely been linked to estrogen.

Dr. Smith says he feels that estrogen therapy is probably too risky a means of preventing bone loss, and he recommends the much safer, more effective, program of regular exercise and modest calcium supplements.

A PREVENTION PROGRAM

The best routine, says Dr. Smith, is an exercise that works all the main muscles and bones. Jogging is not enough. Because women over 50 tend to break wrists and forearms as well as (later on) hips and spines, push-ups and other arm-stress exercises (such as weight-lifting) are in order. Aerobic dancing, Dr. Smith says, "seems to get everything moving." As long as your back and arms are getting plenty of stress, along with your legs, oesteoporosis may be held to a minimum.

A schedule of 30 minutes of exercise a day, three times a week (as recommended in the previous chapter), ought to do the trick. Dr. Smith's mother, age 67, exercises three times a week and is taking 750 milligrams of calcium a day. His wife jogs three times a week, does vigorous arm exercises and also takes daily calcium supplements.

When you go to your doctor to check out this news about osteoporosis, you may not get very far. Osteoporosis can only be detected by X rays after it has reached an advanced state— up to 20 percent bone loss. By the time you're able to see it on the films, you're in bad shape. Don't wait for "proof." Start your prevention program now.

CHAPTER 18

EAT RIGHT
AND ENJOY

The United States probably has more strange diets floating around than any other country in the world. Forever chasing sylphlike figures, we try one diet after another. Some of us slim down for awhile, then chubby-up again. Others seem to be able to eat anything they want and never gain a pound.

The chapter on exercise contained warnings from several experts in the field of physiology that putting all your efforts into dieting simply won't work for people who don't have iron wills. It's the whole self-denial, self-defeat, guilt trip: We hate ourselves for eating too much—but it sure tastes good. While it's true that regular exercise can help you maintain a decent weight and a decent figure, it won't automatically make you *lose* weight in a few weeks or even a few months. You do have to pay some attention to what you eat.

Forget about all the calorie theories you've heard. A statement such as, "It takes a brisk run of 5 miles to burn off one jellied donut" is a lot of nonsense. You can't expect to eat something and then run around with a stop watch to "burn it off." A long-term balance is what is needed. You get your exercise program started, and then slowly, but surely, begin to change the way you eat.

It's pretty hard to get people in their middle years to change their eating habits radically. In fact it's almost impossible without a heart attack or some other health scare to supply motivation. But you can enjoy eating and, for the most part, eat many things you like and still change your habits enough to make a difference in how you feel, how you look and how your health is.

THE PRITIKIN WAY

If you are a food junkie or a prime candidate for a heart attack, you might want to investigate the supertough diet control espoused by Nathan Pritikin at his Longevity Center in Santa Monica, California. Pritikin takes on people who are suffering from heart and artery disease, hypertension, diabetes, arthritis and other maladies. He's done wonders with these "walking wounded." They are run through a diet and exercise clinic for the better part of a month, for which they pay several thousand dollars. Pritikin has put all his ideas, diets, exercise tips (even ways to cheat on the diet) in a book called *The Pritikin Program for Diet and Exercise* (Grosset & Dunlap).

Even if you can't stick to the Pritikin system—and not many people can—it's interesting to study his methods and adapt some of them to your own, less stringent diet. One of Pritikin's main principles is his emphasis on drastically cutting down on fat. His overall diet only allows 5 to 10 percent fat in one's total caloric intake, compared with 30 percent allowed by the American Heart Association. If you are an "average" American, and a beef addict, your fat intake is probably closer to 50 percent.

The trouble with Pritikin's approach is that unless you are

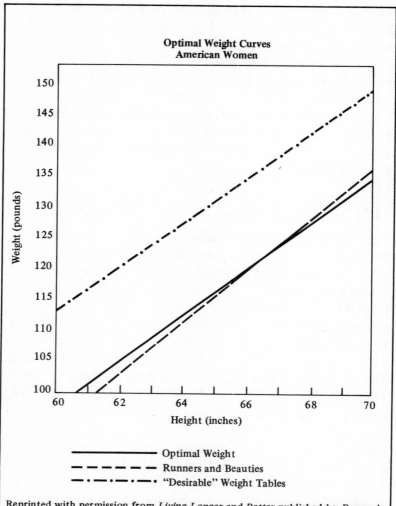

Optimal Weight Curves
American Women

Reprinted with permission from *Living Longer and Better* published by *Runner's World* Magazine, 1400 Stierlin Road, Mountain View, Calif. 94043.

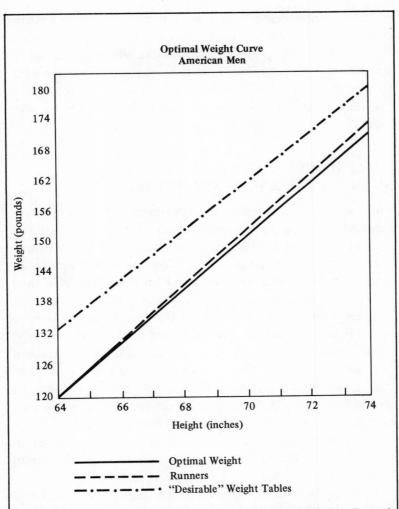

Optimal Weight Curve
American Men

Optimal Weight
Runners
"Desirable" Weight Tables

Reprinted with permission from *Living Longer and Better* published by *Runner's World* Magazine, 1400 Stierlin Road, Mountain View, Calif. 94043.

in agony or near death from disease, you're just not going to be able to comply with the harsh, self-denial his regime requires. You'll have to take a box lunch with you when you eat out. If you have the motivation for medical reasons, you might want to give it a try. You'll have to live with a sparse, almost vegetarian diet, but you may be the healthiest person on your block.

COMPROMISE DIETING— MODERATION AND SUBSTITUTION

For the rest of us, maybe a compromise will do. Dr. Mark Hegsted, a former professor of nutrition at Harvard, and currently head of the Human Nutrition Center at the United States Department of Agriculture, recommends moderation in dieting. It's his belief that too much emphasis on self-denial won't work for any significant length of time.

Hegsted agrees with Pritikin that fat is the big item to watch in any diet. At the top of your list of dieting rules should be this item: CUT DOWN ON ALL FATS. By limiting your intake of red meats and dairy fats and concentrating more on fish, chicken and turkey (without the skin) you can reduce much of the fat in your food. When you do eat meat, stick to the lean cuts as much as possible. Don't indulge in gravies with fat in them. Hegsted believes that fat in food influences serum cholesterol in the blood more than the actual cholesterol content of some foods.

If you have to cut back on meats, such as fatty beef and pork, you can make up for them by eating more whole grain bread and more potatoes. There was a time when we thought that the way to diet was to cut out bread and potatoes. Researchers today say we should have more of these complex carbohydrates in our diets, a lot less fat, and somewhat less protein. For awhile, it was all protein. High protein diets were commonplace. Now, experts are recommending less protein and more of the right kind of carbohydrates.

Heavily processed white bread is frowned on by many nutritionists because vitamins and roughage have been all but removed from it. The processors are putting back some of the vitamins and minerals, but it's still not as valuable nutritionally as whole grain bread. One nutritionist likens overprocessed white bread to "edible napkins."

Most supermarkets now carry a wide variety of whole grain breads. They're tasty, and you can eat several slices a day without feeling guilty. With potatoes, you get necessary, complex carbohydrates, plus a nice assortment of vitamins and minerals. Whenever possible, eat the potato skin, too.

Another good way to cut down on fat is to drink skim milk. From it you get nutrition without butter fat. If you haven't already done so, switch from butter to margarine (except for an occasional buttered bread or pancake splurge). But don't go overboard on margarine, either, or on the other polyunsaturated fats. Dr. Hegsted says, "These should be taken in moderation as well." Cut down on the use of *all* fats, including the polyunsaturated margarines and oils.

As once-a-week or twice-a-week meat substitutes, you might want to try combinations such as: Cuban rice and black beans (using brown rice for extra nutritive value); grated, natural cheese and potato casserole; Italian pasta (try lasagna, kidney beans, natural cheese and tomato sauce); Mexican tortillas and beans (you can buy frozen tortillas); and New England bean chowder (with potatoes, green peppers and milk). These regional dishes are delicious and can help you to reduce the amount of meat in your diet. For recipes and ideas for "meatless days," you might want to read *Recipes for a Small Planet* by Ellen Ewald, a Ballantine paperback.

The next item on your checklist of dietary *don'ts* should be sugar. You can't eliminate it completely, but you can try to curb your sweet tooth. Also, train yourself to read labels and keep a sharp watch for "hidden" sugar in processed and convenience foods. By cutting down on fat and sugar (the latter is the less harmful one to cheat on), Dr. Hegsted says "you cut a lot of calories without cutting much of the quantity or quality of your meals."

Salt is another item you can ration. You needn't cut it out (unless you've been told to by your doctor), but you can use it with a much lighter hand. Watch out for salt in canned and preserved food. That's how a lot of it gets into your diet. As a substitute for salt in cooking you can use herbs such as basil, tarragon, thyme, and garlic and chives. According to Dr. Donald Ware, medical officer for the United States government's High Blood Pressure Education Program: "Studies show that salt intake is associated with high blood pressure. People, and even whole countries like Japan, who have a lot of salt in their diet tend to have high blood pressure problems. You get plenty of salt in your food without adding any. Unless you live in a hot, tropical climate or play continuous, heavy sports in the heat and sweat a lot, you don't need extra salt. Don't add anymore to your food. If you do, make it moderate. All we need is one gram of salt a day and we get much more than that in our regular diet."

Roughage is another item for your good-diet list. For awhile, we seemed to be sliding more and more toward processed foods that were stripped of fiber and cellulose roughage on the way through the processing factories. Supposedly, this meant that bowel movements weren't frequent enough and stool was staying too long in the lower intestines, creating a potential danger of cancer of the colon and all sorts of possible stomach disorders.

So we were told to eat more roughage and fiber. One of the easiest kinds of fiber to find on the market is bran (the material that's refined out of wheat.) Advertising would lead one to believe that bran for breakfast will cure everything from cancer to corns. Sure, some bran is good for you. But, you can—and should—get fiber roughage from other foods such as apples and carrots, whole grain breads and cereals and fresh vegetables. With more roughage in your diet, be sure to drink plenty of water.

WE'RE ALL DIFFERENT

When you start making changes in your diet, remember that we all have different chemistries. For example, do you know a person who is as slim as a reed and has always been that way? No problems—pass the second helpings. Then, there's the other kind of person who has always struggled with weight. The goodies that spend ten seconds in their mouths settle for a lifetime on their hips.

Dr. Hegsted says that our genetic differences make our inner food processing simple for some people and difficult for others. Some of us just seem to have faster engines than others—our combustion systems work differently.

My doctor, Oscar Mann, says you can check various individuals' metabolism by measuring cholesterol. Too much cholesterol in your blood (serum cholesterol) is supposed to be dangerous because it can act like sludge, sticking to blood vessels and eventually clogging them. The clogged vessels precipitate a heart attack.

So, just cut out food that contains a lot of cholesterol—right? It's not always that easy. Dr. Mann says some patients can eat all kinds of food loaded with cholesterol (beef, bacon, eggs, butter) and their serum cholesterol (in the blood) remains normal or below normal. Others diet with great self-denial, eating practically no beef, eggs, bacon, or butter. And, guess what? Their cholesterol levels are high.

"This means we synthesize our own cholesterol at various

rates," says Dr. Mann. How you can control your own cholesterol production is still somewhat of a mystery. You need some cholesterol as part of your blood chemistry. It's thought that stress causes us to produce more cholesterol, and this is under study. Meanwhile, Dr. Mann tells me I should continue my regular exercise because it has raised my high-density lipoprotein level. (HDLs help clean out artery clogging components in cholesterol.) He advised me to eat prudently when it came to foods that were high in cholesterol but he did not recommend my making a fetish of it.

EATING CAN STILL
BE ENJOYABLE

Eating right and enjoying it comes relatively easy for me because of my wife, Vida. She does most of the meal-planning and cooking although I cook dinner once a week. Vida's meals are interesting, well-balanced, and satisfying. The emphasis is on poultry, fish, rice and beans (and all sorts of other nonmeat, Latin American combinations), potatoes, vegetables, and salad. We have beef during the week, but it's usually lean meat or low-fat veal which, unfortunately, is very expensive.

Having a partner who is an expert in producing balanced meals can be a lifesaver. If you are single, you're responsible for your choice of meals, whether eaten at home or in a restaurant. Eating frequently with friends can be a good way of helping you to take care of yourself. If you and your friends are concerned about eating right, you can share the responsibility of feeding each other balanced meals.

Living alone, especially for people in their forties, fifties, and sixties, can present a potential, long-range nutrition problem. The extreme case, is the lonely widow who no longer has anyone to cook for or the widower who may not be able to cook for himself. Such a person easily might slide into the "tea and toast" syndrome. A solitary person often eats less and less because it's a bother to cook for just one. This can lead to depression, and depression can lead to the pits.

If you're a hardy individualist and love whipping up good, nutritious meals on your own (freezing the leftovers to use later), that's fine. If you're not, then seek out others to eat with. Organize a round robin "eat-in" arrangement with good friends. You'll not only eat better, you'll save money. Cooking for two, three, or four is cheaper than cooking for one.

It's not always *what* you eat, but *how* you eat it that counts. In their book, *Living Longer and Better*, Dr. Harold Elrick and his associates suggest methods of eating that can help to stifle the urge to overdo it. Their advice: Eat slowly, sip beverages slowly, drink a glass of water before each meal, drink more fluids during the meal, enjoy a lot of mixed salads (but watch out for those high-calorie dressings.) Use raw vegetables (carrots, cucumbers, cauliflower, celery, radishes, cherry tomatoes, and the like) as predinner snacks.

GOOD READING

You can get a large poster called "New American Eating Guide," published by the Center for Science in the Public Interest. It's big and colorful and can fit on a kitchen wall or refrigerator door or wall. It's all spelled out: Things You Can Eat Anytime (whole grain breads, potatoes, vegetables, skim milk, fish, chicken or turkey); Things You Can Eat in Moderation (waffles and pancakes, french fries in vegetable oil, ice milk, flank steak, pork loin); and Things You Can Eat Now and Then (sticky buns, cheesecake, ice cream, commercial fried chicken and french fries, cheese omelets, bacon and salami). These are just some of the items listed. You get all sorts of other suggestions, cooking tips, the latest advice on additives, fat and cholesterol, etc. For more information, write: CSPI, P.O. Box 7226, Washington, DC 20044.

CHAPTER 19

THE VITAMIN CONTROVERSY

The subject of vitamins is almost as controversial as religion, sex, and politics. On one hand, proponents claim we are lacking all sorts of vitamins and minerals. This group scoffs at the daily supplemental pills that children and menstruating women are supposed to take. That's not enough, they claim. This group believes you should be taking large doses of vitamins C, B-complex, E, and a whole list of minerals, including the latest wonder—selenium. You could easily be taking as many as fifteen to twenty pills a day, just to stay even.

Then, you have the smug folks who say: "What—me worry?" They wouldn't touch vitamins. "If you have a balanced diet," they say, "you don't need any vitamins." But, that "balanced diet" phrase rolls around in your brain, making you wonder if you are, indeed, getting every possible vitamin and mineral you need. Was that "hamburger and shake" balanced? How about the beer and popcorn? This anti-vitamin bunch might condescend to allow daily, small-dose, multivitamin pills for "people who eat poorly."

These are the two extremes in the Great Vitamin Debate. In between, perhaps, lie the rest of us. We have our secret vitamins that we pop surreptitiously when nobody is looking. Vitamin C is, by far, the favorite. Linus Pauling, the Nobel Prize winner, has done much to make vitamin C the biggest selling vitamin by far. They can't crank it out fast enough. Pauling contends that massive daily doses (thousands of milligrams) will help prevent colds and make them go away faster when you do get them. Pauling says he has all the proof he needs, but food scientists and pharamcologists say there is no conclusive, clinical evidence as yet.

In my many interviews for this book, I asked various scientists and others about their diets, including whether or not they took any vitamins or minerals. Most would reply only if I promised anonymity. The consensus was that vitamin C is probably okay to take as a sort of semiscientific, semivoodoo, preventive medicine—if you don't overdo it. The recommended dosage was around 500 to 1,000 milligrams a day. The more astute pill poppers were quick to explain that it does very little good to take vitamin C in one, large dose every morning. They suggest "time-release" capsules as an alternative to taking small doses (100 to 200 milligrams) of the vitamin four or five times a day. The timed release of the special capsules lets the vitamin C seep into your system over a period of about eight hours. The pills cost more than the standard type, but are worth it.

If vitamin C is just dumped into your system in one blob in the morning, it's mostly wasted. It's excreted through your urine and stool and goes down the drain into the sewers. This is why you should always tell a doctor or lab technician that you're taking vitamin C when you have urine or stool tests. It could distort the results.

Why bother taking vitamin C? After all, we get the stuff in such commonplace things as orange juice, potatoes and other fruits and vegetables. But, the question always comes up: Do we get enough? Aside from the vague possibility that it cuts down on colds and makes them less severe, vitamin C keeps popping up in research literature on cancer, aging and other scientific subjects. There is no clinical evidence yet, but some scientists believe that vitamin C can prevent cancer of the colon by causing precancerous lesions, called polyps, to disappear. The *Washington Post* quoted Dr. Jerome DeCrosse, head of surgery at Sloan-Kettering Memorial Cancer Center in New York, as saying that a continuous flow of vitamin C (through a time-release mechanism) over damaged cells in the colon appears to counteract the progression toward cancer.

In various studies of the aging process, vitamin C is mentioned as possibly playing an important role because of its anti-oxidation qualities. In his fascinating book, *Prolongevity* (published by Avon Books), Albert Rosenfeld talks about scientific speculation that longer-lived people seem to have had more access to vitamin C. Rosenfeld, who is science editor for the *Saturday Review,* spent several years investigating research on aging. Other antioxidants such as vitamin E and selenium may also affect the aging process, but nobody is sure just how they work. Rosenfeld says that the combination of vitamin C *and* vitamin E seems to work together to produce a greater antioxidant effect. Mice that were fed vitamin C didn't live longer than other mice. But, mice that were fed combinations of antioxidants did live longer.

Eleanor D. Schlenker, professor of human nutrition and foods at the University of Vermont says a longitudinal study in California over a four-year-period found "higher mortality among older subjects who had reported lower intakes of vitamin C, and vitamin A and niacin (part of the B-complex)." Dr. Schlenker also points to a Michigan longitudinal study which showed that the taste buds of some older women coming in for clinical evaluation had atrophied. Others' had not. The women who had taste bud problems, she says, had been receiving a significantly lower intake of vitamin C.

Of course, none of this is conclusive proof of anything. But, still, bits of evidence keep flashing in the distance, like heat lightning. There seems to be something there. Rosenfeld reports cases of animals deficient in vitamin E showing cell damage similar to that found in the aging process. But, he says, overdoses of vitamin E could conceivably work in the opposite direction to speed up aging. More is not necessarily better. You need a balance.

Selenium is something we're supposed to get in our food, along with other trace minerals. Just a little bit works fine. Too much can be toxic. But, scientists wonder whether food from some areas of the country has enough selenium. It depends on the soil mineral content. Selenium is intricately related to vitamins C and E in its antioxidant (antidecay) properties. First comes vitamin C. Then comes vitamin E, which works with C as an amplifier. Finally, comes selenium which works closely with vitamin E. Selenium can be found in such things as bran, wheat germ, broccoli, onions, tomatoes and tuna fish.

WARNINGS, CLAIMS, AND COUNTERCLAIMS

According to the *Nutrition Almanac*, edited by Nutrition Research, Inc., and published by McGraw-Hill, "In areas where there was high content of selenium in the soil, lower cancer incidence was reported." The *Nutrition Almanac* makes for intriguing reading, but you have to take it with a grain of salt (or a grain of wheat, if you're on a salt-free diet). As you read through it, you find that almost all vitamins and minerals can cure or prevent some dread disease. Vitamin E, for example, is supposed to prevent heart disease, but no clinical proof is offered to back up this supposition.

The almanac warns readers not to overdose on vitamin E because "it has a tendency to raise blood pressure when given in large doses." It's best to keep your daily intake of vitamin E down to 100 or 200 international units (IUs). Selenium, if you can find it as a supplement, should be avoided. It can be toxic at levels as low as five to ten parts per million, and you're already getting some traces of it in your food.

Vitamin C is a lot safer to fool with than selenium or vitamin E. But massive doses have been known to plague some people. Marianne Ivey, clinical pharmacist at the University of Washington Hospital, reports that it's possible to get kidney stones from taking large amounts of vitamin C over a period of time. Ivey, who wrote the chapter on vitamins and minerals for the American Pharmaceutical Association's *Pharmacist's Handbook*, says: "Everybody is different . . . One person may be able to tolerate a lot of vitamin C and another person may not." She recommends moderation in vitamin C dosages, stating there is no clinical evidence to back up claims that large doses have any special benefit.

After hearing all the claims and counterclaims for vitamin C and other vitamins and minerals, I asked science editor Rosenfeld what he, personally, takes on a daily basis. He said, after his talks with dozens of scientists and physicians, he decided to take vitamin C, vitamin E and vitamin B-complex. He said he occasionally takes very small amounts of selenium. He advises against overly large doses of both vitamin C and vitamin E until more is known about them. His original daily dosage for vitamin C, as reported in his book, was 500 milligrams. The original amount for vitamin E was 100 IUs. Since the book was published, Rosenfeld says he has slightly increased the amounts of vitamin C and E he takes.

Rosenfeld admits he has no hard evidence to back up his vitamin selection or dosage. "But," he says, "I found a number of doctors taking these vitamins for the first time, and I also found quite a number of scientists who are working on aging process research taking them... It's just a hunch."

If you take megadoses of vitamin C and E regularly, you should monitor yourself. If diarrhea, headaches, urinary problems or any other unusual symptoms ensue, reduce the doses or stop for awhile. Some people suffer from diarrhea with heavy doses of vitamin C.

For what it's worth, I take 500 milligrams of vitamin C daily (in time-release capsules), 100 (and sometimes 200) IUs of vitamin E, and two tablets of brewer's yeast (natural vitamin B-complex) with each meal. I also put some wheat germ on my breakfast cereal because it tastes good and it contains some B-complex, vitamin E and minerals. (My wife takes a combination of vitamins C and B-complex, plus calcium for bone strength).

Have my vitamins done me any good? I haven't the faintest idea. It's like a witch doctor's ritual. I pop the pills in the morning, sprinkle a little wheat germ on my cereal and Think Good Thoughts. Kaazzaam! I feel better already. Because of the mystique surrounding vitamins, we are probably getting a certain amount of placebo effect from taking them. And this isn't bad. If you believe they will work, maybe they will. Each of us has our own little world of magic, ritual, and incantation.

CHAPTER 20

MAJOR WORRIES

As you move beyond your middle years, you are more exposed to the law of averages. You become more susceptible to such things as heart attacks, cancer, and strokes. This is not necessarily a part of the aging process. It's because the longer you live, the more chance a disease has to develop. Many types of cancer, for example, are triggered after your body's cells have been exposed to various carcinogens (cancer-causing chemicals) over the years. After a cell has been hit four or five times (which could take 30 years or so), it might become mutated and part of a pre-cancerous lesion. This lesion can do one of three things: It can turn into cancer, it can grow so slowly it won't bother you, or it can disappear. All this takes time. After you reach age 50, you may have been exposed to many carcinogenic "hits," and therefore, have more of a chance of contracting some form of cancer.

The same goes for heart disease, high blood pressure, and strokes. The longer you eat a lot of fatty foods, keep gaining

	Mortality for Leading Causes of Death: United States, 1976			
Rank	Cause of Death	Number of Deaths	Death Rate Per 100,000 Population	Percent of Total Deaths
	All Causes	**1,909,440**	**889.5**	**100.0**
1	Diseases of Heart	723,729	337.1	37.9
2	Cancer	377,312	175.8	19.8
3	Stroke	188,623	87.9	9.9
4	Accidents	100,761	46.9	5.3
5	Influenza & Pneumonia	61,666	28.7	3.2
6	Diabetes Mellitus	34,508	16.1	1.8
7	Cirrhosis of Liver	31,453	14.7	1.6
8	Arteriosclerosis	29,366	13.7	1.5
9	Suicide	26,832	12.5	1.4
10	Diseases of Infancy	24,809	11.6	1.3
11	Homicide	19,554	9.1	1.0
12	Emphysema	17,796	8.3	0.9
13	Congenital Anomalies	13,002	6.1	0.7
14	Nephritis & Nephrosis	8,541	4.0	0.4
15	Septicemia & Pyemia	6,401	3.0	0.3
	Other & Ill–defined	246,087	114.7	12.9

Source: Vital Statistics of the United States, 1976.

weight, continue smoking, don't exercise, and become involved in stressful situations, the more you become a candidate for some cardiovascular crisis (heart attack or stroke.) On the plus side, the longer you live, the more you seem to have going for you as far as resistance to some diseases is concerned. You've gotten by the dangerous early heart attack or early breast cancer periods.

CANCER OF THE COLON

Cancer is the disease that strikes the most fear in people's hearts, especially those of us over 50. We've all had friends or family members who have had brushes with cancer, or have

1979 ESTIMATES

Cancer Incidence by Site and Sex†

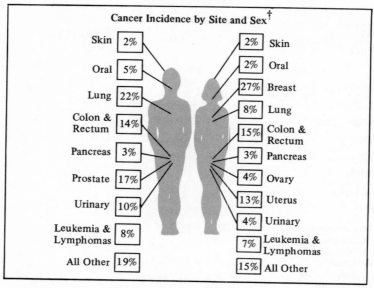

Skin	2%	2% Skin
Oral	5%	2% Oral
Lung	22%	27% Breast
Colon & Rectum	14%	8% Lung
Pancreas	3%	15% Colon & Rectum
Prostate	17%	3% Pancreas
Urinary	10%	4% Ovary
Leukemia & Lymphomas	8%	13% Uterus
All Other	19%	4% Urinary
		7% Leukemia & Lymphomas
		15% All Other

Cancer Deaths by Site and Sex

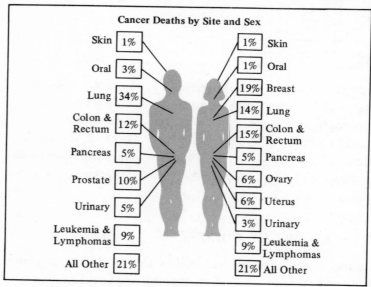

Skin	1%	1% Skin
Oral	3%	1% Oral
Lung	34%	19% Breast
Colon & Rectum	12%	14% Lung
Pancreas	5%	15% Colon & Rectum
Prostate	10%	5% Pancreas
Urinary	5%	6% Ovary
Leukemia & Lymphomas	9%	6% Uterus
All Other	21%	3% Urinary
		9% Leukemia & Lymphomas
		21% All Other

†Excluding non–melanoma skin cancer and carcinoma in situ of uterine cervix.   Source: American Cancer Society

died from it. Heart attacks kill more people every year than cancer, but we don't seem to fear them as much.

Colon cancer strikes more of us than any other internal cancer. According to the American Cancer Society, this may be due to the things we eat—high-fat, high-protein, low-fiber diets. The disease strikes both men and women—there's no discrimination. And, there aren't really any noticeable symptoms in the early stages. When you do get symptoms, they're much like those of other ailments which are relatively harmless. You might get cramps or temporary pain, constipation, diarrhea, or some rectal bleeding (imitating hemorrhoids).

In the past, the usual way in which doctors checked for cancer of the colon was to insert a metal tube in your rectum and examine the inside with a light. This required a previsit enema and was a particularly unpleasant procedure. Doctors still do this, but usually only when they suspect something. Now, they often use do-it-yourself stool tests to see if they can find minute traces of blood.

You get six small cardboard packets that contain test paper treated with guiac, which can pinpoint microscopic blood particles. You take a small sample of your stool with a little stick and spread it on the sensitized paper. You fold up the packet, seal it, put in a special envelope and mail it back to your doctor, or to a designated laboratory. You do this for six different bowel movements. It's very inexpensive. In some cases, you can get free test kits through your local chapter of the American Cancer Society. These tests should be done at least once a year. If you catch cancer of the colon early, you have a 75 percent chance of beating the disease. Get some test packets and put them in your bathroom as a reminder. The test should also be done any time you have persistent cramps, pains, diarrhea, constipation, or signs of blood.

BREAST CANCER

For many women, breast cancer is a major worry. It seems to be everywhere, attacking a neighbor, someone at work and national figures such as Betty Ford, Happy Rockefeller and Marvela Bayh. Half of all breast cancers are diagnosed in women aged 60 and over. For some reason or other, older women seem to feel they don't have to worry much about breast cancer because they've gone past the worrying age. This may be why older women don't seem to discover breast cancers as soon as younger women. It's most unfortunate, because the earlier you discover cancer of the breast, the better the chance that it can be treated successfully.

If you're a woman in your middle years, make a pledge to take a course in self-examination of your breasts. More and more universities, community colleges, and local health agencies are conducting seminars in self-examination. Learn how to do it the right way, then examine your breasts at least once a month. Keep notes and a "map" of where any suspicious lumps are found. The vast majority of these lumps are probably cysts or fatty tissue. But the name of the game is *change*. If there's a change, if one lump begins to get bigger or become hard, or if you find a new one that seems "different" from the others, then go in for a careful checkup with a doctor who specializes in breast cancer. Don't let a gynecologist put you off with "it's probably nothing." If it feels different or strange to you, have a cancer specialist give another opinion. Even a surgical biopsy might be necessary.

Apparently, breast cancer is likely to strike some types of women more than others. In the book *Uncharted Territory: Issues and Concerns of Women over 40*, published by the University of Maryland's Center on Aging, the authors describe higher risk and lower risk women this way:

"It would appear that white women of Northern

European descent who are overweight, have histories of cancer in their families (mother, sister, grandmother), began menstruating early, and had a first child after they were thirty-five (or had no children), are the most likely to develop breast cancer. The least likely candidates are Oriental and American Indian women with no history of breast cancer in the family, late onset of menstruation, and motherhood before age twenty. A short reproductive life because of an early menopause, surgical or natural, helps lower the risk for everyone."

The book explains that the incidence of breast cancer is almost twice as high in families where mothers, grandmothers, or sisters have had the disease. And, women who have had cancer in one breast have considerably increased chances of having it in the other. Women in the higher risk group are most likely to get breast cancer from age forty on up into their seventies.

If you think you have a suspicious lump, it's wise to have your doctor introduce you to a good breast cancer specialist in your area. More tests can be made. If surgery is suggested, make sure you get a surgeon experienced in breast cancer. While many general surgeons can do a good job, you should look for a specialist, someone who has done many operations on the breast.

Techniques for mastectomy are changing fast, so you want to be working with a topflight breast cancer surgeon. There is increasing evidence that it may not be necessary to cut out the entire breast and adjoining muscle. An Italian cancer surgeon, Dr. Umberto Veronesi, head of Italy's National Cancer Institute, says he has had considerable success with partial removal of the breast. But, he warns, this modified surgery technique only applies to women with breast cancers that are quite small. He says around one woman cancer patient in three has this type of tumor.

By no means rush into surgery, giving the surgeon carte

blanche to do anything if cancer is found. A biopsy may be done, and then you can have time to think about it. You'll want another opinion, maybe, and will want to know all the risks, all the options. Some surgeons are still doing the radical mastectomy, in which the entire breast and the muscle around it are removed. This is a brutal, disfiguring, and disabling operation. The majority of surgeons are now doing a modified radical, where just the breast is removed.

You should also be aware that an increasing number of women are combining mastectomies with plastic surgery, so they will still have a breast when the operation is over, or they have a breast rebuilt later on. The plastic surgeon works with the cancer surgeon to leave enough material so the breast can be rebuilt. They can even put on a nipple and give it some color, to match the other breast. This type of plastic surgery is one of the few kinds that is reimbursable under Blue Cross/Blue Shield, some company insurance plans, and Medicare.

PROSTATE CANCER

If breast cancer is a nightmare for women, prostate cancer is its counterpart for men. It's called the "silent killer" and is the major cause of death by cancer for older men. More often than not, prostate cancer's symptoms don't become noticeable until it's too late. The symptoms are similar to those of common prostate ailments. You might have urination problems— starting and/or stopping. Usually these symptoms are related to irritation or enlargement of the prostate. But all urinary difficulties of men over 50 should be checked out by their physicians.

To protect yourself, have a rectal examination at least once a year. Your doctor should examine the prostate gland carefully to see if it's suspiciously enlarged or shows other possible cancer symptoms. This examination is a must. Don't put it off. From age 50 to 60, the risk of prostate cancer rises. After age 60, it rises even faster. The older you get, the more chance you have of getting prostate cancer. The rectal exam is your main means of protection.

The University of Minnesota's Department of Epidemiology is studying prostate cancer cases, trying to find out if some men are more inclined than others to get the disease. As yet, there is no solid evidence as to whether frequent or infrequent sex influences the incidence of prostate cancer. Some studies have gone into the histories of men who have had operations for prostate cancer. It was found that many of these men had less sex than was considered average, but the evidence is sketchy. The lesser amount of sex, the researchers say, might have occurred because the men had embarrassing urinary problems coupled with their disease. They ask: Did the lack of sex cause the symptoms, or did the symptoms cause the lack of sex? Nobody knows.

With prostate cancer and with chronic, enlarged prostate (a benign disease), surgery may be in order. Surgeons have advanced techniques at their disposal, and a man's sex life can be spared in all but the most advanced cases of prostate cancer. The prostate's only function is to supply the ejaculation fluid during orgasm. Most, if not all, of the prostate gland can be cut out and a man can still have an erection and orgasm. He won't have the ejaculation fluid, and this might present a psychological problem. If a man is prepared for the "shock" of not having any fluid, he can learn to enjoy his orgasm without it.

If surgery is in order, you'll want the best prostate specialist (uro-oncologist) available. After all, your future sex life is at stake. If the collection of sensitive nerves next to the prostate are left intact, there will be enough sensation for a satisfying orgasm.

SKIN CANCER

Skin cancer is, by far, the most common form of cancer. Fortunately, the most common types of skin cancer are not all that dangerous. Skin cancer hits blue-eyed, light-skinned people most often, and it begins to show up more frequently as they move up into the years after 50. More than 400,000 cases of skin cancer are reported every year, but the vast majority are handled in doctors' offices or through minor surgery. The majority are slow-developing basal cell or squamous cell cancers. If attended to early, they can be stopped and there's usually no more problem. If you let them go, they can disfigure by eating up the skin and underlying tissue.

According to Dr. Frederick Urbach, director of the Skin Cancer Hospital at Temple University, melanoma is the skin cancer to watch out for. It's a mole, a spot, or a lump that changes color, grows, or does both. This cancer moves fast and is a killer—one of the worst. Once it gets going, your chances of survival are only fifty-fifty. But, if you catch it early, your chances may be as high as eighty-twenty. If you spot the melanoma early (it's usually blue-black or brown), it can be removed before it spreads. The thing to look for is something that changes. A melanoma on the legs might be spotted before it becomes too dangerous. But, Dr. Urbach says, a person might miss a melanoma on the back, where it is hard to monitor.

Dr. John F. Potter, Director of the Vincent T. Lombardi Cancer Research Center at Georgetown University Hospital, says the most frequent symptom of melanoma is a mole that changes color or size. The mole gets darker, thicker, bleeds, and may break down into an open sore. This is why any change in a mole should be checked immediately. People who have already had a squamous cell or basal cell cancer should be especially watchful for moles that change. The fact that you had one type of skin cancer should put you on warning to watch for the development of others.

Blacks and other darker-skinned people have a lot less to worry about. Skin cancer usually develops in people who are blonds (all shades), redheads, blue-eyed and have light skin. These people would benefit by being wary of the sun during the highest radiation hours of the day—from 10 A.M. to 2 P.M.—especially during summer or during outings in tropical areas. People who work in the sun a great deal should be cautious. Sun radiation has a cumulative effect.

Besides being a potentially dangerous cause of cancer, excessive exposure to the sun also decreases the elasticity of the skin and causes premature wrinkling and aging. So do your sunning in the morning and late afternoon. Stay away from sunbathing during the midday period, and wear protective clothing if you have to be out in the sun.

CANCER OF THE THROAT

Throat cancer (cancer of the larynx) primarily hits people who smoke and drink. It doesn't seem to hit people who drink moderately and don't smoke. Dr. Gary R. Burch, a Washington, D.C. otolaryngologist (ear, nose, and throat specialist) says, "Almost all the throat cancer cases I've ever seen or have treated have been people who both smoked and drank . . . this combination increases your risk a hundred times." Dr. Burch says scientists don't put much emphasis on possible hereditary causes of throat cancer. "We do see it in families," he says, "but when you check further you find that everybody in the family is smoking and drinking." If you smoke and drink heavily, he says, you should have your throat checked by a specialist at least once a year. General practitioners and internists might miss the early signs of throat cancer. Here are some of the danger signals:

Hoarseness lasting more than 10 days.
Pain in the throat
(especially pain that goes to the ear).
Pain in swallowing, difficulty in swallowing.
Blood in sputum.
Unexplained lump in throat or neck.

American Cancer Society figures show that throat cancer caught in the first stage can be controlled by a biopsy and the use of X-ray therapy. Your chances of cure are 91 percent. If it's caught in the second stage, your chances drop to 82 percent, with radiation and some surgery needed, but you retain your voice. In the third stage you usually have to have your voice box, the larynx, removed, and you have a 49 percent chance of survival. After the fourth stage, the cancer has spread and you only have a 9 percent chance.

PREVENTIVE MEASURES

The National Cancer Institute has sponsored studies on the use of vitamin A-type substances as preventive medicine for certain cancers. It is known that people with vitamin A deficiences have a higher incidence of cancer. But big doses of vitamin A are toxic. Apparently, vitamin A helps rebuild the cells that have broken down. The institute says that vitamin A has been synthesized to increase its potency and lower its toxicity to the point where it can build up the damaged cells without having any serious side effects. Studies have shown that modified vitamin A, called synthetic retinoids, can fend off cancer in animals that have been exposed to heavy doses of cancer-causing chemicals (the kind that break down cells).

This roundup by no means covers all the forms of cancer (the links between smoking and lung cancer will be covered in the next chapter); but some of the major cancer worries have been explored. You can get more information on any type of cancer by calling the National Cancer Institute's toll-free number: 800-638-6694. If you live in Maryland, you should call: 800-492-1444. Alaska and Hawaii, 1-800-638-6070. You can get quick answers to questions about prevention, warning signals, diagnosis, treatment, and community resources.

HEART DISEASE

Heart disease doesn't seem to get quite as much publicity as cancer, but it's the nation's number one killer. In the chapters on exercise and diet, we learned that it's possible to change the odds of having a heart attack by the way we eat, exercise, and handle stress. The highest risk person is usually male, eats too much fatty foods, smokes heavily, drinks heavily, is overweight, doesn't exercise, and encounters considerable stress in his work. The risk of heart attack is a lot less for women until menopause, and then it increases with age.

Unlike cancer, which appears to be killing as many people now as it did ten years ago, the heart attack rate has dropped by 20 percent in the past ten years. According to Dr. John W. Farquhar, Director of the Stanford (University) Heart Disease Prevention Program, the reason the heart attack rate has dropped recently (from 1940 to 1967, it rose 40 percent) is because there are fewer adult smokers, more people are watching their diets (less fats, less cholesterol), more people are exercising, and more people have controlled their high blood pressure.

HYPERTENSION

The number of stroke deaths, which are related to high blood pressure (hypertension), has dropped dramatically since 1972. That was the year a national campaign was started to alert people to the danger of hypertension and to urge them to have their blood pressure checked. Hypertension is another "silent killer" because without a blood pressure test, you don't know you have it. You should have your blood pressure checked at least once a year.

There are any number of medications that can effectively lower blood pressure. Exercise will also help, but for people with really high pressure, it won't be enough by itself. Transcendental meditation (TM) can be used to unhook one's mind from daily stress, and lower blood pressure. You should read *The Relaxation Response* (Avon Books) by Dr. Herbert Benson of Harvard Medical School. Dr. Benson says nearly one million deaths a year can be traced to problems with hypertension. He identifies the causes of these deaths as: bad diet, lack of exercise, family history (of cardiovascular problems), and *stress*. In pre-historic times, man was programmed to a "fight-or-flight" response. Attack or run. However, today, if the boss or a spouse gets our blood boiling, we usually can't attack, and we can't just run out the door. We stick it out, and our insides churn. Up goes the old blood pressure.

All sorts of things cause stress. Death of a spouse, divorce, and marital separation are the top three. Retirement (another form of separation) is right up there. To handle stress, Dr. Benson suggests the "relaxation reponse." Basically, it goes like this:

1. Sit in a quiet environment after waking in the morning or before going to bed at night.
2. Get into a comfortable position, but don't lie down.
3. Use a hypnotic word, such as "one", and say it over and over again in your mind while inhaling and exhaling slowly.
4. Adopt a passive attitude. Make your mind come back to the word and to the rhythmic breathing.
5. Do the procedure for 20 minutes, once or twice a day.

I have tried this and it works. It's great for calming down before going to bed, and it can put you to sleep. Dr. Benson says TM can help keep blood pressure from getting high, and it might even lower blood pressure if it's already too high. In England, doctors have found that they can sometimes take patients off hypertension medication by working on a combination TM, exercise, and dietary program.

If you are taking medication for high blood pressure, check to see what's in it. Reserpine, the generic name for a widely used drug to control high blood pressure, has been found to cause cancer in laboratory animals. Get another medication (unless your doctor has a very good reason for keeping you on reserpine). There are many other drugs for high blood pressure. Unfortunately, your prescription probably won't have the word "reserpine" on it. The drug is concealed under at least twenty different brand names. Ask your doctor or your pharmacist to tell you what's in the medicine you're taking.

Some medications for high blood pressure can also cause impotence in men. If you have any problems with your sex life and you're taking a medication for high blood pressure, ask your doctor or pharmacist if it's the kind that can interfere with sex. If so, ask to be put on something else.

If you have high blood pressure, or fear it, and want to buy an arm-cuff test device with a stethoscope, have your doctor recommend the right kind to get. Don't order some bargain test device advertised in the Sunday supplements or a magazine (unless your doctor or hospital recommends it). Also, ask your doctor to train you, or have some qualified person show you how to use the device correctly. Actually, a blood pressure checkup once or twice a year should be enough, and you can be tested in all sorts of clinics, and even some dentists' offices. If you're always checking your own blood pressure, you might become a "hypertension hypochondriac."

DIABETES

Diabetes mellitus is related to cardiovascular disease (arterio-sclerosis) and often runs in families. It can cause all sorts of havoc (some of it fatal), and the risk rises as you grow older. One major problem for older people is diagnosis. As you age, your body chemistry changes, and you might have a higher "norm" for diabetes tests. The danger here, doctors admit, is that you might get a false positive on the test and start a course of potentially dangerous medication. According to the National Advisory Council on Aging, "It becomes critical not to err on the side of overdiagnosis... Be sure to get other opinions and have everything checked carefully before you embark on a diabetes medication program."

You can give yourself a screening test quite easily and inexpensively with a special litmus paper tape. You put a few drops of your urine on the paper to see how the changing color matches up with a chart. If you get a "danger" reading, you go in for further, more sophisticated testing. Ask a pharmacist for one of these diabetes test tapes and leave it in your bathroom as a reminder.

GOOD READING

The Breast Cancer Digest published by the National Cancer Institute, Bethesda, MD 20205. This excellent, 165-page book is free and should be read by every woman. It's a guide to medical care, emotional support, educational programs and resources in the field of breast cancer. It covers everything from risk factors, importance of self-examination to types of treatment and follow-up care (medical and psychological.)

CHAPTER 21

THE PRICES
OF VICES

By the time you're in your middle years, you may have some pretty well ingrained vices. The big ones—the subjects of the chilling statistics—are *smoking, drinking, pill popping*. There are others, but they're neither as widespread nor as harmful.

Smoking, of course, is the big one. As we've seen in the previous chapter, the vast majority of smokers also drink considerable amounts of alcohol. Put the two together and you've got a doubly bad combination. The smoking scene is clearing somewhat—at least for adults. More people are quitting, and others are using milder cigarettes, or are changing to less dangerous types of smoking (pipe and cigar). More and more laws are being passed to prohibit smoking in public places, making it tougher for smokers to smoke.

SMOKING YOUR
LAST CIGARETTE?

For some people it seems very hard, if not impossible, to stop smoking. I have a dear friend who smokes incessantly. He tried to quit once, and made it for nine months. Pressures of work and family problems piled up, and he fell back into the fumes. He knows it's dangerous, but he says he can't think straight or work right without cigarettes. He's really hooked.

There are some breakthroughs in therapy that can unhook even the most addicted smoker. Some people are having success with self-hypnosis and biofeedback, but these methods should be carefully supervised by a trained psychologist or psychiatrist. One of my relatives was smoking very heavily. He was coughing a lot, and his doctor told him he was entering the red alert danger stage. A self-hypnosis expert was recommended and a program begun. I hear that he has cut his smoking drastically, and soon might be able to quit entirely. I'm praying for him. At the end of this chapter, I'll list some sources of information on how to stop smoking, how to deal with problem drinking, and what to do about problem pill taking.

To find out what smoking can do to a person over a fairly long period of time, I talked to Arthur H. Norris, at the Gerontological Research Center in Baltimore. The center, which is part of the National Institute on Aging, has been studying 650 men over a period of 20 years. Here's what Norris says about the smokers in the study:

"Current cigarette smokers have significantly lower vital capacities. Heavy cigarette smoking gives evidence of the lung function of a person at least 10 years older. Cigar and pipe smokers (if they don't inhale) have lungs that are similar to those of nonsmokers. We found that the people who quit smoking return to lung capacity levels similar to those of nonsmokers. Some time after quitting, the lungs seem to regenerate back to normal (within a few percentage points). The main problem with some of the smokers who tried to quit in our group was the fact that they would slide back, quit again, and slide back again."

It appears that the damage done to your lungs can be reversed when you quit. Quitting could add 10 years to the life of your lungs. Of couse, if you develop emphysema or cancer, the chances of your lungs reverting to normal are almost nil. The smokers in the study Norris described did not yet have diseased lungs. But, as you may already know, smoking can be the prime cause of all sorts of diseases. If you're a smoker, you have a two to three times greater chance of dying from a heart attack; *twenty-five* times greater chance of dying from lung cancer; and, with time, emphysema (destruction of lung tissue) is almost a sure thing.

There are different types of smokers. In order to be able to stop, you have to know what kind of smoker you are. "The best way to stop," says Dr. Jerome Schwartz, a consultant with the California Department of Health Services, and an expert on the subject, "is to do it on your own." Dr. Schwartz says that, with a few exceptions, people who get the necessary information and then install their own plan to stop smoking have the highest success rate. Clearly these people are highly motivated. "Stop-smoking programs can help certain kinds of smokers, but not others," he says, explaining that basically there are four types of smokers:

· **1.** *Habit Smoker.* This person lights up a cigarette when he's having a cocktail, a cup of coffee or at certain times of the day. He can be helped by a ritual that involves breaking the routine. Wrapping the cigarette package in plastic and rubber bands, putting cigarettes in different pockets, not carrying matches and other such barriers might help the habit smoker.

2. *Positive smoker.* This person enjoys smoking and relates it to relaxation and good times. Substituting some other pleasant activity for smoking will help. Some walking, jogging, tennis lessons, sex, music—anything that's pleasant and occupies one's interest will do.

3. *Negative smoker.* People who are anxious or depressed by their work, their home situation, or whatever, use smoking as a crutch. Programs or devices might not help these smokers until their life problems are straightened out. Psychiatric help or family counseling might help.

4. *Addicted smoker.* People who get the "crazies" when they can't have a cigarette might be addicted. The addicts rush out at intermission during a concert and light up as they walk up the aisle. Stop-smoking programs won't help these people. But, a psychiatrist, psychologist or trained hypnotist might be able to train them in self-hypnosis and biofeedback methods to kick the addiction.

Dr. Schwartz says if you feel you just can't conquer the smoking habit on your own, there are two things to look for in a stop-smoking program:

1. Continuing maintenance and support after the main course is over. Programs aren't much good if they dump you on your own after the final lesson or group therapy session. If there is a follow-up program, find out how much it costs.

2. Special attention to individual needs. If, for example, a smoker is concerned about gaining weight after he quits smoking, a diet and exercise program should be a major element.

ALCOHOL IS A DRUG

We shy away from the word "drug" when we talk about smoking and other vices. Drugs are things like heroin. But, alcohol is a drug, and a powerful one at that. Alcohol accounts for many of the approximately 45,000 fatal automobile accidents that occur every year. It devastates potentially brilliant careers and breaks up families. Alcohol can slowly, but surely, burn out your brain, your liver, your heart—you name it. Eventually both smoking and alcohol will put a damper on your sex life.

We're not talking about having one smoke or having one drink a week. That would never hurt anybody. But who stops there? How much you drink and how much it means to you are the important questions. Are you controlling the drinking, or is the drinking controlling you? Doctors say that they usually double the amount of drinks a patient admits to, when filling out a history. Those of us who drink often drink more than we'd like to admit, even to ourselves.

One—possibly two—drinks a day, wine with dinner, or a cocktail before, seems reasonable. When you start drinking more—day in and day out—the trouble begins. Over a long period of time it can damage your health and mess up your life. And, if you become involved in an emotional upheaval—the drinking habit is waiting there to engulf you. In his book, *A Good Age*, Dr. Alex Comfort has this to say about alcohol: "Your tolerance for it decreases as you grow older. You don't need to change stable drinking habits unless you find those habits changing, or you had an unacknowledged drinking problem all along. For people who are lonely, sick, or have life problems, alcohol is a far more dangerous drug than heroin because it's around everywhere and all your well-meaning friends are pushers."

Once you get into an exercise program, you might find that drinking may continue to be enjoyable, but you can get along nicely with less. It's a good idea to monitor your drinking. Keep count. Keep track of your alcohol intake like a bank balance. If you want to keep to one drink a day, and suddenly you have three at a party, don't drink any alcohol for the next two or three days. This way, *you're* in charge—not the alcohol. I find that on the "off" days a glass of sparkling soda with a slice of lime in it makes a refreshing cocktail substitute. The extra-light beers with 70 calories or less (compared with 140 calories in regular beer) also make a refreshing drink that has less alcohol. My sister, for years, has enjoyed a couple of ounces of dry vermouth with soda and a lemon peel as a low-alcohol drink. The idea is to tune down and stay away from too much alcohol.

How much is too much? A lot depends on the amount you drink at any given time and how frequently you drink. Here's what Dr. Donald M. Vickery of the Community Medicine Department at Georgetown University Medical School says about it: "In my opinion, if you are averaging more than two cocktails or beers per day, you have crossed the line and alcohol is a problem. You may not be an alcoholic in the usual sense, but alcohol is decreasing your chances for a long and healthy life. Alcohol damages almost all tissues of the body, but is especially damaging to the liver, brain, spinal cord and stomach."

Dr. Vickery says if you have a drinking problem in your family or a close friend has a problem, don't try to go it alone—get help. Alcoholics Anonymous and other groups can provide professional help. A nagging spouse or nagging friend makes things worse. The person who *doesn't* have the drinking problem should get some professional advice on how to handle the situation. The same goes for the spouse or friend of a smoker who just won't quit. Nagging won't work; it just makes things worse. Sometimes providing a drinker or smoker with some other pleasurable activity will work. Sometimes drinkers have "too many" for simple reasons such as dinner always being late because a spouse or friend is constantly tardy. Loneliness and idleness, or just having to wait, can make the drinks multiply.

Remember, as you grow older, you may still be able to

"hold" as much liquor as you did in your youth, but your intellectual functions, such as memory and decision making, as well as reaction time, will show a marked decline.

The classic case of alcohol overwhelming a person in later years was related to me by a Boston psychologist. He described a salesman with a large firm, who couldn't wait to retire to Florida. He was a golfer, and he and his wife purchased a condominium apartment right on a golf course. Paradise, the ex-salesman thought. He played golf everyday and, naturally, at the end of each game he would head for the "19th Hole" tap room in the clubhouse. Drinking in the middle of the day and at the end of the day became a habit. The salesman's intellectual functions, as predicted, began to get soggy. He was drinking heavily and eating heavily. Within two years after his retirement, he was dead. Here was a man who was a fairly moderate drinker when he was an active salesman (he always wanted to be sharper than his customers), but when he had no more challenging work to do, the drinking drowned him. If your mind is being stimulated everyday by something more than golf, your chances of falling into a bottle are greatly diminished.

COLORFUL LITTLE PILLS

Finally, there are all those colorful little pills—the uppers, the downers, the tranquilizers, the sleeping potions. How we love them. If you're taking more than a few of these mind benders in any given year, you'd better take stock of yourself. All too many physicians dispense tranquilizers as if they were gum drops. They may have forgotten how many times they've renewed your prescription (or don't realize you're getting a similar pill from another doctor). You just go on taking one after another.

Marilyn Block at the University of Maryland Center on Aging is particularly concerned about the lonely, middle-aged women who have been widowed or divorced. "We've found," she says, "that a good number of these women are hooked on tranquilizers, such as Valium. When this drug was first prescribed for them, they didn't realize it could become addictive." Some doctors feel that a middle-aged woman may have nothing really wrong with her, but she's anxious, and seems to want something for her "nerves." So, a tranquilizer is prescribed, and she's sent home. Out of sight, out of mind. The woman really needs some rearranging of her life—an interesting job, some regular exercise—not just another pill.

Sleep—or lack of it—is the thing that hooks some people on pills. They worry about their sleep. A pill is an easy answer. "It won't hurt you," a doctor might say, "if you take it now and then, when you need it." But the "now and then" blurs into every night. According to the Panel on Biomedical Research for the National Advisory Council on Aging, you may have different sleeping habits than the ones you had during the earlier part of your life. According to the panel's experts:

"Patterns of sleep measured by electroencephalography (EEG) show pronounced changes with increasing age. These include increases in the number of awakenings and the percentage of time spent awake. The increased percentage of time awake is most noticeable between the ages of 40 and 60."

As for trying to combat a natural sleep pattern with pills, listen to what the Institute of Medicine has to say about it:

"The older you get, the more harm can come from sleeping pills. The effects of pills taken at night can throw you off balance during the day. Treatment of insomnia with sleeping pills, or tranquilizers, has never proven effective in controlled studies.

"As many as 38 percent of adults claim they have some sort of sleep problem. When analyzed, most of their sleep patterns do not differ significantly from persons without complaints.

"Drugs should be prescribed for sleep disorders only after complete medical and psychological appraisal, and only for a few nights at a time. Most prescriptions for sleep lose their sleep-inducing effect (but not the harmful side effects) after two weeks' use—yet millions of people keep on taking pills for months."

Sleep is a strange thing. I find myself waking up earlier than I used to—6 A.M. or so, and my wife finds herself going to sleep later—midnight or 1 A.M. Sometimes, we're like two ships passing in the night. She likes to sleep late; I like to go to bed early. But some nights, we compromise. I stay up late some nights and she gets up earlier some mornings. You have to adjust to your sleep rhythms. Your body will tell you how to tune in. Don't fight it. When you're out of tune because of some social event or work call, you can make it up with a nap before dinner or during the weekend.

It's okay to have a tranquilizer for the occasional, emotional upheaval, the sudden bad news, or fright—but underline the word *occasional*. And, remember, never mix tranquilizers with alcohol. The combination produces a magnified effect and could be lethal. Some special drugs don't mix with other drugs or with certain foods. Wine and cheese, for example, produce a toxic, even fatal effect when mixed with certain mood-altering drugs. Any time you have a prescription for a tranquilizer or other mind-dulling drug, ask your pharmacist or your doctor about problems that might arise from its interaction with other drugs, alcohol, or food. Many home medicine cabinets contain potentially devastating drug combinations.

GOOD READING

Clearing the Air: A Guide to Quitting Smoking. This free booklet is an excellent starting point for smokers who want to quit. It cuts through the myths and nonsense and evaluates various stop-smoking programs such as SmokEnders, Seventh Day Adventist Plan, and others. You can get the booklet and more information on stopping smoking by writing: Office of Cancer Communications, National Cancer Institute, Bethesda, MD 20014.

How to Choose a Stop Smoking Program. This booklet, written by Jerome L. Schwartz and Alan Rice, describes the various methods (hypnosis, five-day plans, group methods, aversion therapy, live-in programs, yoga and acupuncture) and evaluates them. For more information, write: St. Helena Hospital and Health Care Center, Deer Park, CA 94576.

National Clearinghouse on Alcohol Information, Box 2345, Rockville, MD 20852.

You Can Drink and Stay Healthy: A Guide for the Social Drinker by Dr. Robert Linn, published by Franklin Watts, 730 Fifth Ave., New York, NY 10019. This book tells you why and how you should treat alcohol with the respect that is due all potentially poisonous substances.

National Clearinghouse for Drug Abuse Information, Room 10-A-53, Rockville, MD 20857.

CHAPTER 22

DOCTOR/TEACHER

The old meaning for the word *doctor* is "teacher," from the Latin verb *docere:* to teach. In working with patients, doctors used to do a lot more teaching than they do now. In the old days (actually, not so long ago), a doctor with a "good bedside manner" would make "house calls." I put these phrases in quotes because they're so quaint. Today, you drag your sniffling, coughing, enfeebled self through the rain or snow to see the doctor, at the doctor's office, and at the time the doctor finds convenient (unless it is an emergency).

Then, at the doctor's, you sit in a waiting room—which is aptly named. You wait, and wait. You catch up on your magazine reading. Finally, you *see the doctor*. What happens? You get a brief look-see from the doctor, you give a quick explanation of symptoms and how long you've had them. A quick check of your records by the doctor, and a quick prescription. "Take these three times a day for 10 days and call me at the end of the week if you're not feeling better." Smile, handshake, out the door.

This little scene is a tragicomedy that's played out millions of times a week across the country. It's not the usual encounter between my doctor and me. My doctor truly is a teacher and has forced me to be a student of my own body and my own health habits. To work out a good teacher-student relationship, as opposed to the stereotyped doctor-patient relationship of "prescribe and pay," you have to know a lot about yourself and you have to know a lot about your doctor's inherent limitations.

As a comparison, a good teacher at a university can help stimulate ideas, can be an inspiration and a guide. But a teacher can't tell you what career path to take, or guarantee that you'll get a specific job. You have to assume the responsibility of testing, probing, and finding out what you want to do with yourself.

THE DOCTOR/
PATIENT RELATIONSHIP

The same is true with the doctor (teacher)- patient (student) relationship. You have to assume the ultimate responsibility for your own health care. The doctor can't do it alone. Unfortunately, all too many people believe it's up to the doctor to provide magic pills and potions. They feel they have no responsibility, except for passive pill popping.

Dr. Herbert Benson of Harvard Medical School, says quite bluntly: "Medicine as it is now evolving, is increasing its potential to do harm." We are being compartmentalized into specialties of organ systems, ages, stages, brains, bones, and bellies. Your mind and body should not be disassociated.

They're each a part of the other, and you can't tinker with one without affecting the other.

As you might surmise from all this, the quality of medical care you'll receive can depend on your choice of doctor. If you already have a doctor you like, perhaps you can discover a "new" doctor inside the one you see all too fleetingly during visits and checkups. If you don't have a doctor you particularly like, then you can do some homework, spend some time and find one. A good doctor might mean the difference between life and death later on in life. It's a good idea to build a relationship with a doctor over the years so your health can be viewed as a continuum. This way, changes and danger areas can be spotted soon enough to allow for effective action to be taken.

The main thing is to have rapport with your doctor. If you don't have rapport, try other doctors. Don't stay with somebody just because of habit, or convenience. If there is never enough time to talk and listen, then move on. You have to have some trust. You have to believe in the doctor's ability to educate you, to make you change destructive habits. The powers of belief and faith are important.

According to Dr. Donald N. Vickery of Georgetown University Medical School, author of the book *Life Plan for Your Health* (Addison-Wesley Publishing Co.), "Physicians are the ultimate placebo because the attitudes of physicians strongly affect the results of treatment." What Dr. Vickery really is talking about is the old "bedside manner" of the doctors who used to make house calls. The bedside manner, which engendered faith, which in turn engendered willpower in the patient, probably cured more people than may of the so-called wonder drugs of today. Half the battle is getting the patient to have confidence that certain advice or prescribed procedures will work.

Just because the dictionary defines a placebo as "a substance containing no medication and given merely to humor a patient," don't knock it. Actually, the dictionary definition is not very good and may well be out of date. The "placebo effect," wise doctors will tell you, is vitally important. Without it, without the power of the patient's own mind, there would be few cures. The placebo effect is similar to the learning effect which superior teachers inspire in their students. Dr. Vickery explains it further: "Placebos are capable of affecting a broad range of mental and physical processes, including the pain of angina pectoris (heart pain), insomnia, the common cold, coughs, headaches, blood pressure, heart rate, stomach function and mood. It has nothing to do with being stupid or suggestible. Indeed, some investigators have found that the placebo effect is likely to be more marked in persons of higher intelligence."

My own doctor, Oscar Mann, says he agrees with Dr. Vickery, explaining that a doctor should be able to see a patient on a fairly regular basis, once or twice a year, to talk things out. The patient has potential curing powers within him, but the doctor has to channel these powers. Dr. Mann explains: "If you can convince someone to stop smoking or start exercising, you can really make an important contribution to that person's health. This will effect much more of an impact than looking at X rays of the lung. By the time you see signs of lung cancer, it's usually too late.

"You should take time to discuss the whole person, the living habits, and the risk factors. You should show what could happen if the patient drinks too much, eats too much, smokes too much, doesn't exercise, and has too much tension and stress on the job. This kind of person, in his [or her] forties and fifties, is at a truly dangerous stage.

"Just giving people results of tests and occasional prescriptions is not adequate. You would be much better off spending the time designing a personal health line. But it's very difficult to change a patient's habits and, as you know, many of our habits are self-destructive—far more so than the aging process. People must be motivated to change. Doctors must give patients a substitute for destructive habits, such as a good exercise program the patient can become enthusiastic about. You start with this and work to ease the job stress. When positive results can be seen (weight loss, feeling better, looking better), you build on it by altering the diet. Finally, after more positive feedback, you may be able to get the patient to quit smoking and reduce the drinking.

"The trouble is it takes time to motivate patients to change their habits, and neither the doctor nor the patient seems willing to take the time."

Of course, we spend far more time and money running around chasing laboratory tests and purchasing prescription drugs. We make ourselves sick, but we don't want to take the time to find out how to prevent our mind-and-body machine from self-destructing. Doctors have invested a lot of money in testing equipment, but using testing devices may not always be to the patients benefit. For example, too many X rays may be slowly killing you. X rays can be of enormous help when you have some threatening illness, or a bone problem. But, according to Dr. Vickery, "X rays are of little value when the illness is minor, or when they are used merely as a screening tool." He says it's not known what level of radiation is safe, or even whether there is a safe level. Radiation levels we thought were safe in the past have turned out to be dangerous.

As Dr. Mann, Dr. Benson, and others have advised, a regularly scheduled visit with your doctor is a good idea. Spend more time on the teacher-student relationship and less time on the multiplicity of "screening" tests. A routine physical and a half-hour talk should keep you going in the right direction.

YOUR YEARLY CHECKUP

When you're in the second half of life, certain things ought to be checked at least once a year. Unless you have some specific problem, many doctors say you can dispense with the multi-phase screening procedures that are so costly. They're even occasionally dangerous, because you might get a false positive on a test and embark on a potentially toxic medication program. Also, some patient might get back scores that, by themselves, are meaningless. If the tests are within the norms, your health still may be in danger because you're smoking, drinking, and overweight. But, you think you're fine because "the tests were all normal."

Still, there are certain tests and certain items that should be checked once a year. You don't need an elaborate physical, including a battery of wasteful and costly tests, but you should attend to the following:

1. Blood pressure and pulse (inexpensive and simple).
2. Breasts (emphasis on self-inspection, with occasional inspection by a physician).
3. Pap smear (to check for cancer of the cervix).
4. Rectal exam (to check for prostate cancer).
5. Tonometry test (to check for glaucoma in the eyes).
6. Skin test for tuberculosis (easier than X rays).
7. Test for HDL and cholesterol levels (if this is a potential problem).
8. Test for traces of blood in stool (simple procedure you do yourself and mail in).

Some doctors like to see an occasional electrocardiogram if you're under sufficient stress, especially when you're starting on an exercise program. Others like to see an occasional—once every three years—X ray of your stomach and intestine to see if anything bad might be developing. After one of these barium enema, X ray sessions, my doctor discovered that little sacks were developing in my intestinal lining. I changed my diet (he persuaded me to change, armed with the X ray films) to try to avoid the potentially painful and disrupting problem of diverticulitis.

The main thing is to have a regular relationship with a good teacher-doctor. This way, the doctor can spot any changes over the years—changes that ought to be checked. Again, the emphasis should be more on teaching and motivation, and less on tests and medication. The basic checkup, as outlined, shouldn't be all that expensive and shouldn't take much time. The talk-time after the examination could be fairly expensive on an hourly basis. But it could eventually save you some money, and perhaps, even your life.

IS A PRESCRIPTION NECESSARY?

A good doctor should be reluctant to prescribe drugs, and should of course know what you are already taking. You may think a doctor is good because he or she always comes up with some magic formula via the prescription pad. Unless this procedure is aimed at creating a temporary placebo effect, to get you turned around in the right direction, it's not a good idea. Don't assume that a doctor is not functioning because you don't automatically get a prescription at the end of a visit.

If a prescription is absolutely necessary, your doctor should explain why, and should also explain any possible side effects or things to watch out for. Your question should always be: "What will happen if I don't take this medicine? Can you wait a few days to see how things work out?" More often than not, if you're willing to wait and see—so is the doctor.

A really good doctor who recognizes a personal lack of expertise about the vast array of pharmaceuticals available, might have a working relationship with a top-notch pharmacist. The pharmacist can be consulted about the pros and cons of any particular drug. Pharmacists are, nine times out of ten, more knowledgeable than a doctor about the dangerous side effects and combination effects of drugs. If your doctor doesn't have this kind of relationship with a pharmacist, you might consider getting to know your own neighborhood pharmacist. It's a good idea to frequent one pharmacy and have all your medicines on record there. Sometimes a doctor may prescribe a drug and when the pharmacist looks up your record, he can tell you that the drug could be dangerous when taken along with something else you've had already.

FINDING A DOCTOR

If you're looking around for a new doctor, check with nearby university medical centers, or hospitals affiliated with medical schools. These medical facilities maintain active relationships with many doctors in your area and their recommendations will usually be excellent.

Once you've established a good relationship with your doctor, you should not try to pick your own specialist if an emergency arises. Use your doctor as a consultant when you need to select a surgeon, eye doctor, gynecologist, urologist, whatever specialty might be called for. You might even ask your doctor who he or she uses.

Here are some of the specialties you may have to call upon at some time during your middle and later life:

1. *Surgery:* Your own physician should always work with you in selecting the best surgeon for the job. Don't try to do this on your own. A prominent midwestern surgeon had this to say about surgery and surgeons:

"I've tried all my life to eliminate surgery if it means high risk and crippling effects. Take cancer. I've often felt that there are some surgeons who view cancer the way people in the Middle Ages viewed the devil, as something to be exorcised right away, and at any cost. There is really no time, except in an emergency, when surgery is immediately necessary. Every operation involves a calculated risk."

That surgeon and a growing number of others in the medical world are recommending second opinions, with due promptness, of course, when surgery is suggested. Your doctor can help you find the best person in the field. Most specialized surgeons are connected with university medical centers, or with teaching hospitals.

If, after all your checking and second opinions, surgery appears to be the best route, then you should pick the surgeon and the hospital with the utmost care. George Wilson of the *Washington Post* wrote about his coronary bypass, revealing that he and his doctor chose a well-known, midwestern medical center because it specialized in this type of operation. The center had an excellent track record.

Another surgeon points out that smaller hospitals only do a few coronary bypass operations during the year, while a big center, such as the one George Wilson used, does hundreds. Because of this, the smaller hospitals that do not specialize in cardiac surgery have many times the mortality rate of the larger facilities. The same is true for other types of major surgery. Once it has been determined that you really need a certain major operation, then go to the place where they do it best—even if it's hundreds of miles away.

2. *Vision:* After age 50, you should have your eyes checked regularly for glaucoma and possible onset of cataracts. Optometrists, who are trained to prescribe corrective lenses, can also give tests for glaucoma screening. So, if you're going in for a vision checkup, or change in your lenses, be sure to get the simple glaucoma test. Every year, it might not be a bad idea to have a complete eye checkup with an ophthalmologist (a medical doctor trained in eye pathology).

3. *Hearing:* By the time you reach middle age, your ears may be suffering a hearing loss due to years of bombardment from noise pollution. You may not notice it, and it may not bother you yet. But, after awhile, if you find it hard to catch what people are saying, you should have a hearing checkup. When you go to an ear, nose and throat specialist for a sore throat or sinus trouble, ask for a hearing check while you're there.

If you do suffer a hearing loss, don't hold off having a hearing checkup and consultation for a hearing aid. It's unfortunate, but some people avoid being able to hear well because they think hearing aids have a stigma attached to them. It's like someone not seeing well because they think there's a stigma attached to glasses. You're missing a lot when you don't hear well.

For a hearing checkup, you should go to a hearing and speech center. Your doctor, local hospital, university medical school, or health department can supply some addresses. If you have any problems finding a center, write: American Speech, Language, and Hearing Association, 10801 Rockville Pike, Rockville, MD 20852. By the way, these centers do not sell hearing aids. They act as consumer consultants to help you get the right equipment for the right money.

4. *Dental Care:* Obviously, you should see your dentist at least once a year. In your forties, fifties, and sixties the big thing to watch out for is periodontal (gum) disease. During the early years, it was cavities; now it's the gums. If bacterial placque (hard, white stuff) goes after your gums, it can irritate them so they separate from the teeth, and eventually you can lose your teeth. Using dental floss between the teeth, and proper brushing helps keep gum problems at a minimum. If you don't already know how to do this, your dentist can show you.

Even more important is how your teeth meet when they bite. They have been banging away for some time now, and might be out of line. If they are off center, the jarring bite might be irritating the bone that supports your teeth. When this happens, the bone can slowly erode, causing you to end up with no teeth. This bad bite alignment can be corrected.

Spotting and correcting an improper bite is not easy. Not all dentists can do it. To find out who specializes in this kind of work, check with your dentist, or ask your nearest university dental school for names.

5. *Your Own Medical School:* You can be your own, part-time doctor if you know what to do. You don't have to go to medical school, but you do have to do some homework. Your doctor, of course, can help by being your "professor" and, as learning aids, you might want to get these books for your own medical library:

GOOD READING

Take Care of Yourself—A Consumer's Guide to Medical Care, by Donald M. Vickery, M.D., and James F. Fries, M.D., published by Addison-Wesley, Reading, Massachusetts. This book may also be available through local Blue Cross/Blue Shield chapters. You are shown how to monitor yourself for temperature, pulse, and sudden change in weight, moles and lumps.

How to be Your Own Doctor—Sometimes, written by Keith W. Sehnert, M.D., founder of the Center for Continuing Health Education at Georgetown University School of Nursing (Grosset and Dunlap). Dr. Sehnert shows how to stock your own "black bag" and your medicine cabinet (after you throw out some of the junk that's already in there.) You are shown, step-by-step, how to check out various ailments to see if you can handle them yourself, or whether you should see the doctor.

Man's Body—An Owner's Manual. Woman's Body—An Owner's Manual. These manuals are easy to read and come with charts and diagrams that cover every bodily function and possible disorder. They show all your "parts" and how your various "systems" work. You are told what can go wrong and how it can be fixed—just like an automobile mechanic's manual. These body manuals, available in bookstores, are published by Paddington Press Ltd., London. If you have a relationship with someone of the opposite sex, it's not a bad idea to exchange manuals now and then to see how the other person's body functions.

CHAPTER 23

HEALTH INSURANCE

If you're working or your spouse is working, chances are you have adequate health insurance. The employer usually pays for it, or you pay a relatively small premium under a group rate plan. You may have had your health or medical coverage for so long you've taken it for granted. It's always been there to pay most, if not all, your medical bills.

THOSE LURKING CONTINGENCIES

But at this stage of the game, you cannot take health insurance for granted. It could be taken away from you overnight. If you are laid off your job because of a "reduction in force," or you are arm-twisted into retiring early, you'll find yourself without any health plan. For the housewife who relies solely on her husband's health plan, a loss of coverage could be devastating. If her husband dies or divorces her, where is she going to get coverage? She can try to get a job, but without recent work experience she may not be able to get anything that provides adequate health insurance. If you are a housewife and do not have a job that provides adequate medical coverage on your own, you'd better start thinking about what might happen if your husband leaves home or dies. It's not a nice thought, and you may reject it at first. But think about it. Make a plan and hope you'll never have to use it. Activist Tish Sommers tells what happened when she got stuck without a medical plan:

"When I was divorced at age 57, I lost my health insurance. (Her husband took it with him) I tried to get coverage through a variety of possible group plans. I was turned down at first because I had had a bout with cancer. Some colleges have group medical plans, but you have to be taking a full course load in order to get in on it. I also found it's not always easy for an older woman to get a job that offers decent medical coverage. I still don't have coverage, but I'm 64 and have less than a year to go for Medicare. I'm keeping my fingers crossed."

The thing to do, Tish Sommers urges, is to get a job or join some sort of association group plan before anything happens to your marriage. Then, you'll have something when you need it. Sommers has testified before Congress in an attempt to get legislation passed which would provide some sort of medical coverage for "displaced homemakers."

Whether you're married or single, you should take a look at your medical insurance coverage and figure out what might happen under various contingencies, such as loss of job or loss of spouse. Some employers—albeit, very few—have health insurance which provides continuing coverage for a spouse if the employee dies. This could be a lifesaver for a widow in her fifties who has to wait until she's 65 to be covered by Medicare.

MEDICAL INSURANCE
AND DIVORCE

What about divorce? If you become separated or divorced, will you be covered? Medical insurance can be a vital issue in a divorce settlement. Here's how insurance consultant, Ben Lipson, explains it:

"A settlement or decree may specify that the wife is entitled to equal medical benefits. For the husband, this could present some problems because the wife, on her own, may not be able to get good medical coverage, or any medical coverage (because of a preexisting health condition). If this happens, then the husband might have to pay out large sums of money to cover his ex-wife's medical bills. Based on the divorce agreement, if the wife goes to work, her employer might take up the medical insurance slack with equal coverage or even better coverage, letting the husband off the hook. If the wife gets less coverage than she had before, the husband might have to make up the difference."

The trouble is, a divorced woman might find that it's difficult to get her ex-husband to continue paying for her medical insurance without constant legal maneuvers, which cost money. Even if a woman gets a provision for medical coverage in the divorce agreement, it doesn't necessarily follow that the payments will always came in on time or that they might not cease after awhile.

"That's why I always tell divorced women to run for coverage," says Ben Lipson, explaining that they should get "some kind of job that provides an employer medical plan, or failing that, get into some association or organization that provides group coverage." Divorced women, widows, single men and women, married men, anyone who loses a job, or a spouse, and ends up without health insurance, might be able to join an organization that will provide bare minimum medical coverage. A college or university alumni association, a volunteer organization, a professional association, or a club might do the trick

SOURCES FOR INSURANCE

One reference source for names of possible associations to join for health coverage is *The National Trade and Professional Associations of the United States and Canada*. It's published by Columbia Books, 734 15th Street, N.W., Washington DC 20005. If your library can't get it, write to the publisher. This annual guide lists thousands of associations, institutes, societies and the like, that cover every conceivable kind of subject matter. If, for example, you had been a secretary, an accountant, a social worker, a seller of antiques, a gardener or whatever, you'll probably find a listing in the yearbook under the "key word index." Of course, not all associations have group insurance plans for members, but a good number do. You may have to pay some dues to the association but, if it's something you're interested in anyway, it might be worth it.

When I left my job to start my own business, I was faced with the problem of finding some kind of group medical coverage. I could have continued with Blue Cross (which my employer had provided) on an individual basis. But at the time, this type of individual coverage was too expensive. So, I cast about for some sort of association to provide coverage. I had served overseas as a news correspondent, and a friend told me the Overseas Press Club in New York had a group medical plan. I joined the OPC and was able to get into a group medical plan. It wasn't the best, but it was a lot better than nothing, and it was relatively inexpensive. Later, I was able to join a very good union medical plan through the American Federation of Radio and Television Artists (AFTRA).

Sometimes, suppliers or franchisers have group medical plans for the people who do their selling. Some companies that sell kitchenware, cosmetics, and various other household products have health plans for their independent sales representatives.

YOUR FALLBACK PLAN

The trick is to start working on your fallback plan now. Don't wait until you're fired, retired, divorced, or widowed. It might not be a bad idea to keep a membership in some organization even though you're still working and don't need extra group coverage. Jean Strong, a former insurance salesperson whom we met in the chapter on life insurance, keeps her membership active in a professional businesswomen's association, even though her current employer has a medical plan. Whenever Jean is in between jobs, or is unable to work, she can reactivate her association's medical plan.

If worse comes to worst, you can get the bare minimum, major medical coverage with as large a deductible as you can afford ($1,000 or so). You pay for all the smaller medical bills, and the insurance company pays for the really big ones. Ask an insurance expert how much it would cost for you to get the barest, minimum major medical coverage. It might tide you over until you can get into a group plan, or until your sixty-fifth birthday, when you become eligible for Medicare. Some of your problems may be solved by a national health insurance plan that covers "catastrophic" medical bills. Congress has been working on this, but, at this stage, it's not clear exactly how you would fit in if you were out of a job, divorced, or widowed.

MEDICARE PLUS...

Once you reach age 65, of course, you become eligible for Medicare, which covers most major medical bills. Medicare gives good primary insurance coverage and should keep you from being wiped out by a medical crisis. But, as you've no doubt heard, Medicare doesn't pay for everything. The Urban Institute reports that the "gaps" in Medicare force beneficiaries to pay as much as 36 percent of their health care bills. Medicare doesn't pay for prescribed drugs (except in rare instances), and it doesn't pay for physicians' charges that are above stipulated norms (as most are.)

These and other "gaps" in Medicare have spawned an insurance industry offshoot aimed at providing supplementary coverage. Various associations sell this type of insurance to members, as do Blue Cross and many insurance companies. The "gap" insurance business (at least some segments of it) has come under fire for scaring older people into buying policies they didn't need at greatly inflated prices. Before you buy any supplement to Medicare, check it out carefully with someone who knows the insurance business. You might, for example, talk to someone at your local Blue Cross chapter for an explanation of the ins and outs of supplemental coverage before you buy. If you have any kind of backup capital and moderately good health, you probably won't need insurance to supplement Medicare.

And, if you continue working past 65, your employer must provide health plan coverage to fill the Medicare gaps. Under amendments to the Age Discrimination in Employment Act (reviewed in the MONEY section), an employer must give older workers the same benefits younger workers get. When Medicare becomes your primary health coverage plan after age 65, the employer must ensure that you get overall benefits comparable to those given under-65 workers. This means you will probably be getting a Medicare supplement plan at no extra cost. The law says there can be "no disparate treatment" for workers aged 65 and above.

Some employers are even providing Medicare supplement insurance for employees who retire. It's a nice gesture, and it doesn't cost much because Medicare pays the primary bills, and workers over 65 are proving to be a surprisingly healthy lot. If your employer is angling to get you to retire early, and you're not all that much against the idea, you might want to bargain for continuing medical plan coverage for you and your spouse. Because it would be part of a group, it wouldn't cost the employer much, but it could cost you quite a bit to buy it on your own. You might even want to push for this kind of continuing coverage as part of an overall employee benefit plan. If enough employees want them, employers might agree to provide these extra benefits. With Medicare and an employer-paid supplemental plan, you would have excellent health insurance coverage for the rest of your life (possibly the rest of your spouse's life as well.) It's an important employee benefit. Check into it now, while you still have some clout.

Part III
Your
Happiness

CHAPTER 24

FRIENDS
AND LOVERS

Happiness means different things to different people. There was a cartoon series at one time which always started with the phrase "Happiness is . . . ": then, the rest of the phrase would be filled with such things as; A Warm Puppy, An Ice Cream Cone or The Last Day of School. Happiness for a child is, indeed, a warm puppy, because it represents a chance for intimate companionship, and a living, wiggling thing to care for. As you become older, describing happiness is not so easy. It might be, for some, a lack of depression, or a vague, but nice, feeling about one's self.

Pushing further in trying to describe happiness, you might imagine it to be a sort of island of well-being that provides sunshine for the heart and breezes for the brain. Sometimes this island is quite large and encompasses most of our current life. Other times it is a very small, almost nonexistent island, with waves of depression and despair crashing around us. What we must try to do is expand the island of happiness so it gives us plenty of room to enjoy life. It's not always an easy task. But, it can be made much easier if we have someone else with whom to share the island.

TIME FOR AN "INTIMATE OTHER"?

There are all sorts of combinations to help people be together, and care for one another. Marriage is the one we've turned into an institution, and it still works for many people. But there are a variety of living-together arrangements for a man and a woman, two women, or two men—or even several persons of each sex. You don't always have to live in the same house or apartment with your friend or lover. You can be neighbors. Your intimate other might be a close colleague in your work, or a long-time friend from school days. Whatever.

In the second half of your life, more than any other time, you need an "intimate other." Remember the old Spanish toast, *"Salud, pesetas, y amor, y tiempo para gozarlo"*? It means: health, money, love, and time to enjoy them. We've talked about money and about health in two previous sections. They form a vital base for happiness. But money and reasonably good health do not automatically make you happy. You've got to have the love of another person—a mate or a close friend (or a few close friends). This doesn't mean you have to have someone at your elbow all the time. Everyone likes privacy and the right to be alone. But, after you've had a chance to spend some time alone, reflecting, you like to know that you can join another person to share part of your life. In his book, *The Three Boxes of Life* (Ten Speed Press), Richard Bolles says this about the need for another person or persons:

"There's a vast difference between loneliness (the longing to be with someone) and aloneness (the state of singledom or solitude—in which one may be content or even delighted). If in retirement or, earlier, by death, divorce or separation, you who were accustomed to thinking of yourself as a couple, suddenly find yourself as a single, this is not necessarily fatal."

You have to reach out, or you risk becoming isolated. Isolation can follow the death of a spouse, or a divorce. These are times when it rushes at you. Or, it can come slowly, in a marriage. Two people are there, but they're becoming isolated. The bridges are in disrepair, falling apart. It can also happen to a single person who spent most of his or her emotional capital on a career during the earlier years. There wasn't time for lasting friendships. Work was a substitute for intimacy. But, bosses change. Jobs change. And, during one of these changes, you might find that your work, your "lover," has abandoned you. Having interesting and enjoyable work is an important plateau on your island of happiness. But alone, it's not enough. You can't spend all your time up there. You have to be with other human beings, to share your victories and your defeats.

You can't invest everything in your spouse, your work, or even your physical fitness—important as these elements are. You have to invest in what Dr. Robert Butler calls "social fitness." Dr. Butler, who heads the National Institute on Aging, recalls Ralph Waldo Emerson's essay on friendship: "It isn't given to you—you have to work at it. . . ." You have to get out and see people and develop true social relationships—(not just meetings, dinners, and cocktail parties).

Social fitness is not only important for your happiness and emotional health, it can be important for your physical health. Having other people who care about you can serve as a life preserver if the waves are looming rough around your island. Dr. Butler explains how it worked with an older woman patient he encountered once:

"I was examining her in her kitchen as part of a city

government-sponsored neighborhood checkup campaign. She was upset because her family wanted her to move to what they considered to be a nicer neighborhood. But she was very wise. She told me that down the street, they knew her at the drugstore. If she looked a little faint, they would look after her. They were her friends. She could sit and chat and pass the time of day. Then, she'd go to the bank, where they knew her too. She would go on to the greengrocer's, and they would joke and gossip with her. If she didn't show up one day, they would call to see how she was. In her building, she had several close friends, people who really cared. They looked after her. She looked after them."

This older woman, possibly without realizing it, had invested in a rich tapestry of friends and intimate others. Dr. Bernice Neugarten, an expert on aging at the University of Chicago, calls this tapestry a "social network." It's not something that you can take for granted. It doesn't just happen. Dr. Neugarten explains:

"You have to encourage friendships. Neighborliness. But, be sure you don't age stereotype yourself. Build up your social networks with mixed age groups. Not just your own age. If you concentrate on your own age group, they're going to die off. Have young friends as well as older friends. You need a mix.

"You've got to keep yourself from becoming isolated if a spouse dies or friends die. Our house is like a hotel. Our children, their friends, our friends—always people of all ages—keep passing through. If you put some effort into opening up social networks, it will pay you back later. You'll always be in touch and you'll be much happier".

But when you're living alone, and your spouse and, possibly, your job are gone, it becomes urgent to break out and make new bridges to people, or to repair old bridges. Otherwise, it's all too easy to slide into isolation and depression.

LIVING ALONE

Unfortunately there's a powerful trend toward living alone," says Dr. Janet Giele, a sociologist and lecturer at Brandeis University's Heller School for Advanced Studies. She notes, "Living alone is common among older women." She quotes Bureau of Census figures from 1950 to 1975, which show that the number of men living alone stayed the same (16 to 17 percent). During the same period, the number of women living alone grew from 24 percent to 41 percent (and later figures, no doubt, will show an even higher percentage.)

"Obviously," says Dr. Giele, "many people prefer to live alone, and affluence has made it possible. But, for an older woman, she says, it could be a trap." Out of all the married people between age 65 and 75, just a fraction of 1 percent are in nursing homes, compared with 6 percent of the singles. When you look at everyone over age 75, the percentage of married people in nursing homes is still very low, but 17 percent of the singles in this group are in nursing homes—and they're mostly women. The reason for this is the fact that women tend to live longer than men, and they marry older men. This means there's much more chance they will find themselves living alone at a later age.

When you're living alone, it takes a lot of drive and creativity to keep in touch. You have to work at it. Some people are good at it, and they encounter few problems. But, others have to make a conscious effort to build and maintain bridges to other people. In his book, *The Broken Heart* (Basic Books), University of Maryland professor James J. Lynch says: "Our society seems to be deeply afflicted by one of the major diseases of our age—loneliness." Professor Lynch, who is the Scientific Director of the Psychophysiological Clinic at Maryland's Medical School, adds up the price one must pay for loneliness:

"The mortality statistics for heart disease among those adult Americans who are not married are striking. You find the death rate is from two to five times higher for nonmarried individuals (divorced, widowed or single) than it is for married Americans. Mortality rates for almost *all* causes of death, not just heart disease, are consistently higher for divorced, single, and widowed individuals of both sexes and all races. Insurance companies that gamble their money on their ability to evaluate health risks have long recognized that a person's marital status is one of the best predicters of health, disease and death. Living alone can significantly shorten your life. . . . Nourish human relationships for your health's sake, if for nothing else."

The problem of having a close relationship with an intimate other becomes acute for some older women because for years they have relied on relationships which were formed while they were married. When they lose their husbands— through death or divorce—they're often lost. Most of their friends were part of a married-couple network.

Because there are more older women than older men in this country, the next chapter will deal with "The Lonely Woman." If you are a happily married woman, or a husband who loves your wife and wants her to have a chance at happiness if she has to live alone, don't skip this chapter. It's for you too. You don't prepare for living alone after the husband has gone. You start now. It may never happen, but be prepared in case it does.

CHAPTER 25

THE LONELY WOMAN

An older woman who finds herself living alone has to cope with the numbers game. There are simply more older women than there are available men. (see chart on page 244) It's a national, statistical fact of life. But this doesn't mean you won't be able to find a man for company, or for marriage, if you want one. They're around. You'll have plenty of competition, but the average competitor may not be all that tough.

BEAUTY IS AN ATTITUDE

Unfortunately, many older women who have been married to a husband, or to a career, are not skilled in the art of being attractive to men. You do not have to be beautiful, although some degree of attractiveness helps, to get their attention. Once you've struck up an acquaintance with a man, the beauty angle becomes almost irrelevant. If you try to hang it all on looks, you'll have a real problem as you grow older. It doesn't seem

Sex Ratio of Persons Over Age 65 (with estimate of female population)

Year	Female	Male	Ratio (approx.)	Percent of Female Pop. (total)
1900	98	100	1 to 1	51
1930	100	100	1 to 1	50
1970	139	100	3 to 2	51
1977	146	100	3 to 2	52
2000 (est.)	177	100	9 to 5	53
2035 (est.)	224	100	9 to 4	56
2084 (est.)	292	100	3 to 1	57
2127 (est.)	351	100	7 to 2	58
2270 (est.)	547	100	11 to 2	60
2330 (est.)	629	100	13 to 2	62
2380 (est.)	698	100	7 to 1	64
				(approx. 2/3's)

Note: 1. Rates of the past few years indicate these predictive figures may indeed be too low (10–15 percent).

2. The estimated figures above assume no wars, epidemics or natural disasters.

3. This assumes an 18–22 percent stabilization of the over 65 group of the general population in 2032.

4. The ratios and year could be accelerated by a drop or stabilization of the males' life expectancy or the opposite.

Source: 1900-1977 items from "Facts About Older Americans," U.S. Department of HEW, 1977

fair, but society tends to say that women must retain their beauty or fade away, while men can be "gray and handsome." Women have to be attractive, take care of themselves—physically and mentally—and have things to talk about. As you grow older, beauty can become much more of an attitude about yourself and much less of a physical thing. Listen to what activist Tish Sommers says about it:

"We are our age, and we have a beauty of our own, and we had better believe it. Beauty is a cultural factor which can be changed. Until we eliminate this youth fetish from our own hands, we will remain objects of ridicule and pity."

Beauty encompasses a lot more than legs, breasts, waistlines, hair color and other traditional sexist female attributes. As many people already know, you don't have to be beautiful, or even good-looking, to have satisfying sex and/or have a good, warm relationship with another person. You do have to have an attitude of feeling attractive and of caring for the other person. You have to know how to be interesting and interested—two important words. You have to fight off the slide into sedentary dullness. Anita Loos, the creator of the Broadway musical *Gentlemen Prefer Blondes*, described what it takes in an interview on South Carolina Educational Television:

"You can have sex appeal at any age. It's having wit, a viewpoint, tolerance, and your own philosophy. Men adore good company. All too many women don't bother to be good company. They bore men. And women who are boring don't last long. Self-pity is the most boring attitude a woman can have. It will drive people away from you faster than anything. I'm a great believer in a little bit of hypocracy. You have to take account of other people's prejudices. I much prefer a hypocrite to a blabbermouth."

Anita Loos, by the way, was in her late seventies when this interview was videotaped. She has always practiced the art of "wit, viewpoint, and tolerance" to the hilt. It will work for anybody, but it requires special skills that have to be polished and practiced. You can't take other people for granted and expect them to make all the moves. As psychologist Albert Ellis said: "Men are available if you are available." You have to know how to meet a man and what to do once you've made contact.

"THE ART OF THE PICKUP"

How do you meet men? You meet them at the supermarket, at gasoline stations, traveling on planes—everywhere. At least one university (Maryland) has a seminar for older women on "The Art of the Pickup." Dr. Marguerite S. Fogel, psychologist, marriage counselor and sex therapist, explains how the "art" is practiced:

"You have to be open to the contact. Your self-image is most important. Looks don't have all that much to do with it. Sometimes people are so oriented to looks they underestimate the importance of the relationship. You must be open to connecting. You have to have an attitude that you're attractive and have something to offer. It's good to have a common interest.

"Some women, unfortunately feel it would be degrading to initiate a relationship. Their dignity might become offended if they opened a connection with a man. They've been raised to be reserved and try to keep an aura of respect about themselves. If you enjoy the company of men, you have to get out of this reserved pose. You have to want to change. Sometimes it takes some sort of trauma such as the death of a husband or a divorce. Sometimes psychotherapy is the catalyst for change. Until some shattering experience comes along, some women never look at themselves. They're not aware of what they're communicating (or not communicating) to men. Divorce and widowhood offer an opportunity for some women to grow."

CHERCHEZ!

In order to grow, you have to develop a positive self-image. The capacity to feel attractive helps promote growth.

"Attractiveness," says Dr. Malkah T. Notman, a psychiatrist at Boston's Beth Israel Hospital, "has a lot to do with interest, responsiveness, and caring about another person...If you're preoccupied with yourself, someone else can't be interested in you."

But, being attractive as an older woman isn't always easy in today's society. You are apt to be put down by people who equate beauty with youth. And there's always the man shortage. At first glance, it seems that men are either married, or are bottom-of-the-barrel. If attractive men aren't immediately visible, don't be discouraged. If you feel attractive and feel you would like to meet men, you have to find out where they are and how to go about making a connection. Lydia Bragger, 75, an attractive divorcée who works for the Gray Panthers, shares some thoughts on how to get a man:

"You have to be more aggressive. If you like someone, let them know it. Invite them over to dinner or for a drink. Offer to share a trip to a show or a museum. Hobby activities, your work, clubs and associations, religious organizations—are all places where you can meet men on a relaxed, equal footing. You should be able to share something in common such as sports, volunteer work, or whatever. You can't wait for them to come to you (as they might have in your youth)—you have to go out and meet them.

"Singles bars are the pits. Weekend resorts are also bad. Everyone is so self-conscious. Everybody knows what you're there for. It can be demeaning. You have to find a place that's neutral. For example, a friend of mine, age 69, met a man at a church function. His wife was an invalid. They talked and she sympathized, offering him support. The man's wife died, and he eventually married my friend. She loves her new life. She says she never knew sex could be so beautiful. It's a joy to see them together."

What about a man's age? Statistics show that, in second marriages, men tend to marry women who are quite a bit younger than they are. Lydia Bragger offers a warning to women being pursued by an older man. "Watch out for the nurse hunters . . . They're the ones who want readily available sex, a maid, and a nurse—not necessarily in that order."

Having weeded out the nurse hunters and ego trippers, who want younger women, you'll find that the best prospects are usually men within a few years of your own age—up or down. Lydia Bragger describes the age gap situation as it works in reverse: "I like a man around my own age, someone I can share mutual problems and experiences with. However, age is not the main criterion—common interests and the right vibrations are more important. I once had a relationship with a man 20 years younger than I. It was exciting for awhile, but age is not important to me. I have seen too many 'old' 39-year-olds and too many 'young' 79-year-olds." When you have a relationship with someone your own age, you can often share common friends and associates more easily.

Of course it's not necessary to get married. Many women like the company of men, but don't want to make the commitment. Men, much more so than women, are apt to rush into marriage after they've lost their wives through death or divorce. Because of the numbers game, it's much easier for them to find marriage partners.

OPENING UP TO LIFE

Psychiatrist Malkah Notman discusses the fact that some women do not want to move toward another marriage after their husband's death or a divorce. Dr. Notman explains how things might work out for this type of woman:

"It's very surprising when you see women who have been very domestic go through a period of mourning or depression after the death or divorce of their husbands, and come out of it and don't feel at all like considering another marriage. A lot of things are open to them. Jobs. Freedom to travel. Freedom to pursue their own, individual tastes. It's a sort of liberation.

"But for other women, this doesn't work. They find it difficult to cope with the loneliness, the fact that it's not always easy to find someone to do things with. A lot depends on the circumstances. If a women lives in a community with a lot of good friends, and she has established a social network on her own, one not based on her husband and his work, she certainly will have a better opportunity to grow and find her own way."

Many widows say they feel free for the first time in a long time. It's not that they didn't love their husbands. They discover that they can do things that they didn't know they could do, or weren't allowed to do. Marilyn Block who studied a group of women over 40 for the University of Maryland, describes the case of a widow who had been married to her husband for more than 30 years:

"She went shopping for a dress eight months after her husband died and spotted one she really liked. But, she shook her head and kept on looking, saying: 'Harry wouldn't like that one.' She suddenly realized that it didn't matter whether Harry liked the dress or not. So, she bought it and wore it until it was in shreds. Today she still has the remnants of the dress hanging in the closet because it symbolizes the new-found freedom to make her own decisions, without worrying about what Harry would say when she came home."

"SHARING GROUPS"

With many women, this liberation, this chance to start a new life, doesn't come so easy. In some cases, it never comes at all. As an aid in breaking out of the old shell of dependence, a growing number of women are joining "sharing groups." Professor Janet Giele of Brandeis University says that women invest an enormous amount of emotion in a marriage, and when their lives are disrupted by their husband's death or a divorce, they might need outside help. One form of help that's becoming institutionalized in Dr. Giele's area (Boston suburbs) is the sharing group. They are usually located in churches, synagogues, and other community organizations. They don't have an ideological tinge. They're just groups of people who meet regularly to discuss what's happening to them.

A sharing group, if you can find one or organize one, helps you cope with divorce, get a new job, sort out the pain of widowhood, organize your finances, and with all sorts of other problems. The meetings are information exchanges as well as structures for social contacts. Experts, such as lawyers, accountants and investment counselors, answer questions about all sorts of problems. Professor Giele joined a women's sharing group and describes what went on during the meetings:

"We found that we had all sorts of resources to help each other. Everybody who came to the meeting came for something they didn't have. The young women who had children were coming for stimulation and to learn about part-time jobs. The widowed woman whose children had left home was experiencing a belated empty nest. I went because I wanted to know more people in my community who were not necessarily PhDs. I wanted to see the richness of life as other people were living it, and I wanted to make new friends. One woman, who was separated from her husband, left a sharing group made up of separated and divorced women. She said she wanted to meet a variety of people. The widow talked about being isolated and typecast. At parties, she said, the married women would quietly slip their arms through their husbands' arms and say, 'It was so nice to meet you,' and whisk them away. The married women felt the widow was a threat."

This sharing group phenomenon seems to be spreading across the country. It's a group of people who are not your family and not your friends (in the strict sense of the word). It's formed for a specific purpose—to share problems and information, but lasting friendships do emerge from the meetings. It's sort of like an emotional commune. A sharing group is an excellent way to keep from being isolated if you are living alone. Or, it could be an insurance policy if you're married and find yourself limited to friends and acquaintances who relate to you only as half of a "Mr. and Mrs. team." By going to a share group, you can build up a wealth of skills to call on. It can be a real backstop when you're lonely, or things go wrong.

Out of these meetings, and other similar meetings, separated and divorced women meet others in the same boat. They begin to form their own "community" to replace the married-couple community they left behind. They're often surprised to find how large this nonmarried adult community can be. When they were married, they had social blinders on, and they couldn't see the nonmarried community. In the community of the separated and divorced, it's even possible for another type of male-female relationship to emerge. Dr. Robert S. Weiss writes about this special relationship in his book, *Marital Separation* (Basic Books):

"Some among the separated form friendships with someone of the opposite sex in which there is no romantic interest. They are just friends, and each becomes a confidant to the other. There would seem to be no analogue to this sort of relationship in the lives of most married persons. The relationships—and valuable. They make it possible for both men and women to talk frankly to someone of the other sex.

They provide a measure of companionship, and they are emotionally safe."

LIVING TOGETHER

But for some, platonic friendship is not enough. They want to form a more intimate relationship without going so far as getting married. They choose to live together for awhile, which has its advantages and disadvantages. Dr. Weiss sorts them out:

"One of the attractions of living together may be that it can constitute a half-way station to marriage. It can appear to make possible the same intermeshing of lives that characterizes marriage, but not be so committing that retreat from the relationship is a major undertaking. Some among the separated speculate that living together might be desirable as a kind of trial marriage.

"Yet living together may not in reality provide a trustworthy preview of marriage. The assumptions of marriage are more complex than those of living together. Inability to manage living together may indicate an inability to manage marriage as well, but success in living together does not guarantee success in marriage."

When men and women live together in later life, they may gain some short-term companionship, but lose a long-term sense of emotional and financial security. It can be exciting, but also, it can be tinged with anxiety. Younger couples can often pull off living together without too many problems. But older couples may be faced with tougher problems (what if one partner dies?); and, more often than not, a different set of rules (grown children and old friends have trouble relating to unmarried partners).

There may be a heady feeling of liberation in a living-together arrangement. Each partner seems much more willing to divide up the chores and responsibilities. When they were married, the partners were probably cast in traditional husband-wife roles. He brought in the bread, she managed the house. Or, he brought in the bread, she brought in more bread from her own job, and she still had to manage the home. Now, they have to be more willing to share the work, because there is no formal contract—nothing that binds the deal.

For awhile, this can be stimulating. It can make for "born-again" sex. But, says marriage counselor and sex therapist Marguerite Fogel: "Just because you have good sex doesn't mean you have a good relationship with another person . . . But, if you have a good relationship, a loving-caring relationship, chances of good sex are increased 100 percent."

JOINING FORCES

So far, we've talked about breaking out of the loneliness shell through woman-man relationships. Faced with the fact that there are many more unattached older women than there are older men, this type of relationship may not always be possible—at least not on any kind of a permanent basis. This raises the possibility of women living with other women. In some circumstances, it might make sense for two or more women to band together to share a house, condominium or whatever. There can be financial and psychological security in numbers. Activist Tish Sommers talks about her experience with other women:

"When I was divorced at age 57, I lived by myself for nine months and worked on a book project. It's a lonesome thing. There's nobody else in the house. I had to get out. I figured, after nine months, this was no way to live. So I joined forces with three other women. I had enough resources to put some money down to help buy a house. We developed a collective living arrangement for the four of us.

"It wasn't easy. We had to learn to live together. Women tend to clash if they ran their own homes before. But, with patience, it can be done. Privacy is important. Each of us had our own room or room-and-a-half. We had a common dining and living room and kitchen space. You have to talk out differences. You have to work out management, cleanliness, chores—that sort of thing. We had house meetings and it took about six months before we ironed out all our differences. After we got organized, it worked very well. I lived there for four-and-a-half years. I left because I needed more space for my work. We supported each other, and it made living costs much less expensive. It meant that I had money to do other things. This kind of group living can work, but somebody has to take the lead and get it going.

"I'm living now with another woman. She works with me too. The work space is downstairs, and there's an organization that helps pay for that. This was a case where there was another older woman like myself who had managed a home. We had to find out what was important to the other person and to make accomodations the same way it's done in a marriage or male-female, living-together arrangement. You find that you lose something and you gain something."

Although it does present some privacy and territorial rights problems, living together could be the wave of the future for older women who need the economic support and camaraderie that goes with it.

GOOD READING

Living Together Kit, by attorney Ralph Warner, published by Nolo Press, 2220 Sacramento Street, Berkeley, CA 94702. This handy book provides a living together contract (for opposite sexes as well as same sexes). Breaking up a living-together arrangement can sometimes be nastier than a divorce (recall the famous Lee Marvin case). The book shows how to work out money management, credit, mortgages, rental contracts and all the "who-owns-what" legal snarls.

Life After Youth: Female, Forty—What Next? Written by Ruth Harriet Jacobs and published by Beacon Press. Dr. Jacobs defines roles of older women with some revealing comments on such types as: Unutilized Nurturers, Chum Networkers, Faded Beauties, Escapists, and Assertive Older Women.

On Being Alone, published by the Widowed Person Service, 1909 K. St., N.W., Washington, DC 20049. This booklet introduces a national Widow-to-Widow program with 75 chapters around the country. It's all aimed at helping a widow to cope. Also good is *Survival Handbook for Widows*, written by the director of WPS, Ruth Loewinsohn (Follett Publishing Co.).

CHAPTER 26

THE LONELY MAN

Much has been said about the lonely woman. Statistics show that, as we grow older, more women keep on living, while men tend to die off. Starting soon, after age 45, women begin to outnumber men. This trend continues, unabated. After age 65, there are approximately 150 women for every 100 men.

This is why unattached males in their forties, fifties, sixties—even seventies—are so sought after at parties and other mixed gatherings. For a man who happens to be looking for female companionship, the "market conditions" seem ideal. There are many women to choose from, and few competitors. Any man in the second half of his life who wants a woman to live with should have relatively little difficulty finding one, unless, of course, he is pathologically shy, or has some other debilitating hangup.

But, market statistics in the mid-to-late-life male-female numbers game can be deceiving. While there are, indeed, more women than men running around, not all the women are strictly eligible as marriage or live-in partners. According to Dr. Barbara H. Vinick, research sociologist at Boston University, "In spite of their more fortunate statistical and economic position, men appear to need remarriage more than women." Women are more hesitant to remarry. Many, as we have seen in the previous chapter, have started whole new lives based on new careers, new friends, new freedom of choice. For years they have done what one man wanted them to do; now, they can do what they want. Also, most of these older women have run their own households for so long, they have all the necessary skills to manage by themselves. They know how to shop, cook, and keep the place clean.

The men? Many of them hardly know how to heat a can of soup, let alone plan meals and cook them. Laundry machines, kitchen appliances, floor-waxers and other housekeeping equipment loom as complicated to them as outer space gadgetry. In short, men have learned to become dependent on a woman for an awesome range of housekeeping and personal skills. When these skills are whisked away by death or divorce, men often are left floundering.

ODD MAN IN TROUBLE

Because of the male-female market conditions, the newly single man usually runs out and grabs another maid-cook combination as soon as possible. Because some of the better prospects among the single women don't want to get married right away, or are leery of it, men sometimes grab whatever is available—often a much younger woman who likes the idea of financial security and the social advantage of having an official partner. And, without a female partner, a man often finds himself as the odd fellow in social networks based on couples. A man's social network might depend on colleagues at work.

But, if most of them are married, he may feel awkward. Of course, friends are always trying to fix the widowed or divorced male up with older, single women. At first this seems like a nice gesture but, after awhile, it can become frustrating, even nerve-wracking.

One widower I know moved into a community of town houses and condominium apartments for "mature" people (translate: over 50). There was a golf course nearby, a swimming pool, good bus service to the town where he worked and many other amenities. He wasn't there two weeks, before various older, single women started to "look after him." He found home-baked bread, cakes, candy, and all sorts of invitations under his door, or in his mailbox. At the community club gatherings, a number of women called him by his first name, and he didn't even know who they were. When he did dine with one woman, the others seemed almost frantic. When he dined with another, the original hostess seemed crushed. "I had to get out of there," he said. He moved back into a bachelor's pad in town, and eventually married a younger woman he met through his work. Some of us felt he got married almost out of desperation, to take himself out of the available-bachelor market. He seemed relieved that all the proposed dates and attempts to fix him up had ceased. He could now relax and rejoin the quiet community of couples.

A younger woman can be quite appealing to a man who sees quite a number of older women seeking his attention. It's flattering to his ego.

MAY-SEPTEMBER—
THE PROS AND CONS

You have to beware of sexual whims," says Dr. Julius Fogel, a sex therapist and marriage counselor. The initial lively sex life with a younger woman "may come back to haunt you when you're older," says Dr. Fogel. Eventually, he says, an older man's young wife might tire of being a housekeeper and nursemaid, at around the same time his sex drive is slowing down, her sex drive may be at its peak. He may become almost paranoid about his wife's outside activities (is she meeting other men?), and equally concerned about his ability to satisfy her sexually. His concern might make it even more difficult for him to perform, and he's caught in a vicious circle of anxiety.

A younger woman may also be appealing for reasons other than sex. A man might think it would be nice to have someone he could boss around and dominate because of the difference in their ages. Perhaps his previous wife fought back and gave him a hard time when he wanted his way. A younger wife might be much more willing to follow his leadership, or so he thinks. After awhile, though, when his physical powers diminish and he becomes more dependent, the younger wife might try to take over the leadership. At first, his intellectual strength ruled. Now, her physical strength and vivacity rule. It's not a pleasant thought for a man.

Of course, there are partnerships where a young woman and an older man do a lot for each other. But it sure helps if the older man has lots of money. With money and the clout that goes with it, an older man might be able to maintain his leadership role longer.

Marrying a younger woman can be an intriguing, but risky, business. Marrying an older woman, someone within four or five years of your own age, is much less risky. And, it may be just as intriguing, if you look over the available pool of older women from a nontraditional viewpoint. Put more emphasis on skills and experience, and less emphasis on outward physical attributes. An older woman has had more experience dealing with an older man as far as sex and male-female relationships are concerned. She has learned a lot, had more experience handling crises, and, more often than not, has a wealth of conversation and experiences to share.

THE TRUE ROAD TOWARD CIVILIZATION— DISAPPEARING STEREOTYPES

In any kind of close relationship, the key is communication. Obviously, a wide range of common interests will give you more to talk about. Men have been stereotyped to be aggressive, work-oriented, and less interested in household doings. Women have been stereotyped to be interested in cooking, child-care, and other household happenings. But, things are changing. According to Janet Giele, author of *Women and the Future: Changing Sex Roles in Modern America* (Free Press), more men are becoming good cooks, and are learning a lot about running a home. Men are also becoming more emotional, softer, and "caring," she says. Women are becoming more aggressive in the working world, and more interested in things like money management. But, even as each sex expands from its old, stereotyped role, the original role is not abandoned. Women can be aggressive and feminine and men can be soft and caring and still be macho. The sex roles are overlapping, and it's about time. This just could be the true road toward civilization.

Men should know how to really cook, not just make hamburgers. Women should know how to manage finances and succeed in the working place. Sticking to traditional roles of "me Tarzan—you Jane," with the male doing the breadwinning and the female doing the homemaking, makes things much more difficult when something happens to either partner in a marriage.

When a man has been trained to cook well, be an astute shopper for food and household necessities, and keep the place neat and tidy, he won't be so dependent on a wife to take care of him. If a woman is out working at a decent job, and is fully capable of managing the family finances (paying taxes, keeping the checkbook balanced, researching and making investments), then she won't be helpless and confused when something happens to her husband.

When a man is a good cook in his own right, he can talk about the fine points in a meal just served by some hostess. She is flattered because he really appreciates what a fine job she did. They have a new dimension in their conversation. He asks where she got some certain spice or rare vegetable. She asks how he makes a certain sauce. They have a common interest, other than what he's doing at work or what her husband is doing.

When a man can really manage a home, even though it might not be the same as his wife's management, he has earned a certain sense of independence. If something ever happens to his wife, he will grieve her loss but he will not be a helpless mess. He can run his home and be a lot less desperate about quickly finding a housekeeping substitute for his wife. He will also be more attractive to the older women, who are widowed or divorced. They will realize that he is reasonably self-sufficient, and they won't have to play the part of housekeeper or nursemaid. They can become more involved in a career of their own, which will make the partnership stronger financially.

THE NEED FOR EMOTIONAL SUPPORT

While it's all well and good for a man to be as self-sufficient as possible in running a home, there's still a need for emotional support to fill the void after a wife's death or a divorce. Traditionally, men have had a much tougher time finding this kind of emotional support in a crisis. Women, more often than not, have built up social networks of friends who can rally around when a husband departs. Men don't seem to get much of this kind of solace.

If a man has a close relationship with a group of men friends through his religious community, or some other group, he will be able to get the necessary support if he loses his wife. The group can be fairly formal, such as the men's associations related to fraternal or religious groups. Or, it can be informal, such as a long-standing poker club that meets regularly once or twice a month.

I recently attended the funeral of the mother of one of my friends. My friend's father, of course, was grieving. But, I noticed that he had several men friends who were always at his side. One friend in particular seemed to provide a lot of support. These men were his buddies from a Jewish men's club at his synagogue. If need be, club members would take him in to live with them. As a matter of fact, his closest buddy was already making plans to get him moved onto the same floor in his apartment building. Strong support was there. These men are able to weep and let down emotionally with each other. They are quite literally capable of salvaging each other's lives when a crisis hits. When a member remarries, they're there in force, with big grins and hugs of happiness.

If you do not have a group of close friends through your religious affiliation or some other association, you'd better start looking into it. Consider it a form of investment—a social or emotional investment. Meet regularly with men friends and colleagues. See if your church or synagogue has a men's group. If not, consider starting one. I will never forget the support my friend's father got at the funeral. Afterwards, I resolved to look into my own church organization to see if there was any similar group I could join. A friend who is a member of Alcoholics Anonymous says the group he meets with is very close. They support each other in many ways—not just with the drinking problem. They have a true brotherhood. It's great to have this kind of support. It can, some day, be a lifesaving antidote for the destructive powers of loneliness and isolation.

Group support has a proven track record. But, what about two men living together? Men do live together in institutions, such as veterans' homes, but you don't find it happening very often outside this type of setting. I'm talking here about men who have been married and have lost their wives through death or divorce.

You do find homosexual (gay) males living together and coping quite well. In an interview published for physicians by McNeil Laboratories, a well-known sex educator, Dr. Mary S. Calderone, refers to the subject of homosexual males and aging:

"Contrary to popular opinion, data reveal improved adjustment and less unhappiness among homosexuals as they age. In homosexual males over age 45, there is a decrease in the frequency of sexual activity, as there is in heterosexual males. But, because of the high premium placed on youth by the homosexual community, the older homosexual is most likely to be living alone. And, unlike the 26 to 36 age group, the older homosexual has more association with the heterosexual world."

Dr. Clyde E. Martin, a coauthor of the famous Kinsey report on *Sexual Behavior in the Human Male*, says that either an older man with homosexual tendencies, or a heterosexual man who has lost interest in sex, might strike up a very practical, satisfying, relationship with an older woman. First of all, as we have seen, there are many more potential partners available among the ranks of older women. "A man should not feel that an older woman would not want him because of his lack of sexual activity," Dr. Martin says, explaining that "many older women are primarily looking for companionship. These women want a partner to do things with and want to form a bond that provides emotional and possibly financial support. Sex is not all that important—companionship is the main thing."

Take this case of a retired woman who has been living alone for some time. Her family was concerned about her after she had an operation, but she wrote them a letter, putting their fears to rest. Apparently, she had been seeing an old male friend on a fairly regular basis. He had never married, and had given her the impression that he was not at all interested in sex. The retired woman and this man once worked in the same type of business. They shared many memories, mutual friends, and interest. He had his place, she had her place, but they saw a lot of each other.

There is no sex in this relationship, unless you want to call fond hugs and platonic back scratching sex. Maybe these caresses should be listed under the broad umbrella of human sexual responses, but, primarily, these two people are buddies. They support each other. He went to the hospital with her. He made sure all was well while she convalesced. They may even "sleep in" at each other's place from time to time. Whatever it is they're doing it works.

Which all goes to show that there are many ways to stave off loneliness. If you are lonely, or think you might be some-day, don't cross out any possibility that might take you out of this depressing, even dangerous, state of mind. In the next chapter we will take a closer look at that institutionalized anti-loneliness remedy—remarriage.

CHAPTER 27

REMARRIAGE

As our overall population grows older statistically, it's only natural that we're seeing an increasing number of remarriages involving people who are in their later years. Remarriage in later life is not like remarriage in one's early years, which often occurs after a relatively short, unsuccessful first marriage that ended in divorce. The older the partners in a remarriage situation, the more likely it is that one or both are widowed. There are, of course, many divorced people involved in later remarriages, but still widows and widowers predominate.

Dr. Barbara H. Vinick, a Boston University sociologist who has studied older adults who have remarried, says that by 1985, we will have about 9 million widows over 60 and 2.2 million widowers in the same age group. In 1970, Dr. Vinick says, there were only 6 million older widows and 1.5 million older widowers. This means that the pool of eligible marriage partners in their sixties or above is rapidly expanding—with an obvious marriage-market bias in favor of the men.

MEETING AND MATING

In a study sponsored by the National Institute of Mental Health, Dr. Vinick interviewed remarried couples with a man who was over 65 or a woman who was over 60. Most partners were widows and widowers, but a few had been divorced. "Most of the marriages we studied were successful," Dr. Vinick says, adding that "this may come as a surprise to a lot of older people who feel marriages late in life are doomed." After interviewing hundreds of remarriage partners, Dr. Vinick and her research colleagues discovered certain truths about what seems to make a remarriage successful—or unsuccessful. Of particular interest to people in their forties, fifties and sixties who might be contemplating remarriage some day, is how the couples in the study found each other. Dr. Vinick explains:

"The majority met through an introduction by friends or relatives. Some had known each other when one or both were married. Our research strongly suggests that people who are active, who get out of the house, and are involved in social networks, have a greater chance of meeting a mate than someone who stays relatively isolated at home. We even found one 81-year-old woman who remarried. She was in a wheelchair, but she was out and around all the time at social events and religious activities. In most cases, the men took the initiative. Most couples were married less than a year after they began their relationship.

"The couples I interviewed were ordinary people, but in almost every case, the women were interesting people. They were well-groomed. They did not look depressed. They had their hair done, often wore jewelry, and were neatly dressed. Their homes looked tidy and organized. The women said they were active, and they tried to look their best, but they admitted that the key factor was being in the right place at the right time to meet a man. They made a conscious effort to go out and build up friendships.

"Many said that, at first, they had no intention of remarrying. The men were the ones who said they were actively seeking a mate. Many of the women, for the time being at least, said they had found contentment in social activities with other women, such as going on trips, going out to dinner. Many had jobs. These were active people. They weren't people who just sat at home and were depressed. When the women eventually felt that they might like the company of a man, they told their friends and relatives. And, of course, that's how most of them met their partners—through introductions by friends and relatives. This is why I urge people not to be shy about telling friends that you would like to meet a man, that you're ready to enjoy the company of a man. Sometimes friends and relatives might feel that they're pushing somebody on you. Let them know you're interested."

PREDICTABLE REACTIONS

It's nice to have introductions and it's even nicer to find renewed interest in the old "dating game." But what about the reactions of your children and some of your close friends? Will they approve of your remarriage? According to Dr. Robert Weiss, professor in the Department of Sociology, University of Massachusetts, who has studied widowed and divorced women: "The most important predicter of a remarriage's success appears to be its acceptability to other individuals in the lives of the prospective spouses . . . A marriage that not only has the approval of the two partners' children, but also has the support of their kin and friends, appears likely to be successful." Of course, your life is your own, and you don't have to deny yourself the company of the opposite sex and eventual remarriage just because one of your children is pouting or a "friend" may try to talk you out of it for selfish reasons. Dr. Vinick says that, for the most part, the children and friends of the marriage partners she interviewed accepted the union and approved. She explains:

"The couples said that, realistically, one of the main reasons why their children approved of the remarriage was the fact that they would not have to care for their mother or father and wouldn't have to worry about them as much. They wouldn't have to worry about getting a meal or wonder what they were doing alone on Saturday night. The children were relieved of this responsibility. But, we only talked to couples who had actually remarried. We didn't find out how many widows, widowers, and divorced people did *not* remarry because of opposition from their children. Some partners said their children were shocked. They thought their parents would never remarry. They weren't opposed so much as they were shocked or surprised (it's incredible how many young people believe their parents no longer enjoy sex.) Children who felt their mother or father was being disloyal, softened when they saw that the marriage was working out.

"Some of the women who had remarried had been living with, or close to, women friends. When they announced their decision to date a man seriously and eventually remarry, their women friends often felt deserted. One woman who had all her meals with a very good friend said that the minute she began to go out with the man she finally married, the woman friend refused to have anything to do with her. It may have been a question of jealousy.

"In general, the older marriage partners we interviewed encountered more negative reactions from some of their friends than they did from their families. One woman said a friend tried desperately to talk her out of remarriage because the friend didn't have the courage to remarry on her own, although she had had a couple of opportunities. On the other hand, when some other women friends saw that the remarriage was working, it helped them to muster courage to try it themselves. It served as a model to attract others to remarriage."

WHY REMARRY?

It's interesting to hear from the remarried couples just why they remarried—sometimes in the face of opposition, or resentment. Dr. Vinick says that the most common reason given was companionship. The second most common reason, especially for the men, was the fact that they wanted care. The men wanted someone to cook for them, clean for them, whatever. And, in most cases, this care was given willingly, because both partners were getting something out of it. It was a workable contract. Dr. Vinick recalls an old Chinese proverb to explain the point: "An old man starves to death if he doesn't have a woman to cook for him, and an old woman starves to death if she doesn't have a man to cook for." Each partner has his or her practical, and emotional needs. Dr. Vinick elaborates:

"For the women, the most important aspect of companionship was the emotional sharing, having somebody to talk things over with. The women mostly mentioned 'love' as the reason for getting married. Whereas, for men, they most often mentioned having someone to go places with and having somebody there. The psychological aspect didn't seem to run as deep for men as it did for women. The men tended to marry for more practical reasons. The women tended to marry for more emotional reasons."

MONEY IS THE ROOT OF ...

What about money problems? They can determine the success or failure of many early-life marriages, and they can pose a problem for remarriages later on. Money, according to Dr. Vinick, was indeed an important consideration:

"Many couples said they were pooling their current resources. They had made agreements that said money and property brought into the marriage would remain in control of each partner that brought it in. This money and property would go to the children of the partner who controlled it. If, for example, a house was involved, it would go to the children of the partner who owned the house at the onset of the marriage. It's vitally important for people contemplating remarriage to discuss money and property carefully. One couple was on the verge of breaking up because of a money problem. The man was tight with his money. He wouldn't give enough to his wife for living expenses and the running of the home. They had different feelings about money, and they had not investigated these feelings before they were married. Remarriage represents a major change in your life, and it's a good idea to consult with a lawyer, and an accountant who specializes in taxes. A few couples had counseling from lawyers on marriage contracts, or prenuptial agreements, but most did not.

"In the most successful marriages, the women did not marry the men for their money. In a few unsuccessful marriages, this seemed to be the underlying motive for the marriage. When women married men simply because they didn't know what they would do financially, it often didn't work out. They didn't consider other aspects, such as having to live with a person for a number of years. They didn't consider the emotional costs, and ended up being incompatible with their partners."

AROUND-THE-CLOCK COMPANIONSHIP

Related to the money problem is the question of who works, and for how long, in a marriage. If a man who is near retirement, or already retired, marries a woman who is still working and wants to continue working, he might try to pressure her to stop, so they can spend more time together. This is a potentially dangerous subject and should be worked out carefully *before* the remarriage. In one case, Dr. Vinick recalls, a woman quit a good job because her new husband (who was older and retired) wanted her to be with him at home. She became bored with what she perceived as around-the-clock companionship and wanted to go back to work. They wanted her back at her old job, but her husband stormed and refused to let her go. He demanded his "right" of constant companionship. Obviously, he was spoiled, and the remarriage appeared doomed to failure. The ideal in this case was to have worked out a plan before the marriage which called for the wife to continue working and the husband to get off his haunches and investigate the possibility of some part-time, paid work, or an interesting volunteer job.

PRENUPTIAL AGREEMENTS

You can make a marriage contract that spells these basic agreements out and also says who is to get what property in case the marriage is dissolved by death or divorce. Most states will not honor this type of contract if there's a divorce. The contract can serve, in these states, as a sort of moral commitment between the partners, but it's not legally binding. Some states, however, do allow marriage contracts that are binding in divorces. The list of states is changing all the time. If you're interested, ask a lawyer how marriage contracts are handled in your state before you enter a remarriage situation.

With prenuptial agreements, the intent is to sort out what a surviving partner and various heirs will get in case of the death of the other partner. This kind of agreement, drawn up by a lawyer, can calm down children's fears of being disinherited. You can spell out who gets what. But, remember, this is just a document of intention. It's not set in concrete. You can always change your will if you want to. Sometimes, after several years of marriage, one spouse can persuade the other to rewrite a will which, in effect, transfers much of the estate to the new marriage partner. The children can be effectively cut out of most of what they expected to get. Depending on what state you live in, these maneuvers might not be allowed if they disinherit a spouse, or your children. It's somewhat of a legal jungle, and you need a good lawyer to guide you as you make up any kind of prenuptial agreement, or change your will. Sometimes it's a good idea to give your children some things outright before the remarriage contract is made. This way, they can enjoy your gift while you're alive, and there's no chance of a family dispute, or fight with your spouse, later on.

In some cases where you'll need all your money and property because neither partner is that well-off, your children will just have to be told as gently as possible that you have raised them and educated them, and that's it. You are entering a new life, and they're on their own (except for a few things they might get when you die). In this type of situation, family counselors have discovered that the children might be satisfied with just a token gift, something that has been in your family for a long time. Perhaps it's a deceased mother's piece of jewelry, or chair, or a deceased father's watch, or desk. Remember, they're your children, and your new life will be much richer with them on your side. If need be, seek counseling with a family or marriage specialist (along with your lawyer). Bring the children in on it, and have things out in the open. It's a lot better to get everyone calmed down before the wedding. Otherwise, hidden feelings could erupt later on to make your life miserable when you become more vulnerable and more dependent.

CONFLICTING RIGHTS AND RESPONSIBILITIES

Sometimes there are no easy answers to the conflicting interests of your children and your new spouse. Dr. Robert

Weiss, the expert on widowhood and divorce, says, "We're not well set up for second marriages." He asks the tough questions. Who gets the heirlooms? If the heirlooms form part of the second spouse's home for a good number of years, does he or she have the right to them? Do the children? What about a family business? If the new, "outsider" spouse works in the family business, what are the children's rights? You've got to realize that you can have genuine conflicts of interest between your kids and your second spouse. What one gets, the other doesn't get. Some of these questions can be ironed out by good legal and family counseling, but sometimes, you have to learn to live with unsolvable problems. Dr. Weiss explains:

"There are an awful lot of difficulties in life that people manage by ambiguity, by waffling. If you don't fudge on certain decisions, you are threatened with the loss of an important relationship (either your kids or your spouse.) Let's say a man comes up to his prospective second spouse and announces that, okay, he'll be glad to marry her, but he wants to sequester all his property for his own kids. The prospective bride might well reply that if that's the way he feels about it, maybe they shouldn't get married. It's not that she's after his money. She wonders about the relationship they're going to have when she throws in everything and he holds backs."

If there's quite a bit of money involved, what about the older man's responsibilities to his children? There are lots of kids who would say that the money is family money and belongs to them. They would tell their father that he has no right to make an arrangement that will send the money out of the family, money that was generated for them. Or, even worse, in the case of a family business, they wouldn't want control to change hands. If he compromises too much, or cuts out the children, they might desert him. If he doesn't, he might not get the woman as a wife. It's not an easy decision to make, so he waffles. Promise each side something, but not everything. Do the children want him to stay single and come live with them? Probably not. So, they can afford to share something with the new wife. Does the new wife want to grab everything? Probably not. So, she can agree to some reasonable sharing. You have to try to avoid confrontations that demand 'either-or' decisions.

You may have to learn the art of waffling, and a shrewd lawyer, along with a practiced family counselor, can help. Fortunately, the majority of us in the second half of our lives don't have all that much property to fight over. But, for those who do—take heed.

THE ART OF WAFFLING— OR TAKE HEED!

People who are considering remarriage must also consider the possibility that it might not work. If you try to sort out important matters such as money problems, work division, and feelings about sex, it may reduce the chance of divorce. If you live in a state that has community property laws (check on this with your lawyer), you might want to keep careful accounting of all the property you owned before the marriage, or property that you inherited, or received as a gift during the marriage. Keep this money and property in a separate account, if possible. Avoid comingling your own, premarriage money and property with your partner's. You should have joint funds, of course. You can both put equal or specified amounts into the joint account. Depending on the circumstances, this may not always be easy, and you might have to do some waffling, as Dr. Weiss suggests. But, having fairly defined "his" and "her" accounts and entitlements, it will certainly make it a lot easier for both partners when, and if, a divorce ever comes up.

If there is a divorce on the horizon, you definitely should consult with a tax specialist (accountant or attorney), along with your regular attorney. Major tax consequences come out of a divorce. You and your partner can at least agree on making it as easy as possible on each other as far as taxes are concerned. You may both be able to save considerable amounts of money.

Productive negotiation depends heavily on how well your lawyer gets along with the other partner's lawyer. Unfortunately, all too many lawyers feel that divorce cases are like combat. They slash at each other, and their clients end up in shreds. A husband and wife might start out on fairly good terms, but find out too late that their lawyers hated each other. Make sure you get an attorney who has a reputation for working well with other attorneys. Nearby university law schools (family law departments) might have some names to suggest.

GOOD READING

Re-Engagement in Later Life (Re-Employment and Re-Marriage), written by Dr. Ruth Harriet Jacobs and Dr. Barbara H. Vinick, published by Greylock Press, Stamford, Connecticut. Dr. Jacobs is associate professor of sociology at Boston University. The book contains a series of case studies of retired people who went back to work or remarried after the death or divorce of a spouse. Dr. Jacobs is also author of *Life After Youth: Females, Forty, What Next?* published by Beacon Press, Boston.

Marital Separation, written by Dr. Robert S. Weiss, Chairman of the Department of Sociology, University of Massachusetts, published by Basic Books. This book also uses the case history approach to reach some interesting and unusual conclusions.

CHAPTER 28

SEX IN THE
SECOND HALF

How long will you be able to enjoy sex? Probably a lot longer than you think. There have been documented cases of men and women enjoying sex into their eighties and a few into their nineties. In general, the desire and demand for sex gradually diminishes with age. By age 75, according to some studies, men begin to encounter an increasing number of problems achieving an erection, but not all men encounter this problem. Women, in general, seem to be capable of enjoying more sex in their later years than men. But, again, there are all sorts of exceptions.

A man's major worry is his ability to get an erection. Women don't have this worry. Technically, a woman can never be "impotent." She can always "perform." But, a man? There it is. He either has an erection, or he hasn't. There's no hiding it. All too often in later life, men have image problems based on sex myths that have no basis in fact. A man might think that because he can't get the same *kind* of erection he had when he was young, there's something wrong with him. "It's the beginning of the end," he thinks. His female partner may be contributing to this myth by believing that his failure to achieve an erection every time means there's something terribly wrong.

Types of erections change. Types of orgasms change. Lots of things *change* as you grow older. But, this doesn't mean they *stop*. The major cause for declining sexual activity in the later years, according to Dr. Mary S. Calderone, president of the Sex Information and Education Council of the U.S., is: "The lack of an *interested* and *interesting* partner... Normal physiological processes of aging should definitely not be taken as a signal for the end of sexual expression."

If you've got "two to tango," you probably have it made. Still, there are a lot of facts male and female partners should know about late-life sex that can make romancing go a lot smoother. To find out more about specific problems which might lessen a person's chance to enjoy sex as an older adult, I talked with Dr. Julius Fogel and his wife, Dr. Marguerite S. Fogel. Dr. Julius Fogel is a gynecologist, psychiatrist and sex therapist. Both he and his wife are members of the American Association of Sex Educators, Counselors and Therapists. They work together as a clinical team for sex, marriage, and family counseling in the Washington, D.C. area. Dr. Marguerite Fogel is a clinical psychologist and an expert on older women's sex problems. Both Julius and Marguerite are over 60, which gives them a certain degree of wisdom to go with their technical knowledge.

FACTS AND FALLACIES

Let's start with male problems, because a man's erection (or lack of it) seems to be a major cause of concern for many middle-aged and elderly couples. Why are many men so anxious about "performing?" Dr. Julius Fogel responds:

"Men at this stage in their lives have a lot of image

problems. They somehow feel that a strong, erect penis—a pipe—is important. It's not. As a matter of fact it may be a detriment if the man's partner is a postmenopausal woman. At a certain age, perhaps some time in the fifties, a man's erection will become softer, and the angle will be straight out, or even partly down, instead of straight up. This is normal, and allows for perfectly good sex. This kind of erection, almost by design, can be more pleasurable for an older woman because there's less chance for pain (her vagina has shrunk somewhat, and is less elastic.) As you know, pain can kill off an orgasm for a woman. The softer penis fits better and feels better. It gives just as much pleasure for both.

"After age 50 or so, it takes longer to get an erection. And, of course, too much alcohol at this stage (more than one drink) might make an erection difficult, if not impossible. As a youth, a man could get an erection in a few seconds. Now, it takes a few minutes, sometimes several minutes. And, it often takes more direct stimulation. You won't get that automatic, quick response. This makes some men worry a lot, and worry has killed more erections than anything else. Taking a little more time to get an erection is normal and can even be quite pleasurable. Of course, the female partner has to understand this and has to know how to help stimulate the penis to erection. There are all sorts of sex books that can show women how to do this in a variety of ways.

"Because there is less tension in the erection, a man tends to have some staying power. He can take a lot more time before coming to ejaculation. This makes sex a lot more pleasurable (a power he wished he had when he was younger.) Taking more time, of course, is a lot better for his female partner, who usually takes longer to achieve orgasm. As he grows older, the man will find that his ejaculation is not as strong. There will be less fluid. But, unless he develops some sort of hangup over this change, the sensation and feeling of pleasure won't be lessened. In some respects, he may have a better, overall sensation of well-being and pleasure. In his youth, he got much more release in a big rush. But, now, there's a deeper emotion and an appreciation of his partner. In youth there wasn't enough time for these deeper feelings to develop."

Because many men over 50 don't know about these normal changes Dr. Fogel is referring to, they may worry about their inability to achieve an instant erection. This worry feeds on itself and makes achieving any kind of an erection all the more difficult. With women, the worry or concern may be concentrated on achieving orgasm. Presuming the female is skillful and can help her partner get a workable erection, the next test is the orgasm itself. Both men and women sometimes have half-baked ideas about the quantity and quality of female orgasms. It's a great subject for hangups. Dr. Marguerite Fogel addresses this problem and others women face as they grow older:

"A woman can always 'perform.' A man cannot. A woman may not have orgasm, but she can always have sex, and even enjoy it without orgasm. But, if a woman has to 'perform' most of the time without orgasm, just doing her 'duty,' it's a shame.

"A woman has to be in touch with her own sexuality. The orgasm has to come from her. The man provides the connection—the circuit—but the woman makes her own orgasm. She has to release inside, accept her primitive needs and let herself go. Contrary to what some men might think, women often want more sex at this stage of life than men do. Sometimes a woman must understand that a man can't get an erection any time she wants it—on demand. The man must be stimulated, not threatened. If a man feels good about himself and valued by the woman, she can bring out his sexuality.

"An older woman may have fewer orgasms than she did earlier in life, but not always. Sometimes when the children are out on their own and are out of the way—both physically and mentally—there's a release. Women feel liberated, and they can rediscover their own sexuality.

"Because the hormone supply is greatly diminished in postmenopausal women, there is less natural lubrication. Some men feel they haven't done a good job if they can't get a woman to lubricate on her own. But, this is nonsense. Use plenty of pharmaceutical lubricant such as K-Y and don't worry about it. It works just the same.

"Women should also realize that it's not always necessary to have the penis in the vagina to have orgasm. A man can stimulate her to orgasm in many ways without an erect penis. Both partners should be ready, willing and able to have separate orgasms. Each can help the other. And, you don't have to have an orgasm each time to have good sex. People have these myths about perceived male and female roles and they don't know what they're missing. A woman can enjoy sex without an orgasm. She can enjoy the warmth and the closeness. Often, this can make a fine prelude to an orgasm later on."

Apparently, there are many ways to enjoy sex, and there are many pleasurable aspects of sex other than the classic form. The Fogels say you should enjoy as much or as little sex as you seem to need or want. Don't put unreasonable demands on yourself, but don't be afraid to express yourself if you want more. Sometimes this is just a state of mind which can be quickly smoothed out by the other partner. One man in his fifties, who came into the Fogel's clinic, said he was thinking about sex all the time. He never seemed to get enough of it. When his wife had counseling and was opened up more to him and was ready—day after day—he suddenly realized he didn't want that much sex after all.

OTHER AVENUES

In an interview published by McNeil Laboratories for physicians, Dr. Mary Calderone talks about another form of sex that is often taboo among older adults:

"Masturbation is a fundamental part of our sexual expression throughout life, and serves very useful purposes during illness or absence or after the death of the sexual partner (or for singles). It also provides a very good means for equalizing the sex drive between two people when one has a higher sex drive than the other. This can carry on into old age. A lot of older adults have a sense of guilt or shame about release of tension by self-pleasure. This is too bad, because it is safe, useful, and effective, especially when combined with fantasies about a person or persons now lost, but with whom they originally did have good sexual experiences."

And, of course, there's nothing wrong with enjoying the companionship and physical caresses of another person without the need of active sex. Dr. Clyde E. Martin, sociologist at the Gerontology Research Center in Baltimore, says, "Some people can get along without sex for long periods of time and not miss it." Dr. Martin has learned from a study of hundreds of men over a number of years that the ones who are the least active with sex "seem quite comfortable with their lives." The problem, he says, comes when a man is stimulated, really wants sex, and is impotent. A man in this situation can feel terribly deprived, whereas the man who no longer misses sex can readily accept the idea of being impotent. The man who isn't all that interested in active sex may well have a satisfying relationship with someone who puts much more emphasis on other ways of expressing affection.

COUNSELING

Because everyone's sex drive is different—heavy steam, low steam, no steam—it's often a good idea to get some professional counseling when problems or incompatibility occur. A man may have a debilitating, Catch-22 worry about his erection capabilities, or a woman may worry about her perceived lack of orgasms. One partner may be making things tough for the other without knowing it. Perhaps a woman is experiencing pain during intercourse, and some hormonal (estrogen) cream might be prescribed. Maybe there's a medical reason (diabetes, for example) for the man's erection difficulties.

But, where do you get good counseling? All too often your own doctor doesn't know much about sex counseling. It probably wasn't studied in medical school, and the doctor may have his or her own sex hangups. If your doctor puts you off, or puts you down, about sex with phrases such as "at your age this is to be expected," get another doctor. A sensitive physician will at least refer you to someone who is a specialist in sex therapy and sex counseling. You have to be careful. Too many people these days are putting up a shingle and calling themselves sex experts. You may pay good money for nothing. Or, you might even be harmed by some quack form of therapy. You have to be especially careful with prescribed medication in this field. Hormone therapy in the form of estrogen may be helpful to the minority of women who suffer severe pains, flashes, and emotional upheavals from menopause. But, this kind of therapy, according to Dr. Julius Fogel, should be carefully watched, and withdrawn as soon as the menopause problems fade. Prolonged use of estrogen (pills) in females may cause cancer of the cervix. Hormone therapy for men can also be very tricky and potentially dangerous. After making absolutely sure there is no psychological problem, get at least two opinions from the best sex experts available before embarking on the hormone route.

In your search for sex counseling or therapy, check with your local university medical school, or department of psychology. You might also check with religious counselors and established family counseling services in your area.

If you still have problems, you might write for a directory published by the American Association of Sex Educators, Counselors and Therapists, 5010 Wisconsin Avenue, N.W., Washington, DC 20016. It lists some 6,200 certified members by state and city. There is a fee for the directory. Being a therapist-member of this association means there has been a certified amount of specific training. It does not certify competency.

GOOD READING

Sex After Sixty, by Dr. Robert Butler and Myrna Lewis (Harper and Row). Dr. Butler is a psychiatrist, and a gerontologist, and is head of the National Institute on Aging. Myrna Lewis, his wife, is a psychotherapist who specializes in the problems of older women.

A Good Age, by Dr. Alex Comfort (Crown), talks about sex, plus other subjects related to the aging process. Dr. Comfort is also the author of *The Joy of Sex* which describes pleasure techniques.

The Fires of Autumn, by Peter Dickinson (Drake Publishers).

Love in the Later Years, by gerontologists James Peterson and Barbara Payne (Follett Publishing Co.).

CHAPTER 29

GETTING A LIFT

The face-lift is fast becoming the most popular operation for people over a certain age. "Everybody's doing it," says one woman in her fifties, adding that "it's almost like going to the hairdresser." It's true. Face-lifts, eyelid clipping, and removal of bags under the eyes are appealing to many people in their late forties and fifties. Last year, plastic surgeons performed more than 600,000 operations, and the great majority of them involved cosmetic surgery on faces, breasts, stomach bulges, wrinkles, and a procedure called "body contouring." Much of the surgery was done on women, but surgeons say more men are turning to plastic surgery than in the past.

The woman who said a face-lift is "almost like going to the hairdresser" probably has a conveniently short memory. Or, she may want to encourage others: "Come on in, the water's fine." For people who are very concerned about their looks, a skillfully done face-lift might, indeed, provide a psychological lift as well. If you're fairly satisfied with your looks and realize that, as you grow older, you will normally have a few sags and wrinkles, then having a face-lift may not be worth it.

IS THE MOTIVATION
WORTH THE COST?

First of all, there's the cost. It can range from $1,800 on up to $3,000—even $5,000 if a Hollywood "surgeon of the stars" does it. Having the eyes done along with the face-lift can add another $1,500 to $2,500 to the bill. And, worst of all, your medical insurance won't pay for this. You also pay in time, pain, and discomfort. An operation done in a hospital takes around three to four hours. This is not "minor" surgery although to save money, some surgeons do work in their offices or outpatient clinics. If you don't want people to see your face messed up, you'll be out of work and off the social circuit for a month to six weeks. Some patients go back to work within three weeks, but they have to put up with stares and questions. Just having the eyelids and eye bags done doesn't take up so much time. You can be back in circulation within a week to ten days.

Because I have excess skin under my chin called "wattles" or "turkey-gobbler" effect (they don't pull any punches), I thought I could have a quick, cheap, operation to take in a tuck or two and be out working in no time. No such luck. The surgeon I interviewed, Dr. Albert F. Fleury, Chief of the Plastic Surgery Division, Georgetown University Medical Center, gave me the bad news. In order to take up the skin underneath my chin and along the front of the upper neck, I had to have a complete face-lift. Just cutting away the skin, Dr. Fleury, says, would leave a scar that would look as if a tiger clawed you.

You see, cosmetic surgery always leaves scars. Unless you

can hide them along the hairline, as is the procedure with face lifting, the visible scars will be out in the open for all to see. To hide the scars, the surgeon must cut from the hairline in the temple region down the hairline by the ear, and around in back of the neck. Then everything is pulled deftly up, and back, to remove the sagging effect. After hearing all this and seeing the price tag of $2,000 to $3,000, I politely declined. When I went home to look in the mirror, I decided I didn't look so bad after all. At a dinner party, when I mentioned the fact that I had been considering removing the wattled skin under my chin, the woman next to me exclaimed she hadn't noticed it until I brought the subject up.

Dr. Fleury says that although some people may actually appear younger after a face-lift, more often, the impression is given that you look "rested" or "healthy." As a matter of fact, if you have an attitude of well-being, you probably won't need a face-lift. Exercising, eating right, learning good posture and grace through aerobic dancing, or other such activities, might do more for your overall appearance than facial surgery. A graceful figure, reshaped through exercise, can often make you look younger than a redone face.

Still, the temptation is there—the longing for that sagging skin to go away. How many times have you gently pulled the skin up by your neck and jaw and taken another look in the mirror? Lifting with the fingers does, indeed remove those "wattles." But, it also gives you another look, a look that sometimes appears a little too sleek—not "you."

Perhaps you're fairly secure with your life. You have a partner who loves you "as is." You may have interesting work which doesn't require chasing the youthful look. Some motivation for lifting the sagging skin may be there—but it's not enough.

SAGGING SKIN AND
SAGGING MORALE

Others who have relied on their looks to get a job or get the attention of the opposite sex, may be super-sensitive about their appearance. Sagging skin is directly translated into sagging morale. For this type of person, paying several thousand dollars and taking the risk that always goes with any major operation, may be worthwhile. Having a successful operation makes this person feel better. The operation is, technically, physiological, but—in fact—it's also psychological. The scalpel not only cuts away the excess skin or fatty tissue, it cuts away the gloomy feelings about one's appearance.

But, you've got to be careful, Dr. Fleury says. "A face-lift won't solve serious psychological problems," he says, "or fix up a marriage, or make people like you better." You should never have a face-lift to "surprise" a spouse or a close friend. He or she may hate it, thinking you are dissatisfied with your life and, therefore, dissatisfied with your relationship. This is why some surgeons suggest that certain patients have psychological counseling before they consider a major face-lift operation. Actually, a good surgeon should have a long talk with you to explain everything—all the risks—before you decide to have an operation done. Dr. Fleury says you must have realistic expectations. The operation won't transform you into the belle of the ball, like Cinderella. And, you must have the right skin and facial contour to insure reasonable success.

SOME POTENTIAL PROBLEMS

With face-lifts, Dr. Fleury explains, "the best cases are those with a rather thin face and loose, thin skin." The worst cases are those who have fat faces or thick skin and deep wrinkles. Blacks, Dr. Fleury says, have a tendency toward keloid formation (scarring), so plastic surgery results may be unacceptable.

Scarring can also be a problem for people who want wrinkles etched off with acid or by abrasion. This procedure, which is often done in a doctor's office, is one of the most iffy of all cosmetic techniques. It's the one that produces the most "horror" stories. Your skin is literally broken down by acid or the abrasion tool, and it leaves a scab. When the scab comes off, the new skin underneath is tighter. The wrinkles are usually smoothed out. But, if your skin is of a particular type, heavy and/or dark, unsightly scar tissue could form. And, if your skin is too light, you could have a "pinto" look. Some of your skin would tan well, some wouldn't.

BODY CONTOURING

Then there's "body contouring." This is where you have your stomach, thighs, arms, legs and breasts "lifted" or "trimmed." A thigh lift costs around $2,000. An abdomen job for a protuberant pot or stretch marks costs from $1,500 up to $5,000, depending on who does the work and how much has to be done. These are major operations, especially the stomach surgery, and require hospitalization. The operations are also potentially dangerous and can leave scars that cannot be hidden. They're among the most dubious of all plastic surgery operations. Dr. Fleury says the best candidate for "body contouring" might be a patient who has lost a lot of weight and is left with skin hanging in folds, or a woman whose abdominal skin had been severely stretched by pregnancy, and is left with unsightly folds of skin. But, otherwise, these operations should be looked at with a certain degree of skepticism.

There's one form of body contouring of which Dr. Fleury and most other surgeons approve. It's the breast-lift. Some women in their middle years have breasts that are big and pendulant. The weight of the breasts can force bad posture and cause a considerable amount of pain and discomfort. Removing some of the tissue and lifting the breasts can make a woman look a lot better and feel a lot better. This is one plastic surgery operation, Dr. Fleury says, that most medical insurance plans will pay for. It can improve the posture and the overall health of the patient.

SOME DO'S AND DON'TS

As you can see, it's crucial to get the right plastic surgeon. You should never respond to an advertisement or a sales pitch from some surgeon who says you can "be made over to start a new life." Start with your own doctor, who should be able to give you the names of recommended surgeons. You want the best, most experienced, surgeon for the type of operation you're considering. Before seeing the surgeon, your doctor should give you a physical exam to make sure you're up to having an operation. If you have high blood pressure, for example, an operation could be dangerous, and the surgeon will have to turn you down until your condition is under control.

As a rule, your doctor will know how to get the names of the best surgeons. A nearby university medical school might be a good source. At the very minimum, the plastic surgeon should be certified by the American Board of Plastic Surgery. The surgeon should have had up to 5-6 years special training after getting a medical degree, and should have done a lot of work in the area you're interested in. Look for a long history of training, good degrees, and experience.

Don't have a cosmetic operation done as a part of some

other operation. If a surgeon offers to do extra work on your face or body with a "won't-cost-you-much-extra" deal, forget it. Remember, any plastic surgery must be done by the best in the field, and only after you have considered it carefully. Any doctor can hang out a shingle with "Plastic Surgeon" on it. There's no law against it. You must know your surgeon's background.

According to a woman who was taking a consciousness-raising seminar, a surgeon mingled in with the group, striking up conversations with women who were "vulnerable." This doctor, she says, flattered prospective clients by saying they would look ravishing—if only the skin on their face was tightened up. If you encounter this kind of unethical approach, walk in the opposite direction. Good surgeons don't have to hawk their wares.

Finally, there's the psychological evaluation. If you're going to have major surgery done on your face or body, you'd better explore your motives thoroughly. You might be able to do this on your own, with the help of a spouse, or a close friend. Or, you might want to get some counseling from a psychiatrist or psychologist. Here's how psychiatrist Malkah T. Notman, of Beth Israel Hospital in Boston, evaluates the situation:

"Face-lifting and cosmetic surgery depend on the individual. I'm not against it, if it means an awful lot to somebody. If you really feel you'll look your best with cosmetic surgery, it might be helpful. I just don't think it's practical for most people. I've noticed, professionally, and among my friends, that those women who remarry or stay involved with men (after widowhood or divorce) are not necessarily those who have had face-lifts. It really has to do with a quality of vitality, interests, liveliness and, to some extent, overall physical appearance. You don't have to have all this plastic surgery to look attractive. A lot depends on your attitude, your warmth, your vitality, and your interest in things."

GOOD READING

Cosmetic Surgery—A Consumer's Guide, by Sylvia Rosenthal (a physician's wife), published by Lippincott. Gives pros and cons and plenty of detail on individual operations and procedures.

   Consultation with a Plastic Surgeon, by Ralph L. Dicker, M.D. and Victor R. Syracuse, M.D. (Warner Books). Two plastic surgeons answer a series of questions about their business.

CHAPTER 30

THE BRAIN GAME

You can have your face lifted, or you can exercise regularly, and your outward appearance will change. But what about your *inside* appearance? What about your head? Your brain needs as much stimulation, if not more, than your body. Some people, as they get older, let their heads go downhill. They put in time at a boring job (paid work, or unpaid housework), and then plunk down in front of the television set. Day after day, night after night. When the body doesn't move around enough through exercise, it becomes flabby and weak. The same goes for your head. You have to play "The Brain Game" and play it well. If you don't, your fuzzy head could do you in later on.

"BROADEN YOUR PORTFOLIO"

Dr. Robert Butler, head of the National Institute on Aging, puts it nicely when he talks about the vital need for psychological fitness, as well as physical fitness:

"You have to expand your mind. If you're cast in one kind

of a job or style of life, you should broaden your portfolio. Invest in other interests. There may come a time when you won't be working, because of a voluntary decision, or because you're unable to work.

"For example, let's say you've always thought you're going to do deep-sea fishing when you slow down, or retire. It may happen that this dream will be impossible because your spouse becomes ill or you become ill. You may encounter severe arthritis, or some other disabling disease. You won't be able to do the deep-sea fishing. If that's the only 'stock' you bought for the future, you're in real trouble.

"You should have a diversified portfolio with a number of different options. You should have a wide range of interests. Some of them should have novelty or newness to them. Stretch your head. Keep your memory and your mind active. Don't just think in terms of physical fitness, think in terms of mental fitness as well. Falling into a rut at this stage can be dangerous. As you grow older, you'll need all the wits you can muster."

OPPORTUNITIES FOR TUNING-UP

Dr. Hilda Kahne, professor of economics at Wheaton College, says "mind exercise" is of special interest to housewives in their middle years. Husbands may get some stimulation from their jobs, but housewives have to get away from the daily routine to tune up their minds. "Women have to meet new people and exchange ideas," Dr. Kahne says, explaining that "taking a course in some field of interest at a community college is an easy and effective way to get started."

Older women and men seem to be taking Dr. Kahne's and Dr. Butler's advice. "There's been an enormous increase in education for older adults," says behavioral scientist Bernice Neugarten. "Education," Dr. Neugarten says, "is not necessarily going back to school in the traditional sense . . . There are all sorts of museum courses, encounter groups, church and synagogue courses, television courses, self-teaching programs, and all sorts of unofficial educational exploration going on."

But, for many, the community college has become the center of the revolution in adult education. Some 4.5-million people are enrolled in the nation's 1,240 community colleges. Many of these students are older adults. Enrollment of older students is increasing by 15 percent a year, while enrollment of younger students is on the decline.

The cost of going to a community college for local residents ranges from free to, perhaps, $30 for a course. It's an enormous education bargain. An increasing number of community colleges now have special free or low-cost programs for people 55 and above. Even if you're not 55 yet, there are literally hundreds of courses to choose from and regular fees are very inexpensive.

Community colleges are ideal places to get started with your mind expansion program because they're usually close by and are open at night and on weekends, so you don't have to miss work. In some cases, courses can be taken on your own, at your own pace. You come into the college from time to time for consultations with your professor, and the rest of the time you're on your own (the community is your "laboratory").

What about your capabilities as a student? "Older adults," says Bernice Neugarten, "often have an advantage over younger students because there's less turmoil in their lives—no boy-girl problems, no hassles with parents." Older students know what they want, and they're usually highly motivated. Older students are experienced and aren't worried about making it as a man or a woman. They're over this hurdle and are freer to work on their studies. Teachers and professors often say that some of their best students are older adults. Younger students may be wondering why they're going to classes, while older students know why they're there. "An older man," says Yale psychologist Danel J. Levinson, "is less tyrannized by ambition, more concerned with the intrinsic value of his efforts, and more able to enjoy diverse aspects of living and learning."

It's the diversity of community college catalogs that makes them so appealing. Most community colleges, which are subsidized by local governments, will organize almost any course you want as long as they can get 10 or more people to participate. Because of this flexibility, the community college has become more than a college. It has become a clearinghouse for community activities. "We're a lonely society," says Philip J. Gannon, President of Lansing (Michigan) Community College, explaining that the college has become "a place for people to get together, make friends, and learn something new." (Lansing has its 18,000 students spread out over 52 community locations).

Dr. Gannon says his college is taking in many more people in their forties, fifties, sixties—even seventies and eighties. Because of this influx of older adults, he says, there has been an explosion of interest in the performing and creative arts. Older adults are even going back to study courses they initially took in high school or college. "At 18," says Dr. Gannon, "you may have read Shakespeare and you probably found him somewhat hard to follow . . . But, at 50 or 60, you read Shakespeare again and you find you've lived some of those things he's talking about . . . You're able to appreciate what he's saying."

PUTTING YOUR LIFE
EXPERIENCES TO WORK

Not all of Lansing Community College's older adults are students. Some people have come back to be part-time faculty members. A good number of the college's faculty are in their fifties and sixties. One 62-year-old man was hired as a full-time teacher after he had retired from his regular job. "The man didn't even have a college degree," says Dr. Gannon, explaining, "He had run his own repair garage for 40 years and it was a great opportunity for us, as well as for him." Community colleges often find that people in their immediate area who have experience in some particular field make excellent teachers. There's a lot less emphasis on academic theory, and a lot more on "I'm-doing-it" practical knowledge.

Being a community college teacher is a good way to keep your mind active, and it's a good way to make real use of your life experiences. For a man who has come to a peak in his career, or passed it, imparting knowledge to others can be the highlight of his life. Here's how Dr. Daniel Levinson expresses it in his book, *The Seasons of a Man's Life*:

"Being a mentor with young adults is one of the most significant relationships available to a man in middle adulthood. As he gains a stronger sense of self, and of his own continuing development in middle adulthood, a man is more able to foster the development in other adults. The mentor is doing something for himself. He is making productive use of his own knowledge and skills in middle age." Of course, this advice applies to women, as well as to men.

So, you can be a teacher or be a student. It makes little difference as long as knowledge is flowing and your brain is active, challenged, alert. The longer you can keep it that way, the better off you'll be.

ALTERNATE LEARNING EXPERIENCES

But, some forms of learning are coming in packages that are hardly recognizable as education. They're a combination of group therapy and education. Take est, for example. Most urban areas have experienced visits from est group leaders during the year. Sessions are advertised, and halls are hired. The hopeful come to register for two, weekend, marathon sessions that often last on into the early morning hours. You pay several hundred dollars for the course, which automatically places it beyond the community college tuition range, and you're packed into a hall with hundreds of others.

Group encounter sessions such as est (there are several competing varieties) are supposed to work like a catharsis, something to get your true feelings out on the washline for airing. A friend of mine, a science writer, gives his impression of an est session:

"It's like cold water in the face. You take a good look at yourself. You come away feeling that you can be more direct with people. It's a sort of psychological cleaning out. But, you shouldn't do it as an alternative to therapy. As a matter of fact, if you're in therapy, you must get permission from your therapist before you're allowed in. You sit in a chair for 12 hours at a time—four times over two weekends—48 hours. You only get one short meal break at each 12-hour session, and bathroom breaks are scarce.

"You are supposed to experience feelings. You must get things through your feelings, not your head. If you want to understand, you must experience—put yourself into it. You learn that you can't do anything about other people's problems. If you want change, you're the one that has to change things—not somebody else."

Apparently, est and some of its competitors are a hodgepodge of various eastern religions, philosophies, and psychological techniques. Some people swear by the sessions (as did my friend). Others say they paid their money and were just "browbeaten." A few may have been harmed. It's relatively expensive and it can be rough on some people.

Other groups catering to alcoholics, drug victims, widows, widowers, cancer patients, and others with special problems, can provide a backdrop for considerable self-help and mind expansion.

The variety of learning opportunities for older adults is awesome. Check with your community college, nearby university, adult education program (board of education), churches, synagogues, fraternal organizations, community organizations (Red Cross, Heart Association). local clubs and civic organizations, museums, the county agricultural extension service (consumer courses), banks, savings and loan, stock brokers, and other organizations. If you can't find something that catches your interest, chances are it's your own fault. You've been glued to the tube too long, and you need some sort of mental dynamite.

GOOD READING

Directory—Educational and Career Information Services for Adults. For information, write: National Center for Educational Brokering, 1211 Connecticut Avenue, N.W., Washington, DC 20036. Educational brokers, usually sponsored by local governments, can act as guidance counselors to show you where and how to get the education that suits your specific needs.

Credit for Work-Life Experience. Write: Council For The Advancement of Experiential Learning, American City Building, Suite 212, Columbia, MD 21044. For a fee, you can buy this guide that lists colleges and universities around the country that give credits for things learned through your work or life experiences. Valuable for college degree programs or advanced degrees.

How to Get College Credit for What You've Learned as a Homemaker and Volunteer. Write: Educational Testing Service, Princeton, NJ. For housewives planning to work for a degree.

Learning Vacations, written by Gerson G. Eisenberg (Acropolis Books). The book lists colleges and universities where you can take courses and vacation at the same time (trips abroad, across the country, archeological digs, museums, concerts, history, the arts, sciences).

CHAPTER 31

GETTING AWAY

You have to get away from time to time. There's a basic need in all of us to get some distance away from work, family problems, and home management hassles. Some older people get away by traveling to a new spot once a year, or even more often if they can afford it. Others like to head back to the same place year after year. Wherever you go, the change of scenery and climate can act as a tonic.

Sometimes, in middle life, we institutionalize our getting away by officially looking for a nice place to retire. This is an interesting rationalization for the urge to travel, and it won't do any harm as long as you're just "looking." If you really do plan to retire—to unplug completely—you'd better think twice before you pack up and leave some city, town, or neighborhood where you've lived for a long time. Of course, if you've lived a semi-gypsy life—moving here and there every few years—your roots won't be very deep in any given spot, and you'll be well versed in the art of adaptation.

If you've read this far, you'll realize that a lot is involved in the "retiring" or "unplugging" process. A case was made for *not* retiring in the classic sense. As inflation burns up your savings, you may find that you simply cannot afford to retire. You may slow down, or change careers but, somehow or other, you may have to make money for as long as possible. With this thought in mind, you will have to choose your "getaway" place with a lot of care. There are many "sun and fun" places that, in the past, have attracted the retirement crowd. But, these semi-resort communities are often tough places in which to find the kind of work you want to do. There are a lot of people along the beach or in the mountains chasing too few jobs. If you have a high-demand, portable skill, you'll be a lot better off.

RECOGNIZING YOUR "SOCIAL NETWORK"

Aside from the money angle, there's the whole business of leaving friends, neighbors, colleagues, and familiar places. The academics call it your "social network." It's the rich tapestry of relationships that you've built up over the years. You know your own home and your hometown. You know your doctor, you know the people who do your banking, your repairs, and all the other services you take for granted. You can't just throw all this over without paying a price.

Dr. Robert Butler, the head of the National Institute on Aging, spells it out:

"Let's say you have lived in a certain city or neighborhood for years and you think, by God, you're going to move to some sunny spot on the beach, or some cool place in the mountains. You went to one of these beautiful places once or twice on trips and loved it. So, you plan to sell your home in the old neighborhood and move to the sun and breezes. But, you might find that the neighbors aren't the same—not your kind of people. You don't know the pharmacist, the doctor, the lawyer, the accountant, the hospital, barber-shop, or hairdresser. They're all strangers.

"Before you break with your old social network, slow down. Take time to investigate your chosen spot thoroughly. Some people swear on a bible that a beach, mountain, or desert hideaway is just the place they want when they retire. I tell them to investigate first. You can't just go to someplace for a vacation and really know if it's going to be the right move. If you can work it out, move to the selected spot for at least six months. A year is even better. Don't sell your old home. Rent it furnished, or put your furniture in storage. Rent a small place in the new area, and live there just as if you had made the big move.

"You'll get a good idea of what living there is really like. You'll see if you can set up some new social networks—friends, pharmacist, doctor, stores, and the like. You'll see what fuel costs are, and how much you might have to pay in taxes. You can get a job and see how it goes. After living there awhile, you can decide whether you want to sell your old home and make the move permanent. As a matter of fact, your old home will probably appreciate in value and you might get some tax benefits out of being a landlord for a year."

SOME HIDDEN FACTS
AND BENEFITS

If you do decide to move, here are some factors you should consider:

1. Be sure you can handle the off-season. Some places get cold in winter and hot in summer. Few people stick around when the weather is bad. Can you live comfortably in your new home all year around?

2. Check the availability of services. Some people are lured into buying a beautiful place in the woods or mountains. It seems like a good idea at the time. They forget that some day, when they're older, they might need a hospital within easy transportation distance. Will your new home be near hospitals, a pharmacy, and doctor's offices?

3. Investigate possible part-time or full-time job opportunities for both you and your spouse. You may or may not feel you want to work right away. Later on, it might become a necessity.

The trouble is, your current employer is not going to give you a year off to "practice" living and working some place else. It would require a formal break through retirement. But, your employer might give you more and more vacation time as you get older. With this extra time, you might be able to do some extensive experimenting with living in a new area.

Or, you might be able to build up certain high-demand, portable skills that can be used in your hometown or the new place. With marketable skills, you might be able to keep your old home and build up in another area a part-time life that gets you out of the winter cold or out of the summer heat.

It might involve supporting two homes (owning or renting), and this could be expensive unless you can be sure of renting out the "empty" home while you're away. It may become more affordable when you sell your home in the old neighborhood. If you wait until you're at least 55, you get up to $100,000 in a tax-free bonus from the profit you make on the sale of your old home. With the profit, you can buy a condominium apartment or much smaller house in or near your old neighborhood (where all your friends and services are), and buy another apartment or cottage in your place in the sun.

At first, you can rent out the retreat home full-time in

order to get all the tax benefits—and they can be considerable. You have to make sure that your retreat is not in some area that has a short season and then goes to sleep. The winter-summer season or year-around places are probably the best investments, because they bring in steady rent and they're easier to visit any time of the year. You may even want to move there full-time some day.

When you buy your vacation home in your high-earning years, you can make a business out of it and reap some tax benefits. As long as you don't spend more than 14 days during the year in your second home, the Internal Revenue Service says it can be classified as a business. You have to actively put it up for rent through agents or your own advertising. You can visit the place for a long weekend to open it up at the beginning of the season (if there are two seasons, you can make two visits.) Then, when the season is over, you can visit it again to close it down or fix it up. These extra "business" days plus the 14 days IRS allows for your own vacation can add up to a total of about three weeks. If you keep within your tax advisor's guidelines, you can get a depreciation allowance and tax deductions that could, conceivably, take a lot off your income tax. It doesn't always work out this way, and you should have a tax accountant at your elbow to show you all the figures. You need to get all the facts about operating expenses, local taxes, realistic rental income, everything, before you make a purchase.

Of course, if you're not that pressed for money, you can buy a place and not try to rent it all the time. Or, the place you originally purchased as a full-time rental property can be converted into a regular vacation home for you. You can still get some tax deductions (for interest on the loan and local taxes), but they're not as big as the ones you get when you rent out the home full-time.

In some vacation areas, homeowners band together to form a rental pool. If you want to pay a visit during the height of the season and your own unit is occupied, the pool tries to find you some other place that's open. You can even make a reservation in advance. If you pay a fair rent, there's no problem with IRS. You don't stay in your own place, but you might stay next door, down the hall, or down the street.

THE FINAL DECISION

After awhile, you might find that you're spending more and more time in your getaway place. Maybe you've made a deal so you can take as much as one, two, even three months off to live near the beach, lake, river, woods, mountain or desert. Then, in effect, you have two getaway places—one here (your old home) and one there. Each place is nice to come home to. Over the years, you may even build up two sets of social networks—one in each place. You have close friends in both places. Ideally, you go back and forth with the climate. You might even decide, after long and careful thought, to spend considerably more time in the "second" home than the first. You might even get rid of the first home and make the move complete.

This is what happened to my sister, Charlotte Jones and her husband, John. He had been a school teacher and then the head of a school. Early on, he would spend his summer vacations working in a boys' camp on Lake Champlain near the little town of Westport, New York. John and Charlotte Jones bought a summer house in Westport. Over the years, they built up a group of friends that slowly, but surely, became as important (or more so) as their friends back at the school.

When John and Charlotte Jones retired, they moved to Westport permanently. It wasn't a sudden, disruptive move—

the kind Dr. Butler warns against. It was a move that really took 25 years or so. They had a home they'd grown to love, they had a group of old friends, they had their doctor, pharmacist, grocer, lawyer—everybody—all in place when they finally made their second home into their first. The winters are cold, but not that much colder than where they were, and they'd learned to love the beauty of the snow on the Adirondack Mountains while spending Christmas vacations in Westport. Their home on the lake, with the mountains behind them, has become a magnet, attracting visits from their children and friends the year-round.

OTHER OPTIONS

The gradual move that John and Charlotte Jones made and the "test" move that Dr. Butler suggested are just two of a wide variety of options you have. Some people, in spite of the high cost of gasoline, still like to follow the sun with big mobile homes or elaborate trailers. They shut down their main home in winter (saving on heating fuel) and drive to the southwest, Florida, or California. They hook up in special camp sites and spend the winter there. Many have skills that bring in extra money (repairs, secretarial, bookkeeping, sales). Then, when it gets too hot down south or out west, they move back to the cooler northlands. Obviously, this type of life is not for everybody. You have to like living in a mobile home or a trailer. But, if you're considering it, be sure to rent a unit first, to give it a try before you make a hefty purchase commitment. You may like the life, or you may not.

Others like to "swap" homes with people in other areas of the country, or even abroad. This way, there's no need to buy a second home or a mobile home. There are several agencies (listed at the end of this chapter) through which you can list your home for swapping. You can work out exchanges for just a few weeks, several months, or even a year or two. If you can arrange your home so you won't be nervous with someone else living in it, this can be a fascinating and inexpensive way to get a much needed change of scenery.

Living abroad part-time or full-time has its good points and its bad points. In some cases, like living in Mexico where a number of Americans have retired, you can enjoy a good climate, low-cost living, and beautiful surroundings. But, if you are 65 or older and rely on Medicare for your health insurance, all bets are off. Medicare won't cover you abroad. You might not be covered on an extensive foreign trip, either. It's something you should look into.

If you're looking for some getaway spot for eventual retirement, *Money* magazine published a list of the "Ten Best States" as far as low-cost living and overall surroundings (for people over 65) are concerned. They are: Utah (low living costs, good job opportunities); Louisiana (warm and inexpensive); South Carolina (low living costs); Nevada (good jobs, no state income tax); Texas (good jobs, housing costs moderate); New Mexico (fair jobs, low-cost housing); Alabama (few jobs, but inexpensive and warm); Arizona (warm, but rapidly rising living costs); Florida (warm, no income tax, living costs high on the coasts); Georgia (mild climate, low living costs, but slow job market).

GOOD SOURCES

Lower living costs: Write to the Bureau of Labor Statistics, Office of Information, GAO Building, 441 G Street, N.W., Washington, DC 20212. You can get a copy of the latest budgets for various levels of income in various cities and regions around the country.

Retirement State Tax Guide: Write to the American Association of Retired Persons, 1909 K Street N.W., Washington, DC 20049. They publish this booklet which gives information on taxes across the country, including special breaks for people over 65.

Home Swap Association: Write to: Vacation Exchange Club, 350 Broadway, New York, NY 10013; Inquiline, Inc., 35 Adams Street, Bedford Hills, NY 10507; Adventures in Living, P.O. Box 278, Winetka, ILL 60093; Holiday Exchange, Box 878, Belen, NM 87002.

Woodall Publishing Company, 500 Hyacinth Place, Highland Park, ILL 60035. This company is a clearinghouse of information for people who are interested in mobile home and trailer living. It has *Woodall's Campground Directory* with all the special sites around the country for these vehicles—listed, described, rated. It also publishes *Woodall's Retirement and Resort Communities Guide*, which lists prices, climate, taxes, medical facilities, services, and other pertinent information.

Part IV
Your
Parents

CHAPTER 32

EMPTY NEST REFILLED

"The next old people are us."
Dr. Alex Comfort

Because people are living longer, especially women, you're going to see a lot more "children" in their forties, fifties, and sixties growing old with parents who are in their seventies, eighties, and nineties. With any given married couple, you're almost sure to find that one or both partners have at least one aging parent who could become increasingly dependent as the years roll on.

The famous "empty nest" situation that follows when your children leave home could have an ironic twist. Just when you think you're free from the responsibilities of supporting your own children, along comes an invalid, frail, or confused, aged parent who needs your help. Suddenly, you ponder the possibility of the *empty nest refilled*. This is why it's not a bad idea, as you plan for your own security and serenity in later life, to have a contingency plan for an aging parent or parents.

CHANGING STATISTICS

You're not automatically going to have a problem taking care of a mother or father. Many older "children" have parents who do not have financial problems, who live full, independent lives, and die peacefully. But, the odds are increasingly going against having this kind of idyllic relationship with parents. Parents are living longer, and in so doing, are becoming more fragile and in need of care. In times past, chances were a parent would become ill and die. Now, medical breakthroughs and a better environment are combining to allow many more people to live to a very old age.

According to Dr. Harold Sheppard, an economist with the American Institutes of Research, "The proportion of Americans in their early sixties who have older parents still alive is increasing at a dazzling pace." Dr. Sheppard points out that, in 1960, there were only 34 very old persons (80 and above) for every 100 persons between the ages of 60 and 65. In 1970, he says, there were 46 "old-olds" to every 100 "young-olds." By 1990, the proportion of very old persons will increase to 63 for every 100 persons aged 60 to 65, and by the year 2000, the proportion will be almost 80 for every 100. With further progress in the biomedical field, you might even see the number of "old-olds" reach 90 for every 100 persons between 60 and 65.

In six years, the population of people between ages 40 and 65 increased by 1.9 percent while those over 65 increased by 14.8 percent. People over age 75 (when medical problems are apt to be more frequent) increased in number by 16.1 percent. And, listen to this: People 85 and above grew in number by 40 percent, making this the fastest growing segment of the U.S. population. This means more people will have one or both parents still living when they themselves are in their fifties, sixties—even their seventies.

Increasing dependency needs of the elderly often come at a time when sons and daughters are beginning to encounter their own problems with aging. The so-called "filial crisis" might start during your forties and fifties, when your parents can no longer be counted on for support. As a matter of fact, your parents may be calling on you for aid and comfort at the same time that you, yourself, are a grandparent and feel the same needs.

HOW MUCH IS ENOUGH?

You want to do what's right for your parents. Your parents don't want to be a burden on you, or your brothers and sisters. You have a continuing call from your own children for assistance with grandchildren, buying homes, career problems, and, perhaps, the hassle of their separation and divorce. We all have this idea that we want to be independent. But, it can be overdone. As we were once dependent on our parents, now our parents are dependent on us. It's a delicate situation. As the ones with the economic and physical power, we have to be careful not to get carried away and, in trying to "do the right thing," become just a bit tyrannical with our parents. We sometimes are tempted to treat our parents as children; and they are not children.

On the other hand, some parents have an almost pathological concept of their own independence. Mrs. Elaine Brody, who specializes in the problems of families with aging parents at the Philadelphia Geriatric Center says: "The cultural value which emphasizes independence as the desirable goal often obscures the psychological truth that interdependence is normal and healthy throughout the life cycle...Total separation and total independence are as pathological as overinvolvement and overdependence." You've got to be flexible.

You have to guard against reacting to each new calamity without a contingency plan. Every one of us has the urge, the need, to do something for our parents. It's part of human growth. But, how much is enough? And, how much is too much? In the following chapters you will be introduced to problems you might face with your parents. Some guidelines will be suggested for handling such contingencies as: Should mom or dad live with me? What happens when a parent remarries? What's the best option—nursing home, in-home care or day care? Where can one find community and other resources for assistance? How do you handle the guilt feelings of "not doing enough"?

A CASE STUDY

I've had to find answers to some of these questions myself. My father, Robert A. Weaver, remarried at age 70 after my mother, May Weaver, died. Her death was what some of her friends said was "ideal...the way to go." She was riding horseback at a ranch in Arizona and was felled by a stroke. She had been healthy and happy up to that point. There was no lingering—no hanging on as an invalid. She had always feared that—the hanging on.

My father married a younger woman and enjoyed an active life until his late seventies. Then, he became disabled by Parkinson's disease and suffered a serious decline. A new type of medication partially freed his body from the shuffles and shakes that typify this disease.

But, the highly potent medication and the fact that he was approaching 80, weakened him and left him increasingly dependent on his new wife. It was not always easy for her to cope with this onslaught of heavy dependency, and my brother, Robert, my sister, Charlotte, and I were called on to provide more and more help.

My father was still living in his home—our old home. That's where he said he wanted to remain until he died. He made us promise that we would do all we could to let him remain in his home, where he had raised the family and had so many memories of past happiness and success.

Because I write a syndicated newspaper column called "Your Retirement Dollar," which deals with the money and medical problems of growing old, I was assigned to help find local resources that might help my father remain in his home until he died. It wasn't easy, as, perhaps, you have already found out in your own attempts to help your father or mother. All too many doctors are simply not equipped to handle the special problems of the aging patient. Until recently, not one medical school had a full-fledged department or chair assigned to the science of gerontology (the study of aging).

When my father's condition worsened, it was necessary to find massage therapists, home health aides, and others to come in to relieve the physical and psychological burden on his sometimes frantic wife. Toward the end, in his eighty-sixth year, it was difficult for him to leave his bed, and his health was failing fast. His doctor, seeing that his wife was becoming fearful of not being able to cope, suggested a transfer to a nursing home.

But, remembering my father's repeated request "to die at home," I persuaded his doctor to enlist more help. A nurse from a nearby hospital was brought in to show my father's home health aide what to do to make a dying patient comfortable. Eventually, he died in his own bed. He had seen his children and wife shortly before, and he seemed at peace.

My brother and sister and I felt that we had helped fulfill

our father's wish to stay in his home. Of course, this is not always possible, but it's a worthwhile goal. When I spoke to my own children about their grandfather's death, I said, "That's what I want—to die at home." Again, I may not be able to die at home, but I know my family will try to make this possible.

The lesson I learned was this: Family communication and closeness are essential for living out one's years in dignity and peace. An aged parent's own wishes must be heard. Perhaps some wishes are impractical. But, both sides—the aging parent and the adult children—must work it out together. You can't impose decisions on either generation without investigating and discussing all the alternatives.

The goal is to permit as much independence as possible for your parent, for as long as possible. How this can be done will be explored in upcoming chapters.

CHAPTER 33

THE DAUGHTERS

When a parent needs special care, the person usually tagged for the job is the daughter. If there is no daughter handy, then a son's wife—the daughter-in-law—is the chosen one. There are exceptions. You sometimes hear of a son dutifully caring for his mother or father. Chances are this son has no sisters, is a bachelor, or has a wife who refuses to take on the job by herself.

Ideally, all the children should share equally in the job of caring for an aging parent. But, this is not always possible. One child might live in the same city with the parent, while the others live elsewhere. When none of the children live in the same city as the parent, then more conflicts arise. Who goes to help? At whose home, or near whose home will the parent reside if long-distance caring becomes impractical?

It's usually the daughter or the eldest son's wife who "volunteers" or is "chosen." This is almost always the case when the daughter or daughter-in-law is a housewife and is not "working" in a paid job. Presumably, this often harrassed homemaker is selected because she doesn't have a job. Her children are more or less on their own, so the rationalization goes, and she has "nothing better" to do.

"If you don't have a paid job," says Dr. Grace Baruch, who is working on a study of older women at Brandeis University, "it's awfully difficult to say you can't care for an older person because you have to attend some garden club function." But, she says, "it's not so hard to report in for work at a job you've been holding for some time... You just say you can't take any more time off than the men in the family."

Apparently, men are more willing to accept the fact that a woman with a good job cannot up and leave it to care for a parent. This means that an acceptable job might provide insulation from the automatic caretaking selection process that goes on in many family meetings. If the daughter or daughter-in-law is working for pay, then something else has to be worked out. But, just having a job might not keep the others from trying to get the daughter or daughter-in-law to do the work all the same. Here's what Dr. Baruch says about the dilemma:

"You have to plan ahead about the caretaking of a parent. It's not wise to just wait until something happens. You have to work out something equitable with the whole family. The job shouldn't just fall on some housewife automatically. Of course, you have more bargaining power if you already have an important, paid job that requires your presence on a regular basis. But, still, some women are brought up in such a way that they might have a problem with this. They might think it's selfish and wrong for them to work if there's caretaking to be done. Some women feel that making others happy is their job, as opposed to making themselves happy. They don't realize that a daughter or daughter-in-law has the right to be happy the same as anyone else in the family."

You find some tough cases where a daughter or daughter-in-law has a real struggle with the feelings of guilt that sometimes go along with a parent's need for care. Mrs. Elaine Brody, at the Philadelphia Geriatric Center, recalls the case of a fragile, 85-year-old woman who will permit no one except her exhausted daughter to do her household tasks. The exhausted daughter (because of guilt feelings) cannot permit a professional service provider in the picture.

I know of another case where an eldest son encountered increasing problems with his mother and father. His mother was crippled with a bone disease, and his father, in his early eighties, couldn't cope with the situation. Unfortunately, this eldest son lived in one city, and his parents lived in another. His younger brother and sister also lived in other cities.

So, he packed up his parents and brought them to his city, where he (or rather his wife) went apartment hunting and found them a place to live. Because this man worked all day, five days a week, guess who had to take on most of the tasks of finding a housekeeper, nurse, and other helpers to make the elderly couple comfortable? His wife got the job by default. Eventually, the man's mother died, leaving his father, in his upper eighties, all alone. But, this time the man's wife put her foot down. She requested a family meeting to discuss the "sharing" of any future work. It wasn't easy to get others, except her husband, on weekends, to handle the constant problem-solving chores. She still didn't have a paid job so the others looked to her as the one "with the time." It must have been quite a family meeting, but things were worked out. She still has some caretaking chores, but not as many as before.

Family meetings are most important when it comes to the immediate or future care of an aging parent. Don't put off the meeting, even if you have to do it by phone on a conference call. The telephone company can arrange this for you and it's relatively inexpensive during the late evening hours or on weekends. It's not a good idea to wait until a crisis hits. You're under pressure then, and it's much more difficult to make rational, long-term decisions. Dr. David Gutmann, a psychologist with Northwestern University Hospital and an expert on the problems of aging, believes that regular investments in family meetings and family contingency planning before a crisis strikes, or before a current problem gets worse, will pay off in better care for the elderly parents and a lot less guilt for the children. Dr. Gutmann explains:

"The best way to handle these things is through the extended family. The load can be shared among the sons and daughters. The parent does not, necessarily, have to live in one of the sons' or daughters' homes. We don't recommend this much anymore. But, you can at least arrange to maintain strong family links, and this is something you ought to work on throughout your life. The modified, extended family can really function well in a situation where an aging parent needs help. But, you have to keep the family alive as a unit to make this work."

Of course, someone in the family has to provide leadership. Family discussions should air everyone's feelings, including the in-laws. And, don't forget the parents themselves. What are their feelings? What do they really want to have done if they become incapacitated? You just can't have some secret family meeting and plot what's going to happen to an older person's life without their being in on at least some of the discussions. How would you like to have your sons and daughters plotting your fate behind your back?

If the tradition of automatically giving the caretaking job to the first available daughter or daughter-in-law is to be broken, then a good series of democratic, one-voice, one-vote, family meetings are in order. But, a family meeting might tend to wander if those who attend are not up on their facts. What some families think might be "best for mom (or dad)," might not be. There are a lot more alternatives today when it comes to caring for an aged parent. To get the facts and to be better able to analyze the alternatives, more and more families are turning to professional counselors. How do you find a qualified counselor? Some resources are reviewed in the next chapter.

CHAPTER 34

COUNSELING
FOR THE
HARD CHOICES

When people have problems with rebellious teenagers, they often seek professional counseling. It's almost commonplace. But, when people have problems with an increasingly dependent parent, what do they do? They often fight with one another. They anguish, and they carry great bags of guilt around. It rarely occurs to families struggling with the care of aging parents to seek counseling. Somehow, because the problems involve adults, instead of teenagers, the need for counseling isn't recognized.

But, in many cases the same issues are there. It's a power struggle for freedom and independence. The teenager struggles to *gain* new independence from parental domination. The elderly parent struggles to *retain* independence, and resists increasing domination by well-intentioned sons and daughters. The same slogan is implied in both cases: "Independence requires responsibility."

If the teenager shows signs of abusing new freedoms, then the reins are pulled in. If the elderly parent shows signs of "forgetting" or "failing," then reins are pulled in (or, at least, an attempt is made to do so.) Often, the middle-aged son or daughter is caught in the middle of two power struggles—one with aging children, and the other with aging parents. It can drive you to distraction with both ends of the generation gap tugging for your attention.

So, you get counseling for the teenager problem. Or, in the case of a single person, you get counseling for other relationship problems (male-female loneliness, boss-career crisis). What about the growing anxiety over a parent's need for care?

One of the problems you would discover right away, if you were to look for counseling, is the fact that there seem to be very few, certified professionals around to handle this sensitive subject. We've got legions of child psychiatrists, child psychologists, education experts, and child and family services. But, where are the older-parent experts? As an officially trained group, they're practically nonexistent, which tells you something about our culture and its preoccupation with youth.

Yet, the counselors are there. They're often just hiding behind other names and titles. Until recently, the vast majority of medical schools and other special training establishments ignored the elderly as if they had some sort of social disease. Cynically speaking, this might have occurred because young people are supposed to have money, and old people are not. Whatever reason, the study of gerontology (problems of aging) was virtually ignored. Now it's becoming popular, even chic, to study aging and the elderly. So much so, you're getting the problem in reverse. You're getting the "instant expert."

Because the federal, state, and local governments, and other institutions are now throwing money at aging and the problems the elderly face, "experts" are popping up like mushrooms. This means your job of finding a qualified counselor for help with an aging parent will be complicated by the task of sorting out who is a true expert and who is a "mushroom."

THE SEARCH FOR
PROFESSIONAL HELP

When problems arise with a parent, or better yet, when you want to avoid future problems with a parent, here are some steps you can take to find professional counseling:

1. Try your doctor or your parent's doctor (with your parent's permission, of course). Chances are you will get kindness and consideration, but not competence. Some 999 out of 1,000 doctors have not had any formal training or even much experience in the handling of parental dependence due to physiological or psychological problems. Nevertheless, the parent's doctor remains an important person with potential powers of persuasion in the task of sorting out the conflicting demands of dependence and independence. Try to get the doctor to suggest people in the area who might provide the necessary family counseling, and by all means, try to enlist the doctor's cooperation and enthusiastic help. If you get indifference or foot-dragging, it might be time to find another doctor.

2. Medical schools are belatedly adding gerontology centers or departments to their organization charts. Call nearby universities and talk with public relations officers attached to the medical schools. Chances are, you'll find at least one or two people who are specializing in the problems of aging, and you might even find a whole bunch of people. If you can't get direct help, you can at least get some recommended names of professionals in your area who have a background in helping families sort out problems with parents.

3. Community mental health centers are realizing that one of the three most mentioned problems that citizens report is the problem of "what to do with mother (father, grandma, grandpa)?" The other two problems are "teenagers" and "loneliness." A mental health center might be able to recommend a trained person to help you and your parent or parents sort out the conflicts. But, mental health centers' capabilities vary greatly around the country.

4. Churches and synagogues have long recognized the need for counseling in the field of older-parent, older-child relationships. Some of the major religious groups have made assistance available to elderly constituents and their families. There are, for example, a good many Jewish Centers on Aging around the country. For the most part, they're excellent sources for information and assistance on counseling, even if you're not Jewish. You can also find excellent Protestant and Catholic expertise on the problems of aging.

5. Family and children's service agencies are trained in dealing with family problems, but not necessarily with the upper rungs of the generation ladder. The emphasis, until recently, has been on children and young adults. But, still these agencies are pros in the counseling business, and if they can't help you, they might know someone who can.

All right. You've gotten yourself a counselor. Remember, the counseling has to be for everybody, if at all possible. You, your brothers and sisters, and your parents. You're all in this. It's ideal to have everybody recognize the problems and be able to understand all the choices—pros and cons. But, this isn't always possible. Sometimes one brother, sister, or parent is stubborn or arrogant ("I certainly don't need any counseling"). Or, perhaps, a parent is frightened or angry, and won't listen to anybody. No matter. Somebody in the family group, preferably somebody with leadership capabilities, has to get solid counseling and be able, diplomatically, to convey factual information to the others. Otherwise, things can get out of hand.

A CASE IN POINT

Take the case of a woman in her late seventies who was terrorizing her family. She insisted on living with her oldest daughter. The older daughter had her own problems with her husband and a rebellious child. The mother moved in, and she wanted more care. She reached out and tried to drag her younger daughter into the emotional net. Through manipulation, the mother threatened to go to her younger daughter's home (where another husband and family problems were spinning on their own.) Everybody was supercharged with guilt, resentment, anger, love-hate—the works. Finally, somebody got to the husband of the younger daughter and talked him into seeking some sort of counseling, for his own sanity, if nothing else. Perhaps, with counseling, this fellow can put some sense into what has been, up to now, a chaotic family confrontation. Reasoning, instead of ranting, may save the day.

Dr. Eric Pfeiffer, professor of psychiatry and associate professor for programs at Duke University Center for the Study of Aging, has this to say about the need for counseling:

"One of the main goals is to assist the family members in determining when their own resources have reached the limit, or when the condition of the aging parent has become so serious that admission to some other kind of care setting is indicated. The optimal arrangement for the largest number of older persons and their families is to have the aging person living in his own home, or other place of residence in close proximity to siblings or adult children. Ideally, the distance should be within 30 minutes of each other to permit frequent visiting. When ill health intervenes, other arrangements might have to be made."

INTERPERSONAL RELATIONSHIPS DETERMINE GIVING

Of course, a lot depends on family relationships. Some are harmonious and friendly, others are strained to the breaking point. Sometimes money and time for caretaking are both needed. As a rule, sons tend to give aid in the form of money, while daughters tend to offer aid in the form of services. The type of giving depends a lot on the sons' and daughters' relationships with their spouses—the in-laws. If a son's wife is working, or otherwise not about to give much personal attention, then the son might end up giving more money. If a daughter's husband is against giving money, she might end up having to give more. But, giving *something* seems to be important to sons and daughters. It's all a part of their own growing, their own maturity. Philadelphia Geriatric Center's Elaine M. Brody, talks about the growing process:

"When filial maturity occurs, the parent is seen in a new light, as an individual, and this is the way in which adult children prepare for their own old age (as in childhood, they prepare for adulthood.) A trained counselor can help the middle-age family member accomplish the task of achieving filial maturity to the best of his or her ability. This is important, because it will inevitably determine how successfully the middle-aged person meets the challenge of growing old. And, this suggests that the way in which adult children resolve their own filial crisis also determines the way in which their own children will, in the future, meet *their* own filial crisis."

In other words, how you work out your own filial responsibility to your parents will, in large part, determine how your own children will treat you when you get old. Unfortunately, not all adult children can accept or meet the challenge of a parent's increased dependency. They just don't have the emotional resources. In this case, a counselor has to get the adult "child" to be able to do his or her best, even if it's just sending a little money, or making time for extra visits. Other members of the family have to realize that the person with limited capacity is trying to do his or her best. This must be accepted. There's no need for scorn because the person with emotional problems already has enough guilt. The thing to do is erase or diminish feelings of guilt wherever possible.

VARYING DEMANDS AND CAPACITIES

More often than not, the whole question of relating well to one's parent depends on how long the parent can maintain a relative degree of independence. Dr. Brody comments on the desire for self-sufficiency:

"The big question for the parent is: 'Can I survive independently without being a burden?' This speaks to the fear of losing control over one's own life, surrendering to the direction of others, and no longer having the sense of mastery that is so essential to the integrity of the human personality. Both the old person, who has extreme difficulty being dependent, and the one who is overly dependent may hamper the adult child's efforts to become filially mature. If the adult child must acquire the capacity to be depended on, the elderly parent must have the capacity to be appropriately dependent and thus to permit such growth.

"The physical care of an extremely impaired old person requires strength, stamina, and nursing, in quite different and more difficult ways than the care of a young child. This may put too great a demand on the adult child's capabilities. So, when the very old person is extremely impaired, and the capacity of the aging child to give care is not equal to the task, the role of the care-giver is not a natural developmental stage of life for this adult child. This is why counseling is so often necessary. Focusing on the very old individual's needs, to the exclusion of the care-giver's needs, disregards reality and places yet an added burden of guilt and stress on the individual in the family who supposedly 'fails.' You may have to accept the fact that you (or some family member) simply can't handle it and find another solution. Counselors need to focus on the capacities, needs, and problems of the entire family—not just the aged person."

It seems that we all have different capacities for handling the needs of an aging parent. The aging parent also has varying degrees of dependency. When possible it sometimes may be best to just support parents with phone calls, visits, and *caring*. It's a myth that older people long to be taken into their children's homes. A parent may want to live *near* you, but not *with* you. In some cases it's best to leave well enough alone and let the older person cope without a lot of outside interference, or "doing what we think is best for you." Sometimes older people do very well on their own, better than you think, and persuading them to give up their autonomy can make them depressed. You can literally kill an older person with kindness.

What most aged parents want from their adult children is not so much money, or caretaking services, but concern, affection, caring, continuing communication and contacts, and the knowledge that their children can be depended on.

Being able to be independent as long as possible is a goal that most older parents want, and most of their children want. But, all too often, continuing independence costs money. The more funds the aging parent has to deal with contingencies, the more he or she can call the shots, and the less the family has to play the role of hovering caretaker. Some older parents continue to earn their own money to supplement pension and Social Security funds. Some people have funds stashed away to buy their way out of having to go to a nursing home. They, or members of their family, can afford to have care brought in, step by step, when it's needed. In my own father's case, he had the financial backup to buy his way out of a final stay in a nursing home. What was needed in his case was an effort on the family's part to find the necessary in-home care services to make him comfortable and to allow the household to function.

THE CHOICES

Very often, you are faced with a single, older parent living alone after the death of a marriage partner or a divorce. You worry: "Can mom (or dad) handle it alone?" Your worries have foundation in the fact that some older people tend to go downhill after being left alone. So, the first question on your checklist is the possibility of remarriage. Two can often live better and more cheaply than one. The partners can support each other, and the family can relax. This is why you should encourage and support a move by your mother or father to remarry. Sometimes this might bother you, especially if you're worried about the "outsider" not being good enough (which might be part of your own mother or father image hangup). Or, more often, it might be that you don't want part of your inheritance transferred to someone else.

Without realizing it, you might start to utter some put-downs such as "act your age," or make jokes about "dating" games. Don't do it. Bite your lip and shut up. If your parent asks about your feelings, or asks for advice, try to be objective. You should be aware of the fact that your mother or father may be ready, willing, and able to enjoy sex with another person—an "outsider." Talk to your parent openly about your inheritance fears and your desire for some remembrance that the deceased parent left. Counseling can be helpful with this delicate situation.

If remarriage is not in the picture, the next choice is helping to keep your parent in his or her own home for as long as possible. The home may not be the place where your mother or father lived while raising a family. It might be some newer place, that's smaller, and easier to manage. But, this newer place is, in effect, "home" and is often extremely important to an older person's psychological integrity and physical well-being. A home with lots of friends and loving neighbors can be a lifesaver.

The next possible step is when your parent begins to have physical or mental difficulties handling the management of his or her home. The difficulties may be real—or imagined. You should sort this out right away with a counselor. Sometimes you might worry because your mother or father has "memory problems." You wonder whether the parent will remember to turn off the gas, lock the door, buy enough food, or whatever. Certain types of short-term memory loss are normal in aging.

You may have noticed it with your own memory. You can't instantly recall certain names or places which are familiar, but aren't used daily. This affliction continues, but usually doesn't get much worse. However, when it happens to your parent, you might become upset, wondering whether the brain is functioning well enough to cope. Remember, if a younger person forgets a name or forgets an appointment, you shrug. It happens. But, when an older person does it, you think: "Uh-huh—loss of memory." If you or your parent becomes preoccupied with worry about possible memory loss, a medically-trained counselor who understands the aging process can make an evaluation and explain the functional limitations, if there are any.

If professional evaluation does, in fact, reveal that your parent is mentally or physically unable to handle housekeeping chores and normal living tasks independently, the next step for investigation is in-home care. A counselor may recommend hiring a housekeeper or home health aide to come by on a regular basis. You may pay more frequent visits, and your parent might be encouraged to pay more frequent visits to various members of the family.

You might want to experiment with such in-home services as Homemakers, Inc. or the Visiting Nurse Association. Also, most communities have "meals on wheels" programs, where meals are brought in, if necessary. Better yet, it's a good idea to get your parent out of the home during the day, at least for awhile. You can investigate the possibility of senior centers in the area (many of which serve tasty, home-cooked lunches, with occasional dinners and breakfasts thrown in.) If you need more structure, you can investigate the possibility of "day care" centers where an older person can go for the day and get a meal, plus scheduled activities, socializing, entertainment, and round trip transportation. This type of service is often vital for people whose parent must live with them. A counselor may know of a convenient day care center (often run with county or city government support, or support from a religious organiza-tion). The centers cost money, but never as much as full institutional care. And, they give the older person some independence, some autonomy, some decision making of their own. The older clients still go home to their own beds, their own dining tables, and their own familiar surroundings. Says Dr. Isadore Rossman, Medical Director of Home Care and Extended Care Services Department of Montefiore Hospital in New York: "We have seen patients in the hospital and nursing home with remediable disorders who have not fared well... But, when they were transferred to the home environment and received the resources of a home care program, they showed striking improvements." Dr. Rossman, whose views have been published in a booklet for physicians by McNeil Laboratories, explains that "there are people who are depressed, even crushed, when they're out of their home environment... Usually, the home is a familiar place where these people tend to function better."

It's important to keep an older person stimulated with outside contacts when they are receiving in-home care. If at all possible, having a pet to care for can provide stimulation and companionship. Cats are easy to care for. A properly selected and trained dog can do wonders for an older person's morale. So can some kind of job, or daily activity. Gardening is great therapy for all of us, but it's especially good for an older person. Flowers, plants, and vegetables need constant care and devotion. And, sometimes home-grown vegetables can be sold or given as gifts, to reaffirm continuing worth and productivity on the older person's part. County and city agricultural extension services, or even a good plant store, can provide booklets and guidelines for types of plants and soil that work best in certain kinds of environments.

In Montefiore Hospital's extended care service program, shut-ins are often coaxed into doing some meaningful work such as assembling and packing small items for manufacturers. When their work is paid for, Dr. Rossman says, "it acts like a potent anti-depressant... When one elderly gentleman got his first paycheck on our program, he leaped into the air, clicked his heels together and, waving the check, exclaimed: 'There's life in the old boy yet.'"

In some communities, older people have been selected to live in what pass as "communes." The Jewish Council on Aging of Greater Washington (D.C.), for example, has leased large, three-bedroom apartments in a suburban building. Selected elderly clients live in the apartments—three to a unit. Their bedrooms contain all their own personal furniture and belongings. The common rooms, such as the living, dining, and kitchen areas, have shared furniture. The residents help each other and get daily help from a professional homemaker who cooks lunch and dinner and does some help with chores. A housekeeper comes in to do the heavy cleaning, and the residents get mini-bus transportation for shopping, visits to a senior center and other outings. Commune residents are not locked into a geriatric ghetto. Their building houses many other adults of all ages, and many children. There's plenty of communication between old and young.

In a few cases, you can find an elderly person who wants to keep the old family home going, but finds it increasingly difficult to cope. One woman in her eighties faced the difficult choice of leaving her beloved home of many years for a nursing home, or some other institution. She needed daily care. Her son worked out a deal whereby graduate students from a nearby university—two secretaries and a young married couple—could move into furnished rooms for free. In return, the roomers helped look after the woman, buy the food, cook it, and clean up. All shared in the food and utility costs, but the net cost of living with the old woman was so low the residents felt themselves lucky.

Naturally, any residents for a joint living project must be carefully screened. There have to be escape clauses. Many older residents can't stand sharing their privacy with others.

Sometimes it works, sometimes it doesn't. A project usually has a better chance of working if there is some structure and administration provided by a church, synagogue, or some other organization.

There are also apartments and villages where an older person can buy "continuing care." Usually these are run by a religious or fraternal organization, and they cost quite a bit of money. You trade most, if not all, of your savings for a sheltered home with food, cleaning, some medical services, and some transportation thrown in. There are often waiting lists for these institutions. If there is an opening and a contract is offered, don't sign anything without having a lawyer look it over carefully. Don't leave any questions left unanswered. (How much do you pay? How will monthly fee increases be handled? What do you get, for how long, and under what circumstances?)

Finally, there's the nursing home. If you have tried all the alternatives, with help from a professional counselor, and a nursing home is indicated, then it's probably the best solution. Yet some feel enormously guilty because they have had to put a parent in an institution.

One way to short-circuit possible bad feelings is to find a home where the parent can become a part-time resident. Maybe the parent can live with a son or daughter for a week at a time, or on frequent "vacations." Or, perhaps, the older person can spend several days a month with various members of the family. If a more permanent home is required, then the older person should be able to have a place where furniture and other memorabilia can be taken. The more the place can function as a little apartment inside an institution—with as much privacy as possible—the better off the resident will be, and the less guilt the family will have to carry. Working with the aged patient on selecting the best place is essential. See as many places as possible before making a choice. Then, everybody will know: "We did our best."

By all means, once a nursing home has been selected, don't just drop communication. The elderly person should enjoy as much two-way visiting as possible. The family should visit, call, send gifts, and write a lot. Whenever possible, the older resident should be able to get out for lunches, dinners, overnight or weekend visits, outside entertainment, and personal care (hairdresser, barber shop and shopping). This isn't always possible, but the closer you can get to maintaining full communication, the better the parent will feel about life, and the better you'll feel about yourself.

GOOD READING

Why Survive? Being Old in America, written by Dr. Robert N. Butler (Harper & Row). This book, awarded a Pulitzer Prize in 1976, gives a comprehensive account of what is being done and what can be done for the elderly.

Tender Loving Greed, written by Mary Adelaide Mendelson (Alfred A. Knopf), talks about the lucrative nursing home "industry" and what to watch out for.

Re-Engagement In Later Life: Re-Employment and Remarriage, written by Ruth Harriet Jacobs and Barbara H. Vinick, published by Greylock Publishers, Stamford, Connecticut. Stimulating case studies.

CHAPTER 35

LOCATING
RESOURCES

When you're dealing with the problems of an aging parent, you need counseling, and you need to know what resources are available. In some cities, there are any number of agencies and organizations that can be of help. In other areas, the resources are scarce.

The first thing you should do is to get in touch with the area agency on aging in the city or county where your parent lives. These agencies can go under a wide variety of names and it's not always easy to find them. The agencies are usually sponsored by local governments, and they act as clearinghouses for information and resources to help elderly citizens. If the older person is having trouble with Social Security, or other government benefits, someone at the agency can help straighten it out (or find someone who can). If the home of an older person with a modest income needs repairs or insulation, the agency might be able to find someone to do the job for a small fee through a program for retired carpenters. If an older person is lonely and wants to get in on a low-cost social dining program at a senior center, the agency can find out if a local program is available. You name it, and they can find it, or find someone who can point you in the right direction.

If you can't locate the area agency on aging (by whatever name) through the local government information operator, then you can write or call: National Association of Area Agencies on Aging, 1828 L Street, N.W., Washington, D.C. 20036. Phone: (202)-223-5010. You'll get the name and address of the agency nearest your parent's home, and the name and phone number of its director. Once you get in touch with the agency, your mother or father can go in for an interview to find out what services are available. If necessary, someone might be able to visit your parent's home to evaluate the situation. It can be determined if your parent qualifies for such benefits as special housing, Medicaid or free legal services.

If it's at all convenient, you might want to get in touch with the agency and make an appointment for a personal interview. Take a pad and pencil and get all the information available. You can also get names of professional counselors, or others who can help you with specific problems.

The next thing you want to do is to look in the Yellow Pages of your local telephone directory under the heading "Social Service Organizations" or "Social Services." You'll find the names, addresses, and phone numbers for local religious, social service organizations (which can be of enormous help), family services, senior centers, mental health organizations, and others.

The local Visiting Nurse Association office (if there is one in the community) could be another good resource. VNA people often know what doctors work with older persons, and they can put you in touch with other organizations that bring care facilities into the home, such as Homemakers, Inc., and Meals on Wheels.

Then there are the national organizations and agencies which can provide answers to questions and supply background information.

CHECKLIST OF SOURCES

Administration on Aging is a part of the U.S. Department of Health, Education and Welfare (HEW) (after mid-1980 known as Department of Health and Human Services), 330 Independence Avenue, S.W., Washington, D.C. 20201. This government agency has a list of publications and booklets on almost every aspect of aging and the elderly. You can find out what special government programs are available in your parent's area.

National Institute on Aging is part of the National Institutes of Health, 9000 Rockville Pike, Bethesda, MD 20014. The institute does research on aging and supports programs dealing with elderly people. You can get the publications list for more information on specific subjects. By working through the public affairs office, you might be able to get names and addresses of universities and other organizations that have gerontology expertise in your area. There's no guarantee that they'll come up with anything, but it might be worth a call.

Veteran's Administration, 810 Vermont Avenue, N.W., Washington, D.C. 20420. If your father is a veteran, or your mother is the widow of a veteran, some benefits might be available. After age 65, more benefits are open to veterans (medical care, possible pension or shut-in stipend, burial lot, and money for funeral expenses). Ask for the booklet: Federal Benefits for Veterans (there may be a small charge).

American Association of Retired Persons, 1909 K Street, N.W., Washington, D.C. 20049. This is the largest membership organization for older people. For a modest membership fee, you get the association's magazine and a newspaper that outlines new programs for the elderly. You can also get the name of the nearest AARP chapter, plus special membership benefits (low-cost mail-order pharmaceuticals, low-cost auto club, and hotel-motel discounts).

National Council of Senior Citizens, 1511 K Street, N.W., Washington, D.C. 20005. It's similar to the AARP, but has different benefits and different publications. It's not a bad idea to join both organizations, because membership dues are just a few dollars. The council has many more local membership chapters than the AARP.

National Association of Retired Federal Employees, 1533 New Hampshire Avenue, N.W., Washington, D.C. 20036. If the older person is a retired federal worker or is the widow of one, he or she might want to join this organization. It keeps its members in touch with changes in federal benefits, and can help with referral services.

National Council on the Aging, 1828 L Street, N.W., Washington, D.C. 20036 (Suite 504). You can write for the NCOA's long list of books, booklets, and newsletters.

National Senior Citizens Law Center, 1709 W. 8 Street, Los Angles, CA 90017. You can get publications on what to look for in Medicare supplement insurance, ins and outs of housing, and the legal rights of the elderly. Good place to call if you have a question involving an older person's rights.

Gray Panthers, 3700 Chestnut Street, Philadelphia, PA 19104. Run by activist Maggie Kuhn, the "Panthers" are involved in all sorts of projects, programs, and causes, including better deals for nursing homes residents, and better housing. Chapters around the country help members with problems such as landlord hassles. Ask for a publications list.

American Association of Homes for the Aging, 1050 17th Street, Suite 770, N.W., Washington, D.C. 20036. This association publishes an excellent booklet, *Continuing Care Homes—A Guidebook for Consumers*. It shows how you and your lawyer (or your parent's lawyer) can, and should, investigate a contract before buying into a "continuing care" home. You can also get the names of nonprofit nursing homes, state by state. Nonprofit homes often provide better care at a better price than for-profit homes—but not always.

As you can see, there are quite a number of resources for the elderly in this country, but some other countries do a lot better. In Sweden, for example, pensioners who remain in their homes are entitled to noninterest loans or nonrepayable loans (grants) for repairs and improvements. The elderly are also able to get low-cost or free care in their homes. The corps of people who take care of the elderly in their homes are called "samaritans." Elderly residents can get help with meals, therapy, cleaning, shopping, cooking, laundering, and transportation. The Swedish government says its goal is to help older citizens live in their homes as long as possible.

In Great Britain, the elderly are also encouraged to stick with their homes. Nursing care, meals, household chores, baths, and errands are all part of an in-home program. Some health districts even pay the older person's friends and relatives to provide assistance. The government has found that this often costs less than providing the older person with institutional care. If institutional care is absolutely necessary, then an older citizen can get day care or nursing home care virtually free of charge.

THE FULL CIRCLE

But, in this country, as elsewhere, the main support of the elderly often comes from their children. And, at some future date, the main support for your care (if needed) might come from your children, or a close relative (if you're single.) An older person's children often can be the key to a successful old age or a bitter one. A single person's nieces and nephews can also be a source of aid and comfort in old age.

Start bringing your children in on your efforts to help grandpa or grandma. Grandchildren should be encouraged to give attention and care to the elderly. This way, your children will be exposed to the problems of aging and will be better prepared to deal with you, when and if the need arises.

People who are in their forties and fifties now should have a wealth of children to help them in old age. For the most part, they are the parents of the famous post World War II "baby boom." But, these children may have fewer children of their own, or even no children. One wonders: Who will be around to take care of them when they grow old?

Meanwhile, treat your own parent with care and tenderness, and let your children know what you're doing. While you have their attention, ask what they think about the possible need for your own care some day. If you start the dialogue now, feelings on both sides can be aired, and you may have a smoother, better-working relationship. You have to work out how you want to live, and where the help might come from if it's needed.

CHAPTER 36

TALKING TAXES

Supporting a mother or a father, or both, can drain finances and strain any relationship. In some cases, a lot of this drain and strain can be removed if a clever tax specialist designs a support plan that will provide adequate deductions and exemptions. Basically, you have to be paying more than 50 percent of the support in order to claim a parent as dependent and get a $1,000 a year exemption ($2,000 if both parents are living). And, if you're single, you might even be able to get a special "head of household" tax break.

If there are several brothers and sisters involved, a multiple-support agreement can be arranged. This permits each brother or sister to take a support deduction in rotation without personally having to pay at least 50 percent support.

A parent might have considerable money—enough to pay most of his or her own support—and you might still get the tax break. You have to pay more than half of the specified support items (rent, mortgage, food, clothing, utilities, medical costs).

Parents can pay slightly under one-half of their own support, and you get the tax break. Parents can also pay the total tab for their travel and entertainment costs, which are not counted in support claims.

If your parent doesn't have much money, you might want to alternate paying the support. You pay more than half the support bills one year, and the following year the parent pays. During the year you pay, the parent can invest Social Security checks in savings. The following year, the parent can use the savings to pay his or her own support. You get a tax break every other year. Also, if you pay at least half of the support and get the tax break, your parent is allowed to give you—free from federal taxes—up to $3,000 a year, which can be used to defray the support costs.

By paying your parent's unreimbursable medical bills, you might also be able to build up your overall family medical costs to the point where they could qualify for a tax deduction. Your overall medical costs must total at least 3 percent of your adjusted gross income in order to get the deduction, and your parent's medical bills can help reach the necessary minimum.

With advice from a tax specialist, a whole series of tax breaks might be worked out by having a parent sell his or her home to you, or to someone else in the family. Perhaps, by this time, your own home has most of the mortgage paid, and you're not getting any appreciable tax deduction from interest payments (which dwindle to almost nothing after the first 10 to 15 years.)

By refinancing your parent's home, you, as the new owner, could get a sizeable tax deduction on the interest payments and local real estate taxes. If you charge your parent a fair rent, you could get even bigger tax savings through a landlord's depreciation allowance, plus deductions for operating expenses.

Remember, you and your parents can give each other tax-free "gifts" of as much as $3,000 a year per person, per donor. This means that you can give each parent $3,000, or your mother and father can combine to give you $6,000. Parents can also give your spouse and your children $3,000 each ($6,000 if both parents are living). By keeping within these limits, you and your parents can work out an arrangement to shunt money back and forth, as needed.

By owning your parent's home, you get a valuable property and a series of tax breaks. You pay the major bills. By paying the mortgage and other home operating costs, which you'd have to pay anyway, you could, conceivably, claim your parent as a dependent for the $1,000-a-year dependent's exemption. If your parent pays you rent, you can reimburse half of it, or, in some cases, all of it as part of your support payment.

A key factor is the definition of "support." It's not based on how much income your mother or father receives in Social Security checks. A parent could be getting, say, $6,000 a year from Social Security and be paying $4,000 a year into basic living costs. You could pay $2,000 of the living (support) costs and claim your parent as a dependent. Your parent could bank the rest of the money. If your parent receives other income from a job, dividends, or interest, that adds up to more than $1,000 a year, then you can't claim a dependency exemption. There's no limit on how much the parent receives from Social Security or other nontaxable income.

PURCHASING YOUR PARENT'S HOME

If your parent owns a home, you may not be able to get a $1,000 yearly exemption for support payments, because his or her income outside of Social Security might be too high. But, by purchasing your parent's home, you'd get a lot of tax breaks.

Let's look at this sample case. Say your mother owns a house which has a current market value of $100,000. Years ago, your father and mother bought the home for $30,000 (in today's market, this is entirely possible.) The mortgage has been paid up to the point where only $15,000 is owed. Your mother is getting little or no tax advantage from home ownership because she is in a relatively low income bracket and there is no more interest being paid on the loan (just principal.)

There's a lot of money locked up in this house which your mother could use. You are in a fairly high income tax bracket now and could use some tax breaks. You and your mother talk to a tax specialist and come up with a plan to have her sell you the home for $100,000. You get a loan for $75,000, and you have to come up with $25,000 for the down payment. Your mother gets $75,000 from the lender and pays off the $15,000 on the old mortgage, leaving $60,000 in cash. She won't have to pay any federal income tax on the profit she made on her home because the amount is under the $100,000 tax-free exemption people get when they sell their homes after age 55.

Because you might have trouble raising the $25,000 necessary for the down payment, your mother could lend you part or all of the money from the $60,000 she has left from the home sale. You can either pay this loan off over the years, or your mother can reduce the amount with $6,000 annual, tax-free gifts to you and your spouse.

Using the loan-gift combination, your mother would eventually be left with $35,000 (providing she made enough gifts to liquidate her loan to you). Your mother will have large monthly rent payments, but money for these can come from the $35,000 she has left. You might even be able to afford giving your mother "gifts" to help pay the rent and other expenses after you've paid more than half her support, because you'll be saving a lot of money in taxes. Let's add up what you might be able to save:

1. Depreciation allowance for the home as a rental property. This will be worth thousands of dollars a year at first but will diminish by a certain amount each year. After 10 to 15 years, there will be few depreciation deductions left. You can either sell the home to another member of the family, or keep it and figure that in a few years you might be in a lower tax bracket because of retirement, or by working part-time. Or, your mother might die, and you could sell the home and use the profits you make to buy another rental property, or whatever.

2. You get deductions for interest paid on the mortgage and for all operating expenses (taxes, utilities, insurance, repairs, and maintenance.)

3. When you sell the home, you will only be taxed on 40 percent of the net profit (capital gains). It's a much lighter tax than you'd have to pay on investment dividends or savings interest.

Speaking in behalf of your mother, it's important that a lawyer draw up a lease allowing her to stay in the home for as long as she wants. This is important because your death or divorce might bring a new person into the picture, and this new person might want to force her out of the home. Your mother, or whatever parent, should have a lawyer, and you might want one too for advice on how the home is to be listed as far as ownership is concerned. Do you want the home in your name only, or do you want the home in both you and your spouse's name? You might even want it in your children's names. A good attorney should be able to explain the consequences of any decision you make.

In some cases, where several brothers and sisters are

involved, a small corporation or partnership can be set up to handle the purchase of a parent's home. This way, everybody can share in the ownership and the tax advantages (and share the initial investment costs). It's a fairly tricky business and needs the guidance of a lawyer.

You don't need a lawyer to help with your initial tax-planning research. You can go to a good tax accountant who will probably cost less in consulting fees. You and your parent can present all the necessary financial papers (recent tax returns, outstanding loans, property appraisal), and a plan might be worked out to benefit both sides. Why wait until your parent dies? You can get the tax breaks now, when you need them most, and your parent can get the use of some of the money that has been locked in the home's long-term capital gain.

These family home-sale deals are not for everybody. Some older people just don't want to sell or give away their property to anybody. Outright home ownership, for them, represents a psychological bastion of independence. If you can't put a parent's fears at ease with a solid lease agreement which guarantees lifetime residency, then let the subject drop. Everyone has their rights. But, the idea should at least be investigated by you and your parent. It could unlock some money and bring some smiles.

Part V
Final
Plans

CHAPTER 37

WHAT IF?

In a book which deals with contingency planning for one's later years, it would be foolhardy not to touch on the subject of death. Without becoming morbid, there are some very practical things you can do now to prepare for the ultimate contingency—the emotional and financial consequences of death.

THE IMPORTANCE
OF A WILL

One way to prepare your mind for the eventuality of death is to play "what-if" games with your spouse or close companions. One of the least threatening opening moves in this game is to discuss the need for a will, a trust, and other legal documents to cover the distribution of your estate in case you should die. Even people who do not want to talk about their mortality can be coaxed into having a will drawn up. It makes sense. There are hard and fast financial and tax-reasons for making a will. You may already have a will, but it could be out of date.

Dying intestate (without a will) is unwise. When you die without a will, the state takes over and decides where your money and property should go. The state has already taken over too many of your decisions, so don't let this big one fall by the wayside.

More often than not, it's the wife who nags her husband about getting a will. Of course, there are exceptions. Some men take great satisfaction in having their final finances all neat and tidy, but the average husband tends to put off writing a will. Sociologist Robert Weiss, author of *The First Year of Bereavement*, explains what's going on in some men's minds:

"You've got to have a will, but a lot of men don't like to make wills. Why should they? It's not going to do them any good. Why plan for your own death? You've got enough things on your mind. But, if you're a wife, you say to your husband: 'Here's a will. Please sign it.' If the wife doesn't initiate the action, get it organized, it may be impossible for the husband to do it. You can work it out together, but it's the wife's initiative that's going to get the job done. If she leaves it up to him, chances are he won't do it. It's not that he's mean or doesn't love her. He's just got other things to do, other things on his mind. The wife has to use diplomacy, take the initiative, talk with a lawyer, make an appointment for an interview and make it easy for her husband."

The same ritual might apply to a couple that has a will which is out-of-date. Lots of things have happened since the will was drawn up. Children may have left the nest to work or get married. Grandchildren may be on the scene. Or you may have moved to another state that has different inheritance and probate laws.

TRUST FUNDS

When you have a will updated, or make a will for the first time, ask the lawyer to explain the various kinds of trusts you can set up for a spouse, children, or anyone else. In a "revocable living trust," for example, you arrange for much of your estate to bypass probate with all the waste of time and money it entails. With this type of trust, not all assets in your will go through probate, and it can save money, time, and aggravation for the heirs. It's not for everybody, but it's certainly worth investigating.

Also worth investigating is a marital trust for a wife or husband. If you have a fairly large estate, it can save money on inheritance taxes. Trusts for children are worth exploring because you can set up money or property for them without their having control until a certain age, or a series of ages (X-thousand at age 25, Y-thousand at age 30, and Z-thousand at age 35.) The kind of lawyer you want for all this is one who has had experience in estate planning work. Your local bar association, university law school, or friends and colleagues can recommend names.

Okay. You've taken the first step; you've drawn up a will. During the interview with the lawyer, hard questions came up. You had to decide who was going to get what, and how much. You had to prepare for the eventuality of your death. You were told that both husbands *and* wives should have wills. So should single people, especially those over 50 who might have accumulated considerable property.

THE EMOTIONAL SIDE

Now that the paperwork is over, do you drop the subject? Not really. The next step, after tidying up the financial side, is an investigation of the emotional side. This is a much more sensitive issue and must be handled with care. As in the case of the will, a wife usually (but not always) brings up the subject. Hopefully, she brings it up when everybody is healthy and not feeling threatened.

The person who brings up the subject usually asks: "What if I were to die this year? What would you do?" Sometimes the subject has to be postponed, because the other partner isn't ready and indicates this with a phrase such as: "Don't be silly, you're as healthy as a horse." But, after awhile, the subject comes up again, and this time the initiating partner goes a step further: "If for some reason I were to die this year, I'd want you to have my antique chair (car, boat, ring, whatever)... and [here's the message] I'd like you to seriously think about the possibility of marrying someone who could look after you."

It's out. It's the beginning of a dialogue about continuing life after a partner's death, and the importance of not going it alone. This is a hard subject for most people to tackle, but I can't overemphasize the importance of broaching these two major subjects:

1. emotional security
2. financial security

It may be safer to start with financial security. Each partner should know what expenses might come up if the other dies, and where the money to pay for them will come from. If a wife can't get an answer to the money question, she had better start providing the answer by earning her own money. If a husband feels he might be strapped without his wife's job income, he'd better get an insurance policy on her life. Each partner should have a good, working knowledge of the family investments, debts, insurance, and home operating expenses. Each partner should also know where the will is located (the lawyer's office is the best place), the name of a good accountant, who can advise on investments (careful here, you need an objective source— not some hungry insurance, or mutual fund salesman). The whereabouts of all important papers and financial information also should be known to both partners.

As for emotional security, the what-if dialogue can be quite revealing. It's very difficult for some couples to cope with this, but genuine love and persistence can bring it out. The big question is the possibility of remarriage. One of the greatest gifts one partner can give to the other is encouragement to remarry, in case he or she is left alone. It's understood that the surviving partner would grieve and feel a lot of pain, but life must go on. The surviving partner should be encouraged to marry again. The whole idea is to drain the reservoirs of guilt. Dr. Weiss cites a case history to explain the point:

"Of great importance to a widow, Mrs. G., was her feeling that she had her husband's 'permission,' even encouragement, to remarry. It's doubtful that so soon after his death she would have been able to go against his wishes in relation to remarriage if she had felt he would have opposed."

In his book on bereavement, Dr. Weiss says that the widows who realized their husband were going to die and had time to contemplate the fact and prepare somewhat for their life afterward, were the ones who were more apt to remarry and rebuild. He says that "there was a positive correlation between longer advance warning and eventual satisfactory adjustment to widowhood... Advance warning seemed to facilitate recovery by making the loss more nearly understandable, and so a bit easier to come to terms with."

BEREAVEMENT AND CHANGE

While you can talk about contingency plans to cover the possibility of a partner's death, you can't really prepare for the intensity of pain that the final loss brings. You can speculate, but nobody knows what it will be like, deep, down inside, until it happens. You can file away information that will be helpful in sorting out the confusion and chaos that follows the death of a partner. But, you simply cannot plan for everything, and you shouldn't try. As Dr. Weiss says, after a partner's death, "you're not the same person you were before."

You might find that this new person will want to stay put and not move out of the home. Or, the new person will want to move away from the memories and start a life in a new home. This is why you can't make any hard and fast plans about selling, or staying on in your current home. When a partner dies, it's best to stay where you are for at least six months (perhaps longer for some widows) to give your feelings a chance to get sorted out.

The main thing to do while you're both still in good health is to give "permission" to your spouse to do whatever he or she thinks necessary to regroup and start a new life. This covers remarriage, selling the home, moving, getting a new job—whatever. But, you can agree that some things will remain constant. Children or grandchildren will be taken care of, and the remaining partner will meet with all of them from time to time to recall the past. This shows each partner that the memories will never completely fade. There will always be something of the old marriage remaining in a surviving partner's mind.

SORTING OUT FEELINGS

When you talk about these things, you'll find that a lot of hidden or repressed feelings can come out. At first, it might be painful. After doing research on the subject, I approached my wife, Vida, with the big question: What if? Since, statistically, men are supposed to die first, and since I brought up the subject, I asked what she would do if I were to die this year or next?

At first, there were a few tears as she talked about our life together and how much our home meant to her. She would hate to give up the place, she said, but wondered if she could cope by herself. She was torn between keeping the house and moving south to live with friends she'd known since childhood. Nothing was resolved, but the sorting out process had started. We let the subject drop.

Then, one evening it came up again. This time the talk was about money and where it would come from if I died first. We talked about the money she would get it she sold the house, and how much income she could expect from insurance and investments. And, for the first time in a long time, she talked about moving from volunteer work into a paid job.

After talking about the financial consequences of my dying first, the conversation moved into the sensitive subject of remarriage. I told her that she should remarry if she wanted to and she had my complete blessing. She wasn't sure that she would want to marry again. I told her that she was a wonderful companion and that it would be a great coup for some man to marry her.

She turned the thing around and said that I should remarry if she were to die first, and that I had her blessing too. I joked about never remarrying—just playing the role of the available bachelor. She didn't think it was funny and scolded me, saying it would be a great mistake for a man who had been happily married for so many years not to remarry. She said I was not designed to live alone and needed a permanent companion. I agreed, and we relaxed with a feeling that something had been accomplished.

If you can sort out feelings like this, it could do a lot for the surviving partner one day. The less guilt a person has to carry around, the better. And, even more important, by discussing these contingencies and related feelings now, you should feel a sense of relief and be able to live an even fuller life. With fears out in the open, the thought of your partner's death—or even your own—becomes less formidable.

You might want to do the same sort of thing with your children, or with other members of your family. Ask the children to think about it. How would they feel about their mother or father marrying again? What would they want as a remembrance? Listen to their thoughts and feelings. Explain that each parent really wants the other to marry again if there's an opportunity. The children are part of the family and they should have a say in where and how a parent is buried and memorialized. They don't have the final say, but they have a say.

CONTINGENCY PLANS

If you can get your feelings out in the open on the subject of death, you might be able to explore other related contingencies such as a long-term illness or disability. Each partner should know that most psychiatrists and psychologists stress the importance of the "caretaker" partner's need for a certain amount of independence and "getting out" on a regular basis. It's to be understood that getting out periodically to clear the mind is important for the caring partner's mental health, and in no way means a lack of love or concern. Someone who is tied to the bedside of an ailing partner can become frustrated, angry, and ridden with guilt feelings.

To avoid the problems of being overly tied to the dependent partner, the caretaker should investigate the possibility of bringing in the help of a professional home health aide or homemaker service. Therapists and nursing help can also be brought in. Some health insurance plans will pay for in-home help, some won't. (For more information on couseling and other resources aimed at helping care for a dependent adult, check source lists at the ends of chapters 37 and 38; "Counseling for the Hard Choices," and "Locating Resources."

While you are in the process of making contingency plans, don't overlook the planning of making funeral and memorial services. Put your plans on paper, and be sure your family, your lawyer, and others know where they are. Know exactly what each partner wants done, where, and more or less how much it will cost (more on this in Chapter 42, "Giving Survivors a Break"). This way, you can escape the sales pressure some funeral establishments bring to bear when there's a death in the family. The same goes for your will and the probate process. Try to get your lawyer to have everything mapped out ahead of time. What will happen? How long will it take? How much will everything cost? How much money will be left? If you can't get hard answers to these questions, get another lawyer.

One widow said she had to go through a year of hell after her husband's death. First, she was hassled by the funeral business (her husband had wanted a simple, dignified, but inexpensive service), and later by the legal business (because the lawyer dragged his feet and kept adding one charge after another).

Finally, a word for single people. You might want to consider making some sort of pact with very close friends. Activist Tish Sommers is involved in forming a mutual care pact and she is willing to share her thoughts:

"I'm working with a group of women, sort of a sisterhood, whereby we will get together to form a collective nursing home for those who might need it. It's called OWLS—The Last

Perch (OWLS stands for Older Women's League). We plan to develop a communal place where we can go before we're pushed. It will accommodate eight to twelve persons—a highly selective group of women who are activists. It would be our last place. We would buy or bring in all the services needed, but all the decisions would be in our own hands.

"Other women might begin to think about setting up their own, collective living organization. Design a place for yourself. If you think about it in advance and work on it, it might be possible. Planning the right kind of ending for yourself is a personal thing. This is really packing your bags."

Everyone should pay attention to "packing their own bags" and, wherever possible, share it with a marriage partner or very close friends. As gerontologist Alex Comfort says: "It's not ghoulish or bad luck . . . It's loving, because each partner is considering the preservation of the other."

GOOD READING

Now Is The Time—To Prepare a Guide For your Survivor. This guidebook is written by Rear Admiral Benjamin Katz (Ret.) and published by: The Overlook Company, 910 N. Overlook Drive, Alexandria, VA 22305. You get information on wills, probate, taxes, location of important papers, funeral plans, death and survivor benefits, death notices, and all the forms needed for the benefits and notices. The price is just a few dollars (changes with inflation).

Giving Through Your Will (free booklet), published by the American Kidney Fund, 7315 Wisconsin Avenue, Bethesda, MD 20014. Good information on wills and a "Fact Summary For Your Attorney."

CHAPTER 38

THE HOSPICE CONCEPT

About 70 percent of all terminally ill patients in this country die in a hospital. Yet most specialists in the subject of death and dying say that a hospital is probably one of the worst places to die. Our medical establishment is directed toward curing. It's all a big battle, and death is the "enemy." When the battle is lost, the medical establishment usually retreats, leaving the dying person alone in the austere confines of a hospital room.

According to Dr. Robert S. Weiss, a sociologist and specialist in bereavement, "Some nurses and doctors have very mixed feelings about death." He explains that they're good people, but their whole training has usually been focused on "winning" the battle with disease. "When it's known that you're going to die," says Dr. Weiss, "these professionals want to avoid you—avoid the reminder of their defeat. And they can justify avoiding you by arguing that their time can be better used by those they can help."

But, there is a growing minority of medical professionals concerned with the quality of life that remains for terminal patients. "Before I took training in the subject of death and dying," says one cancer specialist, "I was frustrated and depressed because I couldn't do anything. . . . Now, I can give a human being a chance to live a fuller life during the time that remains."

RECOGNIZING VALID FEARS

In order to achieve this fuller life, a patient and the patient's family and friends have to understand some of the major fears involved when death becomes a reality, and not just an abstract. Balfour M. Mount, director of the Palliative Care Unit, Royal Victoria Hospital in Quebec, enumerates seven common fears the dying person faces:

"First, there's pain. But, this can be controlled now with drugs that leave the patient alert and free to communicate.

"Second, is isolation. In most hospitals, the dying patient encounters less interest and fewer visits from doctors and nurses and fewer visits from friends. A study of 80 breast cancer patients found that fear of isolation was almost greater than that of the disease itself.

"Third is the loss of control a dying patient often suffers. A formerly active person encounters increasing dependence on others. Hospital regulations take a lot of control away. They practically strip you of your belongings and anything else that's familiar.

"Fourth is the fear of what will happen to loved ones.

"Fifth is the fear that's reflected in the eyes of others. One patient said: 'I never knew what fear was until I saw it in the eyes of those caring for me.'"

"Sixth is the fear of the unknown. Patients often ask What will happen and how will it work?

"And seventh, for some people, there's the fear that their past lives may have had no meaning." (This subject will be explored in a subsequent chapter)

In talking about these fears, Dr. Mount says there's often a "conspiracy of silence" among the family and the professionals who are treating a patient in a hospital. There's a reluctance, he says, to talk frankly about the reality of the situation. "A candid, honest, yet supportive approach," Dr. Mount maintains, "will produce less anxiety in the long run than well-intentioned dishonesty, or lack of communication." If everyone pretends nothing is happening, it can hinder the patient's relationship with the family and close friends.

There's a need for honesty, Dr. Mount explains, but he warns that a patient's initial need for denial should be respected. Patients usually let you know when they want to talk about the probability of death. Doctors and others, Dr. Mount says, should offer some kind of hope for the patient without engendering a misunderstanding of what the hope means. "For many patients," says Dr. Mount, "the hope for cure or longer life gives way to hope for an absence of pain and hope for the family and physician to be able to stay with them until the end."

Near the end, according to Dr. Mount and others in the field, most patients do not fear death itself. They fear the possibility of pain and suffering. "In reality," Dr. Mount explains, "when death comes, it is usually painless and peaceful for a patient dying of a malignant disease." Apparently, mental and physical pain commonly recede during the last few days. Patients must be reassured that this will be the case, and reassurance comes easier in familiar surroundings.

One's own home seems to be the most "familiar" place for people to die. But, dying at home is not always possible, especially when a spouse or other members of the family feel they can't cope with the task. However, the usual alternative— a hospital—can be a grim place to contemplate one's death.

WHAT IS THE
HOSPICE CONCEPT?

This is why the "hospice" concept has taken hold and is spreading around the country. A hospice, in olden days, was an inn or "way station" for people traveling to some destination. Today, a hospice is a "way station" where a dying person can remain in comfortable surroundings until the time of death or "departure" for some other state of existence.

The idea was developed in Great Britain by Dr. Cicely Saunders, who founded St. Christopher's Hospice. A major item in hospice care, Dr. Saunders determined, was the control of pain. Mixtures of drugs that really worked were developed to keep the patient active, alert, and able to communicate fully with family and friends. You don't get the "zombie" effect with these drugs that you get with many pain killers used in regular hospital practice.

Most hospice specialists will advise the patient and family that one's home is the best place for a person to live the life that they have left. In some instances, a patient can be transferred to a special wing of a hospital for treatment and observation, and then returned home. If the home setting is not feasible, then the patient can be set up in the special hospital (hospice) wing, or in a building designed exclusively for hospice use.

The whole idea of hospice care away from home is to allow patients to have whatever belongings they want in their rooms, to dress any way they want, and, within reason, to eat anything they want. There is complete freedom for family and friends to visit, sleep with, and live with the patient. And, most important, the hospice staff team is trained to understand a dying patient's needs and the family's needs. You don't get any of the "sorry-it's-against-the-rules" litany that most hospitals deliver. This is because a hospice is not a disciplined place for "curing." It's a relaxed place for "caring."

If hospice care is to be given in the dying person's own home, then the family or friends who will be on hand must have some training on what to expect and how to handle the patient. This is where the hospice team from a nearby hospital becomes all important. Dying patients rely heavily on their doctors for explanations and moral support. So, the doctor should have some background in the hospice approach. Specially trained nurses, therapists, social workers and others may also be part of the team. Transporting the patient back and forth from the home to a room in a special wing of a hospital may be part of the planning, to cover any crisis the family or friends can't handle.

In some cases, the home setting may not be ideal because the family or friends are not up to the job of coping with a dying person. Or, there may be no family or friends nearby. In this case, a specially designed hospice center might be in order. It might be a wing of a hospital, or a building adjacent to a hospital. Or, it might be a community of buildings designed specifically to function as a hospice. So far, there are very few places exclusively designed for hospice care. But, as the hospice movement takes hold, more special places should be available.

HOSPICE FACILITIES

Hillhaven Hospice in Tucson, Arizona, claims to be the first free-standing facility in the country devoted entirely to hospice care. Patients have their own rooms, with their own furniture and belongings, and are even allowed to have pets. Families are allowed to come and go at will and are encouraged to "live in" with patients who desire it. Diets are completely flexible, and families often eat together in private dining rooms. "One woman," according to a Hillhaven staffer, "wanted Chinese food but was never hungry at normal meal times... So, we arranged for a Chinese restaurant in town to bring her meals around midnight, when she said she was ravenous." Another woman wanted a canary in her room because it reminded her of her early married days. She got the canary.

Hillhaven has a specially trained staff, an emergency arrangement with a local hospital, and draws on a wealth of volunteer workers from a nearby retirement community. A nonprofit foundation, backed by a religious organization, runs Hillhaven.

At first, the national hospice movement ran into problems with Blue Cross, Medicare and other health insurers. These organizations were designed to cover active, medical "curing" costs, not "caring" costs. When it was pointed out that it costs a lot more to maintain a dying person in the average hospital than it does in the average home or hospice center, the insurers began to make special coverage available. Not all insurers are set up to handle reimbursement for hospice costs for the home or elsewhere, but the ranks are growing.

A National Hospice Organization has been set up to establish standards for hospice accreditation. So far, NHO officials say, there are fewer than 200 recognized hospice establishments around the country, and most of them are affiliated with hospitals or religious organizations. According to the NHO, the word "hospice" cannot be used by any nonprofit group or company without specific approval and authorization outlined in this official statement:

"The word 'hospice' is a nationally registered service mark, as determined by the U.S. Patent and Trade-Mark Office. The National Hospice Organization will be responsible for establishing guidelines for licensed use of the name 'hospice.' This includes communicating offers to license, executing licenses, and maintaining the nature and quality of services rendered. Unauthorized use of the service mark is prohibited."

NHO officials admit that policing the burgeoning hospice industry won't be easy. This means you should pick a hospice with a certain amount of care. The best way to find out about hospice care in any given area is through your local American Cancer Society chapter. You may also get information on the whereabouts of hospice services through the public relations office of a nearby medical school, religious organizations, and local hospitals. The NHO also serves as a clearinghouse for information and may be able to provide names and addresses of hospice specialists in any given city or state (see source list at the end of the chapter).

Another good organization to get in touch with is Make Today Count. It was founded by Orville Kelly, a former journalist and cancer patient. MTC now has some 250 chapters around the country devoted to helping cancer patients and others with terminal diseases. MTC chapters also work with the families and friends of people who are threatened by terminal disease. Most chapters are run by volunteers with trained staff supervision. Financial backing comes from the American Cancer Society. Local ACS chapters should know where Make Today Count offices can be found. There is no formal membership, and no fee is involved. Patients and their families can call any time to ask questions or get help with specific problems. There are scheduled meetings to hear doctors, psychiatrists, and other professionals, and there are many informal "sharing" sessions. It's hard to explain, but the sharing of fears and experiences really seems to work wonders with people who know they have a terminal illness.

THE RIGHT TO DIE

One thing cancer patients and others with terminal diseases seem to talk about at MTC sharing sessions is the fear of being kept alive with surgery, machines, and tubes after there is no hope for recovery. This brings us to the concept of one's "right to die." California passed a law which allows a person to sign a directive asking the doctor to suspend life-sustaining equipment or medication after two other physicians have certified that death is imminent. After this certification, the patient must wait two weeks before signing the directive. Even if the patient hasn't signed the directive, but has just expressed his or her desires beforehand, physicians have the power to use their own discretion to decide whether life-sustaining treatment should be maintained or suspended.

Most states don't have this kind of law, but you can still write your own directive, outlining your right to die. The directive won't be legally binding, but it will give the doctor something to go on. You can copy the sample directive on page 369. Keep a copy with your will, and give copies to your doctor and your lawyer. It's also wise to explain your feelings about your right to die with your next of kin.

THE RIGHT TO LIVE

Again, the whole idea behind all these plans and preparations is to allow the dying person the right to live the best life possible for as long as possible without resorting to futile (and inordinately expensive) medical measures. The last months of life should be a time of talking, reflecting, and reviewing past experiences with family and friends. Sociologist Robert S. Weiss has this to say about the need for married couples to use the time left to their best advantage:

"It seems to work out better if the spouse and the dying patient, together, focus their attention on making the married life that remains to them as worthwhile as it can be. They can regard each day that remains as a bonus, a holiday period, a

---

Living Will—a Directive

To my family, my physician, my clergyman, my lawyer:

If the time comes when I can no longer take part in decisions, let this statement stand as the testament of my wishes:

If there is no reasonable expectation of my recovery from physical or mental disability, I (your name), request that I be allowed to die, and not be kept alive by artificial means or heroic measures.

(signed, dated and witnessed)

---

time in which they can express, without interference from other responsibilities, their caring for each other. They may be surprised to find out how rewarding this period can be."

Of course, Dr. Weiss' poignant advice to married couples can be applied to any close relationship with a member of the family or a dear friend. No matter who it is, when you help another person die, you're really helping that person to fully live every possible year, month, week, hour, minute, and second.

GOOD SOURCES

National Hospice Organization, Room 504, 1828 L Street, N.W., Washington, DC 20036. NHO will provide the names of hospices and hospice specialists in your city or state. You can also get a booklet, *Hospice In America*, which explains how hospices work. The NHO also publishes a directory of hospice services around the country, which is available for a fee. You might also be able to get information on how your local religious organization, hospital, or medical center can set up a hospice, and where training can be obtained.

CHAPTER 39

GIVING
SURVIVORS
A BREAK

In ancient Egypt, planning one's own funeral was an art form. Today, what do we have? Except for an occasional wish to be buried in some certain spot, most funeral planning is usually left to the survivors to attend to in a hurried fashion *after* death occurs. This can put a considerable burden on the family or friends of the deceased person, who have to take on a well-entrenched funeral industry without much knowledge of what's going on.

Things would be much better if people could take a tip from the ancient Egyptians and make funeral plans well ahead of time, when the purchase of special services can be contemplated without the pressure and emotion that follow the death of a spouse, family member, or close friend. We don't even have to go back to the ancient Egyptians to find a precedent for planning one's final act.

The making of a will takes into consideration the distribution of a person's money and belongings after death. Life insurance is also part of one's "final finances." So is the naming of a beneficiary for a pension with survivor's rights. All these acts of tidying up, of packing your bags before departure, fill a certain need to "get things in order" so survivors won't have to suffer the task of untangling the mess. Why not add one more item to your contingency planning checklist? Why not find out what you and the person closest to you want to have done in the way of funeral arrangements? You can investigate the wide variety of possibilities, determine what's best for you and your survivors, put it all down on paper and entrust it to your closest relative or friend. A harassed survivor can follow your funeral plan as if it were a mandate and not feel at all guilty if some funeral director feels something more elaborate (translate: more expensive) would be appropriate.

Following the same, cautious method of buying insurance or having a will made, you should get objective, experienced advice before you make your final decision. A good place to start might be the local office of one of the members of the Continental Association of Funeral and Memorial Societies (you'll find the address under GOOD READING at the end of this chapter). A memorial society has a staff, usually volunteers, and members who are well versed in matters funereal. It's a nonprofit organization dedicated to giving consumers honest information on a very sensitive and complicated subject.

The first thing you'll probably have to decide is what is to be done with the remains when death occurs. You may have your own personal feelings on this fundamental choice, or you may want to find out what your spouse, children, or close friends would like. After all, the survivors are the ones who will be around to pay tribute to your memory.

THE TRADITIONAL FUNERAL

So what are the major choices? The great majority of Americans opt for having the body removed to a funeral home in their neighborhood. As a rule, most survivors buy the traditional, adult funeral package, which includes a casket, embalming, presentation of the body for family and friends to view, transportation of the body to a church or synagogue for religious services, transportation of the body and family members in a hearse and limousines to the burial site, and arranging for the burial lot and burial procedure. A funeral home will also help with the obituary notices and will obtain copies of the death certificate and all the forms necessary for various benefits (Social Security, veterans and Civil Service burial benefits, insurance, and surviving widow's benefits from Social Security and pension funds.)

It's a lot of work to arrange a funeral, and it costs money. Just how much money depends on what products and services are ordered. According to a Federal Trade Commission report, the cost of most funeral home packages is determined by the price of the casket that's selected, and caskets can run from a few hundred dollars on up to the thousands. According to the FTC report, this is where sales pressure is often applied. There's nothing wrong with sales efforts per se. Car dealers, insurance agents, mutual representatives—all use various forms of sales pressure (some more subtle than others.) You just have to know that it's going to be there and pay little or no attention to it. Of course, it's a lot easier when you plan ahead of time. Some relative or friend who is in a state of semishock a few hours after a death occurs is usually not in the best condition to play buyer-beware games with a funeral home sales force.

If you plan your funeral in advance, you'll find that some funeral directors, in the calmness of an office visit, are excellent consultants. They know their business, and they can give details and prices to suit your special needs. But, others, sensing that you might want something simple (translate: inexpensive), might politely refuse to negotiate, stating their package price includes all—or nothing. If this is the case, say thank you and depart. More often than not, a local memorial society recommended by the Continental Association of Funeral and Memorial Societies will have names of local funeral directors who will gladly arrange whatever you want, no matter what the cost.

CREMATION

After studying the traditional funeral home method of casket viewing and burial, you might want to investigate cremation as a simpler, less expensive alternative. In some areas, a crematorium will remove the body, cremate it, and return the ashes to you for burial or whatever you wish. Because the ashes are legally "clean," they can be buried in your back yard, at sea, mixed in the loam of a farm field, or sprinkled over some remote mountains from a light plane. In some areas, a body must be taken to the crematorium by a funeral home (an extra cost), but there is no need for embalming, no need for a casket, and really no need for burial in a cemetery. But, a lot of people have ashes buried in a cemetery as a memorial focal point for family and friends.

When you subtract the need for a casket, embalming, and other funeral home package services, the cost drops dramatically. The only major cost after cremation might be the purchase of a cemetery lot and a marker if this type of burial is selected.

DONATION OF BODY

Another way of having a body removed after death is to donate it to a medical school or hospital. Medical schools need bodies for study and research, and many hospitals need organ donations to supply hearts, kidneys, corneas, ear bones, pituitary glands, tissue and skin (for grafting) to living recipients. An increasing number of people like the idea of giving their body or organs for use by the living. If this is done, the family can get the remains back for cremation or burial. Sometimes the medical school or hospital pays for the transportation, sometimes not.

Unfortunately, not all medical schools need bodies on any given day, and not all hospitals are equipped to receive bodies or organ donations. This is why there's a national clearing-house to make sure donations go where they're most needed. It's called The Living Bank (see listing at the end of this chapter). You may want to give your body to a specific university medical school, or a specific hospital, but this might not be possible at the time of death. Survivors should understand that body or organ donation can be transferred to some other medical school or hospital through a quick phone call.

CONTINGENCY PLANS

Finally, if you're planning travel to foreign countries, you should have some contingency plans in case of unexpected death. About 8,000 Americans die abroad every year, and it can cost as much as $5,000 to ship a body home. The deceased person's passport and instructions for burial or cremation are needed in case there's an emergency. The U.S. Consular Service will handle the job if no relative or close friend is along.

THE NEED FOR CEREMONY

Whatever happens, wherever death occurs, a planned funeral ritual for survivors fills a basic human need. It helps to build a bridge between a survivor's past life and the future. Sociologist Robert Weiss sums it up in this sensitive commentary for widows in his book *The First Year of Bereavement*:

"Like other time-honored ceremonies, the cermonies of leave-taking respond to profound human needs. They provide an orderly and proper way of dealing with and disposing of the body, in which there is recognition both that the body is now lifeless and that only days before it was a living, loved person.

"The ceremonies also provide a setting in which the community of kin, friends and co-workers can take leave of the deceased and can express the roles he played in their lives. In this setting, others can support the former wife in the transition to her new status of widow.

"Afterward, there is often quiet approval that communicates to the widow that the ceremonies had been successful. Knowing that they had been able to see to it that the departure of their husbands had been properly accomplished helps many widows begin the first year of bereavement somewhat stronger and more assured."

GOOD READING

Manual of Death, Education and Simple Burial, written by Ernest Morgan, published by the Continental Association of Funeral and Memorial Societies, 1828 L Street, N.W., Suite 1100, Washington DC 20036. You can write for the current price and availability of this excellent book on funeral procedures. One important section includes a checklist of things to be done in making funeral plans and handling duties on the day of, and the days following, a death. The association also publishes a free booklet that describes how memorial societies work and lists member chapters state by state.

The Price of Death, A Consumer Guide for Funerals,

Cemeteries and Grave Markers, prepared by the Seattle Regional Office of the Federal Trade Commission, is available for a modest fee from: Superintendent of Documents, U.S. Government Printing Office, Washington, DC 20402. When you write for information on price and availability, indicate the booklet's stock number: 018-000-00185-3.

The Living Bank, P.O. Box 6725, Houston, TX 77025. This organization serves as a clearinghouse for information on where body and organ donations are needed. Inquiries are answered with a booklet on how body and organ donations are made and a "universal donor card" is included.

Various books by Herman Feifel, who was the first to demonstrate the effects of dying on human behavior. One of his latest books, *New Meaning of Death*, published by McGraw-Hill, is a compilation of writings on the subject of death.

On Death and Dying, by Elisabeth Kubler-Ross, published by MacMillan, was the first easy-to-read book on the subject. It brought death out of the closet for factual, yet sensitive discussion.

CHAPTER 40

THE NEED FOR
SUMMING UP

Perhaps you've heard of some late lamented friend or relative who supposedly had a "good death." By this it's meant that the person was at peace with the world. You may have wondered, as I have, how this type of death is possible. You might have envied the person who has a peaceful death. How can anyone have a "good death?" The two words seem to be the ultimate contradiction.

To learn more about this elusive, somewhat frightening subject, I talked at length with Dr. David Gutmann, a clinical psychologist, who deals with patients facing death. He is professor and chief of the Division of Psychology at Northwestern University Medical School. I asked him about the kind of person who seemed to be at peace when death was imminent. I wanted to know if there is anything the person did during his or her life that made things easier. Is there anything that we can do now, while we're healthy and, presumably, have many years ahead of us? Dr. Gutmann pondered the question and offered this advice:

"You should stand for something—have a sense of integrity at the end of your life. By integrity, I mean you have to be able to say: 'I've paid my dues to my identity. I haven't sold out to the fashion of the times. I've stuck to my guns when I had to, in the defense of what I stood for.' If you can make this kind of statement, it can be tremendously comforting at the end of life. But, you don't wait until then. Start now.

"An example of the kind of integrity I'm talking about, of meaning something, can be seen in the whole Watergate pageant. The overthrowing of the Nixon administration was accomplished essentially by old lawyers who had integrity. Archibald Cox got fired for his integrity. Senator Sam Erwin loved the constitution. Anyone who messed around with it would have to deal with him. Judge John Sirica was suffering from a life-threatening heart condition. He didn't know whether he was going to come out of those court hearings alive. But, he stood his ground."

While we are not all judges, senators and other symbols of power, we do have things we can stand for—things that are important to us. We can stand for patience, understanding, and unity in our families. We can pass on our skills and knowledge to young people, as teachers, volunteers, employers, employees, and as parents, grandparents, aunts, uncles, brothers, and sisters. Changing the life of just one other person for the better could give real meaning to your life. It links you with something constant, something worthy, that will continue after you have gone.

REVIEW THE HIGHLIGHTS—
AND THE LOWLIGHTS

As you grow older, you should keep reviewing what you've done and what you'd still like to do. It's a good idea to keep a scrapbook, notes or even tape recordings of the things you've done for others—your accomplishments. While you're at it, dig back in your life's history and review the highlights—even some of the lowlights. If possible, put names, dates, happenings, pictures, clippings, whatever, in your scrapbook. You might even want to tape an "oral history" of your life—the good times and the bad. It can be part of a family history that your children and grandchildren will appreciate and keep passing on. Get your parents to review their lives, and put it all down on paper or tape. It will not only be a valuable addition to your family history, it will provide certain therapeutic benefits for parents as far as their mental health is concerned.

By looking back into the past with the persistence of a professional researcher, you'll find lots of things you had forgotten. You might well discover that you did, indeed, stand for something. You did mean something to other people. You might have forgotten all about it.

For example, I thought the time I spent in the navy during World War II, was just something that had to be done. I've always felt I didn't amount to much in the navy. Recently, something happened to change my mind. Members of the crew of my old ship, the *U.S.S. Crowley, Destroyer Escort 303*, decided to have a reunion in Washington, near my home. I had mixed feelings about going, but, in the end, my wife and I went. I immediately recognized several faces and the memories that had been buried for years started bubbling up. "Remember when. . . . ?" The question kept coming up, again and again, as crew members exchanged stories. In talking with the captain, I wanted him to know how grateful I was that he handled the ship with such remarkable skill. He took us out—and he brought us back.

But, it wasn't just a one-way expression of gratitude. The captain said he, too, was grateful to have a crew he could count on. While we were talking, it dawned on me that, as a radio operator, the captain counted on me, as did the rest of the crew. The recounting of stories showed that we all relied on each other. There was a bond. I guess this is why everyone was so glad to see each other. The bond was still there.

Afterward, when I got home, I rummaged through an old scrapbook and found some pictures of friends in the ship's crew. At the reunion, I exchanged addresses with several men who had pictures of me and the ship. I want to preserve these pictures and memories for my children and grandchildren. It's difficult to explain, but I suddenly felt proud of something I had done, something I had blocked from memory for many years.

Documenting your own history can mean a lot to your children, their children, and others with whom you've had a close relationship. It's sort of like a mini-version of Alex Haley's *Roots*. You're giving your family a part of yourself, something they can weave into their own personal histories.

When you work on your history, you might notice some gaps, some things that need doing—things you shouldn't keep putting off. Career consultant John Crystal urges his clients to: "Write your own obituary now while you still have plenty of time—then go out and start fulfilling your expectations." When you're gone, asks Crystal, what would you like them to say about you? If you want them to say you were a good parent, or a loving child—then find ways to be one. If you want them to say you stood your ground when some developer wanted to cut down the trees in a neighborhood park, then get involved. Fight the good fight. There are many things in your life that might need doing. Dr. Gutmann offers some suggestions:

"In the upcoming years, you may have some opportunities to stand up and be counted. You might even be threatened by a superior. If you stand up for something and stop being pushed around, you might find that you are less afraid. This can be very sustaining in your later years. You will realize that you have some integrity that carries you through losses or setbacks and you don't have to just keep taking the easiest way out. Some people grow up, become old, and never know if they ever really made a significant choice. They never know if they did what they did because they were too scared to do otherwise."

Stand up and be counted. Do what you think is right. According to Dr. Gutmann, if you can face your life, you can face your death. Dr. Viktor E. Frankl, a professor of psychiatry at the University of Vienna, a man who suffered in a Nazi concentration camp, sums it up beautifully in his book, *Man's Search for Meaning*:

"Man is able to live and even to die for the sake of his ideas and his values... Man is never driven to moral behavior; in each instance he *decides* to behave morally. Man does not do so in order to satisfy a moral drive and to have a good conscience. He does so for the sake of a cause to which he commits himself, or for a person whom he loves, or for the sake of his God... There is nothing in the world that would so effectively help one to survive even the worst conditions, as the knowledge that there is a meaning to one's life."

EPILOGUE

THE METHUSELAH CONNECTION

When I finished this book, I felt there was something missing. Several friends who had been following the book's progress wanted to know about life expectancy and lifespan. They wondered, with all our technological advances, whether we were any closer to solving the mystery of why human beings age and live for just a relatively short period of time. Is there any way we can live longer?

I, too, was curious. So, as an afterthought, I did some research on what was being done about altering the aging process. If the biblical Methuselah lived for hundreds of years, why can't we? When you investigate the possibility of human beings' eventually making the Methuselah connection, you learn that there is a distinct difference between human life *span* and life *expectancy*. The human lifespan, according to Dr. Robert N. Butler, head of the National Institute of Aging, "is somewhere between 100 and 110 years of age." (See chart page 384.) Life span, he explains, is the "natural, inherent life of a

Maximum Recorded Life Span of Species

Species	Years
Human	111
Horse	46
Goat	20
Guinea Pig	7.6
Rat	4.7
Mouse	3.3

Based on information from *Guinness Book of World Records* and *World Book Encyclopedia.*

particular organism." Life expectancy, on the other hand, is the "likelihood of living to a certain age within the limits of the lifespan."

Tinkering with the lifespan is not easy, and it may even be impossible until some time in the future when our brains have evolved to a stage where the evolutionary process will "allow" us to live longer. Much more possible, however, is the expansion of life expectancy. As Dr. Butler points out, the average life expectancy for Americans (when you combine the sexes) is about 72-plus. With the lifespan set at around 100 to 110 years, you have up to 30 years or so to play with. It might be possible, someday, for more people to live to 100 and a little beyond. About 12,000 Americans are there now.

Even more important, it might well be possible to postpone somewhat the effects of old age, and let people live longer in better health. As we have seen, people who exercise regularly, have a minimum of bad habits (no smoking, moderate drinking), and eat moderate but nutritious meals, tend to retain their health longer. While living a sane and sensible existence certainly helps, there's more to it than that.

According to Albert Rosenfeld, author of *Prolongevity*, a book about the research being done on ways to extend life expectancy and lifespan, "Some scientists feel certain that the aging clock is in the brain, that it is located in the hypothalamic-pituitary endocrine-control center, and that whatever is responsible for aging changes that occur there produces a cascade effect of changes throughout the body." Some sort of "death hormones" are released and they begin to slowly, but surely, block off the cells' ability to take up thyroid hormones. Thyroid, says Rosenfeld, may be the rate-controling hormone of both systems. When these systems break down, we age and die.

This may be what happens, Rosenfeld says, when salmon swim upstream to spawn. When the salmon get the call to swim to their ancient breeding grounds, a death hormone may be released. Suddenly, they're getting too little of some hormones and too much of others, especially the adrenal hormone. After spawning, this negative hormone action makes them die fast—within a few days. The same kind of thing happens to human beings, but, instead of a few days, the action is spread out over 20 to 40 years. Our aging may be like the salmon's, only in slow motion.

There may be many other elements involved in the aging process, but our glands have to be at, or near, the top of the list. In talking to Rosenfeld about his extensive survey of longevity research, I asked him if any breakthrough seemed to be on the horizon. He said thymosin, a mixture of hormones from the thymus gland which regulate the immunological system, "could be one of the first important antiaging agents to reach the marketplace." Rosenfeld gave me the name of the scientist who developed thymosin, and I gave him a call.

He is Dr. Allan Goldstein, professor of biochemistry and chairman of the department at George Washington University School of Medicine, Washington, D.C. Dr. Goldstein started his research on thymosin at The Albert Einstein College of

Medicine in New York, continued with it at the University of Texas Medical School in Galveston and the George Washington University School of Medicine. Dr. Goldstein, who spent 15 years working on thymosin, says the thymus gland regulates the immune system by producing lymphocytes which attack disease. As we grow older, the thymus gland slows down and far fewer lymphocytes are produced. Fortunately, we have enough stored lymphocytes to get us into and through much of the second half of our lives. As we grow older, we begin to pick up a chronic ailment here, a chronic ailment there, and are much more vulnerable to attack from serious diseases.

Apparently, thymosin works to reverse this shutting down of the immune system by stimulating additional production of lymphocytes. This new hormone was not initially developed as an agent to retard the effects of aging. It's supposed to be used with children who have genetic immune system deficiencies. How does it work with these children? "Beautifully," says Dr. Goldstein.

As you can see, new agents take a long time to develop. After working for more than 15 years on thymosin, Dr. Goldstein says a marketable product (made by Hoffman-LaRoche, U.S.A.) won't be ready for another couple of years, and then, it will be restricted for use by children with nonfunctioning immunological systems and certain cancer patients.

As for use by older people as a booster for the immune system, Dr. Goldstein thinks this might be possible within the next five years or so. "When it's ready," he says, "thymosin could be taken by people from age 40 up."

Aside from its overall capability of beefing up the immune system, thymosin has worked on cancer patients who are taking chemotherapy. One of the problems with certain kinds of chemotherapy is the debilitating, sometimes devastating, side effects the body has to suffer. Thymosin, according to Dr. Goldstein, can do much to offset these side effects. He says that in the first controlled trial, thymosin has been found to double the survival rate for patients with lung cancer, who are receiving heavy doses of chemotherapy. If this trial can be confirmed by additional trials, it will have a major impact on the treatment of cancer.

People suffering from rheumatoid arthritis might also benefit from thymosin, because it could counter the damaging action of the lymphocytes which are attacking healthy cells and tissue. As a footnote, Dr. Goldstein says the side effects of thymosin are minimal.

According to *Prolongevity* author Rosenfeld, the breakthrough on antiaging elements will take place in piecemeal fashion. One little breakthrough here, another one there. Some breakthroughs might come as a result of research in other areas, that don't seem to be related. For example, the drug L-dopa, which is used to counteract some of the tremors caused by Parkinson's disease, might be used to slow down the effects of aging. Work is also being done on getting rid of lipfuscin (cellular garbage), which damages other cells. Chemicals that work on cells may be available within our lifetime, and these could, conceivably, slow down the wrinkling of the skin and could produce healthier hair that grays more slowly and won't fall out with age.

All these things may alleviate the symptoms of the aging process, but they won't really extend the lifespan much beyond the evolutionary design of 100 to 110 years. To do that, some basic changes will have to take place. Some scientists are fiddling with body temperatures and diet, hoping to push the span up to 120 or 140 years. Experiments with laboratory animals have shown that a warmer body temperature (not outside temperature) in early years, combined with a colder body temperature in adult years, tends to make rats live longer. So does a restricted, low-calorie diet during the early years.

The key to living longer is elusive, but scientists keep probing for it. Dr. Joan Smith-Sonneborn, a professor of zoology and physiology at the University of Wyoming, says she has uncovered a life-extending mechanism in her work on a common, single-celled organism. Dr. Smith-Sonneborn says the cell was bombarded with ultraviolet rays, which hastened the aging process. When the cell was bombarded again with ultraviolate radiation of a different wave length, it stopped aging and, in fact, lived 50 percent longer than normal. This ultraviolet radiation may work with this cell under certain conditions, but what about all the other types of cells? Does each one have to have some special gimmick, some special kick, to slow down the aging process? Nobody knows for sure.

Some scientists feel that we can't effectively lengthen the lifespan. Life expectancy, yes, but not the lifespan. This, it is felt, is part of a secret that's guarded by the entire evolutionary process. Human beings will be "allowed" to live 200 years or more when, and if, the evolutionary process that governs human development sees fit.

In his book, *The Seasons of a Man's Life*, Dr. Daniel Levinson included a most intriguing commentary on senescence—the normal aging process. Apparently, senescence, or aging, as we know it, is not built into the lives of some organisms. But, senescence is very much built into the life cycle of all land vertebrates, including human beings.

To explain why human beings and other animals have a built-in aging clock and other organisms don't, Dr. Levinson cites an idea based on research done years ago by G.P. Bidder, the English biologist. Bidder said humans and other fast-moving land animals, had to have a growth regulator to limit size. Otherwise, the species couldn't survive. Each species has an optimal body size and shape. If we grow beyond that, our adaptation and survival are threatened.

At first, primitive man needed to live only 40 years or so. This allowed enough time for procreation and raising the young to the point where they, in turn, could procreate.

But, Bidder said, when we learned to communicate through language, and to store more information in our brains, the evolutionary process "allowed" longer lives. Why? Because a middle-aged human being could adapt better and live longer, and would help the tribe even further through the communication of ideas and wisdom. Younger members of the species could benefit from information contained in the heads of their elders.

We're at that stage now. The outside limit is set at the 100 to 110 mark. Will we be able to change the evolutionary process on our own and push the limit up further? Nobody knows for sure. Scientists agree that cracking the genetic code through research on DNA, or deoxyribonucleic acid, the enzyme building blocks that form the basis for all life, could eventually lead to modification of the aging process.

The answers, while seeming to be close, are probably a number of years off. Research is going on, but it takes money. For the moment, we have other priorities. Says gerontologist Alex Comfort: "The control of the human rate of aging is going to happen. How soon it happens . . . depends upon the social pressure for research and the wisdom with which that research is applied."

INDEX